George Washington on Leadership

GEORGE WASHINGTON ON LEADERSHIP

Richard Brookhiser

BASIC
BOOKS

A MEMBER OF THE PERSEUS BOOKS GROUP
NEW YORK

Books published by Basic Books are available at special discounts for bulk purchases in
the United States by corporations, institutions, and other organizations. For more
information, please contact the Special Markets Department at Perseus Books Group,
2300 Chestnut Street, Suite 200, Philadelphia, PA 19103, call (800) 810-4145, ext. 5000,
or e-mail special.markets@perseusbooks.com.

Designed by Timm Bryson
Set in 11.5 point Adobe Caslon

The Library of Congress has catalogued the hardcover as follows:
Brookhiser, Richard.
    George Washington on leadership / Richard Brookhiser.
        p. cm.
    Includes bibliographical references and index.
    ISBN 978-0-465-00302-0
    1. Washington, George, 1732-1799—Ethics. 2. Washington, George, 1732-1799—
Military leadership. 3. Leadership—Case studies. 4. Conduct of life—Case studies.
5. United States—History—Revolution, 1775-1783. 6. United States—Politics and
government—1775-1783. 7. United States—Politics and government—1783-1809.
8. Presidents—United States—Biography. 9. Generals—United States—Biography. I.
Title.

    E312.17.B85 2008
    973.4'1092–dc22
                                                    2007044789
    Paperback ISBN: 978-0-465-00303-7

10 9 8 7 6 5 4 3 2 1

For Douglas Lenard

Contents

Acknowledgments   ix

A Note on Style and Spelling   xi

Introduction: Founding CEO   1

I
PROBLEMS

1.   Start-ups   11
2.   Strategy   23
3.   The Future   37
4.   Small Stuff   47
5.   Management Style   55
6.   Communication   71
7.   Timing   81

II
PEOPLE

8.   Unusual People   87
9.   Troublemakers   99
10.   Superiors and Subordinates   113
11.   Failure and Betrayal   121

12.   Enemies   133
13.   Allies   139
14.   Sex . . . and Drugs   147
15.   Courtesy   155
16.   Bringing Out the Best   161
17.   Personnel   165

<u>III</u>

Self

18.   Identify Your Strengths   169
19.   Build Your Strengths   185
20.   Avoid Weaknesses   199
21.   Control Your Flaws   213
22.   Succession   227

      Conclusion: We Must Take Men   235

      Notes   239
      Bibliography   253
      Index   257

Acknowledgments

In 2005 Thomas S. Schreier, Jr. and Cheryl B. Stone of First American Funds invited me to give a series of talks called "George Washington on the Art of Management." I am grateful to them for prompting me to look at Washington in a new way.

Terry Golway, Douglas Lenard, Nicole Seary, and Micheline Tilton helped me with tough points.

I would like to thank my editor, Jo Ann Miller, my agent, Michael Carlisle, and, as always, my wife, Jeanne Safer.

A Note on Style and Spelling

Although there were many politically savvy women in the world of the founding fathers (Abigail Adams, Adelaide de Flahaut), all the leaders George Washington met, and most of the people he led, were men. This tugs my style in the direction of the generic pronoun *he.* Twenty-first-century women will be savvy enough to see that Washington's lessons of leadership also apply to them.

The president did not have a "cabinet" or "ambassadors" in the eighteenth century, but I use the words because they are more convenient than "heads of departments" and "ministers," the terms that were then used. I sometimes use place-names (for instance, Indiana) that Washington never heard of, though when I am following his point of view, I try to use the names he knew. The Republican Party of Washington's day is the ancestor of today's Democratic Party (the modern GOP began in the 1850s).

I have modernized all spelling and punctuation.

INTRODUCTION: FOUNDING CEO

America's greatest leader was its first—George Washington. He ran two start-ups, the army and the presidency, and chaired the most important committee meeting in history, the Constitutional Convention. His agribusiness and real estate portfolio made him America's richest man. He was as well known as any actress, rapper, or athlete today. Men followed him into battle; women longed to dance with him; famous men, almost as great as he was, some of them smarter or better spoken, did what he told them to do. He was the Founding CEO.

Even at a time when entertainers and freaks commandeer so much of our attention, the most important men and women in society are its leaders, whether in politics, business, or war. In politics, the buck stops at their desks; in business, they are responsible for bringing in the bucks; in war, they plan the operations and command the troops. That is why it is always important to know how a great leader of the past navigated his life, and what a leader or aspiring leader of today can learn from him.

When George Washington died, one of his mourners called him "first in war." He got his first taste of the military at age twenty-one when his in-laws got him a commission in the colonial militia. His superiors found him a bit of a pain in the neck; his junior officers adored him, calling him an "excellent commander," a "sincere friend," and an "affable" companion. He saw two debacles, in which hundreds of his comrades were killed, and one great victory, in which not a shot was fired; he was assigned to defend an undefendable frontier. When he was twenty-six, he resigned, went home, and got married.

When Washington was forty-three, he got a harder assignment. Congress named him commander in chief in June 1775; he had angled for the job by showing up to the sessions of Congress in his old uniform. The American Revolution had barely begun. The troops he was assigned to command were local militias that had been renamed the Continental army; turning them into an actual army would be one of his many tasks. During his time on the job, he fought ten battles in five states and oversaw operations from Canada to Georgia to Indiana (then the Wild West). Between battles, he solved a range of problems, from smallpox to treason. Since there was not yet any such thing as a president, secretary of defense, or secretary of state—the government consisted only of Congress—his job as commander in chief embraced some of the functions of these jobs as well: negotiating with Indians and Frenchmen, buying shoes and food. Although Congress had picked him unanimously, and backed him throughout the war, there were times when individual members schemed to replace him and when Congress as a whole simply could not help him; he had to deal with that, too. In December 1783, after the last skirmish had been fought and the last negotiations concluded, Washington resigned in a simple ceremony. "The spectators all wept," wrote one of them, "and there was hardly a member of Congress who did not drop tears." Washington went home for Christmas—the first he had celebrated there in nine years.

His eulogist also called him "first in peace." He left home in 1787 to attend a convention of delegates from across the country that had been called to Philadelphia to revise the form of government. He showed up when he was supposed to, though there were not enough fellow delegates for a quorum ("These delays," he wrote, ". . . sour the temper of the punctual members"). On the first day of business, in late May, he was chosen to chair the meeting. The convention met every day, except Sundays and for a ten-day break in late summer, for nearly four months. Washington attended every session. Fifty-four other delegates attended at various times, of whom perhaps twenty did most of the heavy arguing and heavy lifting. The result was that the United States got a brand-new constitution, including a chief executive ("The executive Power shall be vested in a President of the United States of America" [Article II, Section 1]).

Washington got that job, too, in the spring of 1789. Many private organizations had presidents, including fire companies and cricket clubs, as Vice President John Adams remarked. But no country in the world, and very few in history, had been ruled by such a figure; everything Washington did was, in a sense, being done for the first time. He had more free time in this job than he had as commander in chief, spending his summers at home. But while he was in the nation's capital, he met regularly with his cabinet, and greeted the public at weekly receptions. He also made a point of visiting every state, at a time when travel was not routine (his Air Force One was a carriage). He performed some tasks that the old national government had performed, such as waging war and negotiating peace; other tasks—suppressing a rebellion, collecting taxes, paying debts—were novelties in American history. "Few," he wrote circumspectly, "can realize the difficult and delicate part which a man in my situation had to act." Chateaubriand, a French poet and diplomat, was more effusive. What did Washington leave as his legacy in the "forests" of America? "Tombs? No, a world!" In March 1797, after serving two four-year terms, Washington went home for good.

Home had never been far from his thoughts, for Washington was first in business, and his corporate headquarters was Mount Vernon, his Virginia plantation. Washington's family was prosperous, if not wealthy; his father owned 10,000 acres, most of it undeveloped, and a share in an iron mine, and sent his two oldest sons to England to be educated. But he died when George was eleven; instead of going to England, the boy would have to go to work. The same in-laws who would later put him in uniform hired him to survey their property, which was as big as New Jersey. The money he saved from his survey-ing jobs, and from his militia service, became his stake. When he was twenty-nine, his older half brothers having died, he inherited Mount Vernon, the family's main property, a 2,500–acre tract on the Potomac (marrying a rich widow helped him improve it). Over the next four decades, he added 60,000 more acres in New York, Pennsylvania, Maryland, West Virginia, Kentucky, and Ohio. Most of this real es-tate was held as an investment; he hoped to flip it at a profit to other investors, or lease it to tenants. Mount Vernon, however, was a work-ing farm that was more like a little country: in the 1790s, more than three hundred people lived on it, more than worked for the State De-partment or served in Congress. Washington Inc., or WashCorp, was a complex enterprise that included farming, food processing, and speculation. Its CEO had to cope with overseas customers, changing markets, and deteriorating natural resources. Although Washington was often strapped for cash, by the end of his life he was able to leave legacies to twenty-three heirs and free his labor force, his slaves. He did better than many of his wealthy peers: his friend Philadelphia merchant Robert Morris was imprisoned for debt, and one fellow planter and president, Thomas Jefferson, died bankrupt.

At the climax of his life, Washington had fame and respect, power and honor, wealth and a good conscience. His long career had its share of disappointments and outright smashups, from lost battles to lost friendships, and Washington tended to focus on these shadows more than the average person, for as Jefferson put it, he was "inclined to gloomy apprehensions" (one of the subjects that made him apprehensive was Thomas Jefferson). But Jefferson also said, in his final judgment of the man, that "his character was, in its mass, perfect, in nothing bad, in few points indifferent." How did he get to be this way? How did he learn to do all the things he did? How did he become such a leader?

I have to admit, at the beginning of this book, that Washington never read a book like this. One of his young friends, Gouverneur Morris, the peg-legged ladies' man who wrote the final draft of the Constitution, was quite caustic about the relationship of book learning to leadership. "None know how to govern but those who have been used to it and such men have rarely either time or inclination to write about it. The books, therefore, which are to be met with" on the subject "contain mere utopian ideas." Since *utopia* is Greek for "no place," Morris is saying that books on leadership are good for nothing.

But no one is a born leader. George Washington had a long learning curve that began in his teens and stretched well into middle age. He learned from problems: from situations that he mastered, or that mastered him. They came in every shape and degree of difficulty. On one disastrous day during the Revolution, he watched helplessly as the enemy captured 2,800 of his troops, which made him weep "with the tenderness of a child." On a potentially more disastrous day, he had to talk his own officers out of a mutiny. "On other occasions," wrote one of the officers who watched him do it, "he has been supported by the exertions of an army . . . but in this he stood single and alone." As a political leader, he had to sit through six-hour-long speeches and tiny points of order. "Mr. Madison," wrote James Madison in his notes on the Constitutional Convention, "moved to insert between 'after' and 'it' in Sect. 7 Art. I the words 'the day on which'. . . . A number of members [became] very impatient & call[ed] for the question." As a farmer, Washington had to oversee men and beasts. "Such a pen as I saw yesterday," he wrote testily to one of his employees, "would, if the cattle were kept in it one week, destroy the whole of them. They would be infinitely more comfortable . . . in the open fields." It was the last letter he wrote in his life; how many hundreds—thousands— had preceded it? He had to learn things he did not know, do things he did not do well, and learn not to attempt things he could not do at all. He had to face unpleasant surprises and conundrums that squatted, toadlike, in his path for years.

He learned from people: people he worked for, and with, and people who worked for him; family and in-laws, comrades and colleagues, neighbors and strangers. He learned from a German who could not speak English, a whippersnapper from the West Indies, and the planter down the road. Unlike Benjamin Franklin the cosmopolite, he never went abroad, except for a youthful trip to Barbados, accompanying a half brother who hoped the climate would be good for his health, so he had almost no opportunity to learn from foreigners in their own culture. To compensate, he met many foreigners in America—tourists, diplomats, officers (both friendly and hostile) who came here to fight in two world wars; his best male friend was a Frenchman. Some people of foreign culture lived right here: he met his first Native Americans when he was sixteen, and kept meeting with them into his sixties. There was no person who was the sole model for Washington's life, but he spent decades picking up what he needed from whomever he could.

And, whatever Gouverneur Morris might say, and despite the fact that his own formal education stopped before what we would call middle school, Washington read: rules of etiquette, books on farming, generalship, politics, and history. Although he never read a book on leadership, early in his life he read a book on how to be a good man, by the Roman philosopher Seneca. His better-educated friends read the Renaissance political scientist Machiavelli, who did write a book on leadership—*The Prince*—that is the source of many leadership books today. He learned from Seneca, but was very different from Machiavelli and his modern descendants. He wanted to know how he should behave, and how other men had behaved in positions of power and times of stress.

Action and reflection helped Washington in the most difficult subject of all, learning from himself: what he had, what he lacked, what he might acquire. Everyone makes mistakes; mistakes happen. It requires effort to turn them into useful experience. Everyone has at least some good points. What are they? Can they be made better? Everyone has flaws. Can they be minimized?

This book is not a biography of George Washington but a discourse on leadership, drawn from what he did, who he knew, and what he thought. Since it is organized topically, not chronologically, a moment from his teens may be followed by a moment from his sixties (I will explain how he grew and changed in the intervening years). Since I am looking for lessons in leadership, some events that rightly preoccupy biographers and historians will be passed over. Others will be put under a microscope. Some events will be revisited more than once; a meeting in March 1783 yields four different lessons.

Washington's problems were the same problems that every leader faces now; the details have changed, but not the essence. Very few readers of this book will be revolutionaries or presidents; more will be in politics; many more will be in business or the military. Washington's solutions, and occasional failures, are invaluable to them all.

When George Washington was a boy, he wanted to make his way in the world. By the time he was a man, he was changing the world. History is full of surprises. Here is how a man whose situation in life was in some ways less promising than yours became a leader, and made history.

Part One

PROBLEMS

————

In 1799, at the end of his life, Washington wrote that his mind had been "constantly on the stretch since the year 1753 [when he was twenty-one], with but short intervals, and little relaxation." The problems of those years are voluminous, when described in detail (his most thorough biography, by Douglas Southall Freeman, fills seven volumes; his letters and papers, which are being published by the University of Virginia, are expected to fill ninety). But most of the problems Washington faced came in a few clusters: family groups of headaches, puzzles, and routine tasks.

CHAPTER I

Start-ups

———

ALMOST EVERYONE has some experience working in an established organization, whether it is a business, an arm of the government, a church, a school team, or a local club. But more and more Americans start their own businesses; new organizations spring up (and whither away) like mushrooms. What do you do on day one when there is nothing to do, because no one has done it before?

The Power of the Obvious

Much of the work of a start-up flows from the obvious goals and needs of the organization, but that doesn't mean that any of it will be easy or quick.

When Washington became commander in chief in June 1775, Americans had been fighting in wars for a century and a half—he himself had fought in the French and Indian War twenty years earlier— yet there had never been an American army. Individual colonies made temporary call-ups of militias, or citizen-soldiers, to meet emergencies, from Indian attacks to French raids. Now Britain was the enemy, but the basic situation had not changed. The New England volunteers who had bottled up a British army in Boston had as yet no common organization. When Washington arrived at the beginning of July to take command, his first General Orders cast a wide net.

He named the major generals who would serve under him (Congress had picked them). He asked for an accounting of all supplies on hand, from gunpowder to tents to kettles. He forbade "cursing, swearing & drunkenness," and ordered "punctual attendance on divine service." He announced the court-martial of a crooked quartermaster and the funeral of a colonel. He also discussed latrines. "All officers [are] to take care that necessarys be provided in the camps and frequently filled up to prevent their being offensive and unhealthy."

Congress had created an army of 20,000 men. Given an average diet and average health, they would produce about 20,000 bowel movements per day. There was no indoor plumbing in late-eighteenth-century America, but even if there had been, it would have been of no use to an army, which must live in temporary quarters and be prepared to move out suddenly. That meant there had to be latrines, also known as "necessarys," "necessary vaults," and "sinks."

So much seems obvious. But it was not obvious to Washington's soldiers. Most of them were rural men and boys, because that is who populated America. Though farms had outhouses, on a hundred acres one could be casual. But hundreds of men encamped on every hundred acres couldn't be. In battle, in flight, or in hot pursuit, soldiers do what they have to do. In camp, what they must do is regulate their waste, or disease is the inevitable result. Digging latrines is a matter not of decorum or convenience but of sanitation.

When Washington ordered "all officers" to attend to this problem, he meant, in the first instance, the generals who ranked beneath him, who passed the word to their colonels, the men actually in command of individual regiments, and so on down the line. One of Washington's youngest senior officers was Nathanael Greene, of Rhode Island, who would turn thirty-three at the end of July. He had enlisted as a private in a militia unit, then was promoted, thanks to political connections, in one swoop to the rank of general. Greene now wrote that his men were "void[ing] excrement about the fields," with the result that their health was "greatly dangered by these neglects." Therefore, he "recommended" that the officers of his regiments "put due attention" into digging and maintaining latrines.

Problem solved? Maybe. Washington had addressed the situation of the army outside Boston in the summer of 1775, and that might be enough. Perhaps George III would acknowledge the just complaints of his subjects and call the war off (America was not yet fighting for independence, only against the British government's tyrannical acts). Perhaps the British could be driven out of Boston before winter, by an American assault (the besiegers outnumbered the besieged, and Washington considered various plans of attack). But suppose the war lasted longer? The terms of enlistment under which most of the men served ran only six months, through the end of the year. When their time came up, unless they reenlisted, they would go home, to be replaced by brand-new men, including (in many cases) brand-new officers. Suppose the war moved elsewhere? There were thirteen colonies, every one of them accessible by seacoast or river to the enemy and its splendid navy.

No help came from George III, who declared Americans to be rebels; no attack was made on Boston (Washington's senior officers talked him out of trying). The siege continued, with the result that, after New Year's Day 1776, Washington turned his attention to latrines once again. "The regimental quartermasters, and their sergeants," he wrote in the General Orders, "are to cause proper necessarys to be erected at convenient distances from the barracks in which their men are lodged, and see that those necessarys are frequently filled up." Quartermasters are responsible for the logistics of their regiments, and sergeants are their assistants. But Washington did not leave the responsibility to them alone. "It is equally . . . the duty of the other officers to look into this business, as too much care cannot be used in a matter where the health of the men so much depends upon it." Washington also made inappropriate bowel movements a punishable offense: "Any person who shall be discovered easing himself elsewhere is to be instantly confined and brought before a regimental court-martial."

The British left Boston in March 1776. Washington expected them to attack New York, where he moved his army in April. New location, same problem. Nathanael Greene, commanding troops in what is now Brooklyn, ordered them to bury "all filth and putrid matter," and to fill up and redig latrines every three days. "The general also forbids in the most positive terms the troops easing themselves in the ditches of the fortifications, a practice that is disgraceful to the last degree."

Washington's army moved from New York to New Jersey to Pennsylvania, sometimes chased by the enemy, sometimes striking back. He won battles, and he lost them, but the battle for sanitation never ended. In March 1778, in Valley Forge, outside Philadelphia, he tried shame. "Out of tender regard for the lives and health of his brave soldiers, yet with surprise that so little attention is paid to his orders, [the commander in chief] again in the most positive terms" directed that the carcasses of dead horses be buried, and "old vaults filled and new ones dug once a week," with "fresh earth . . . flung into the vaults twice a day." After shame, he reverted to sternness. "No plea of ignorance will be admitted and the least breach . . . severely noticed."

One thing Washington needed was a structure, a self-replicating set of procedures that would automatically convey his orders about latrines despite changes in personnel and location. He got it from a new officer who had arrived at Valley Forge in February 1778, Baron Friedrich Wilhelm von Steuben, a German soldier of fortune who had enlisted in the American cause. Steuben had useful knowledge of European practices, and a flair for adapting them to American conditions. He and Washington hit it off, and over the following winter, Steuben prepared the *Regulations for the Order and Discipline of the*

Troops of the United States, which Congress approved in March 1779. Steuben told the typical regiment what to do in the course of its daily business. "When a regiment enters camp, the field officers must take care . . . that the sinks [latrines] and kitchens are immediately dug in their proper places." He told them who should do it. "On the arrival of the regiment in camp," the adjutant—an assistant to the colonel— "must immediately order out the necessary number of fatigue men to dig the vaults or sinks." Thereafter, "the quartermaster must be answerable . . . that the sinks are filled up, and new ones dug every four days." And he told them who was responsible for making sure that it got done. "The preservation of the soldiers' health should be [the colonel's] first and greatest care; . . . he must have a watchful eye over the officers of companies, that they pay the necessary attention to their men."

Washington and his army kept moving and fighting, from Pennsylvania to New Jersey and back to New York. Putting down the rules of latrine care in black and white was a useful thing—a word to the wise and a reminder for the careless. But Washington still had to keep a watchful eye on the problem himself, to make sure the written rules were heeded. "The Commander-in-Chief," he wrote in April 1779, two weeks after Steuben's *Regulations* had been approved, "as the hot season approaches, expects . . . vaults to be properly dug . . . and sentries placed to see that the men make use of them only."

What is obvious to you as a leader may not be obvious to everybody; if it's necessary for the health of your organization, then it's necessary for you to keep after it.

THE POWER OF THE UNOBVIOUS

Establishing routine during a start-up can be easier than Washington's experience with latrines: both the goal and the means of accomplishing it are obvious, and people embrace the new job. But sometimes what everybody wants to do is wrong.

When Washington was trying to defend New York in the summer and fall of 1776, he realized he needed a "channel of information" about what the enemy was planning. Britain sent an immense land and sea force to Staten Island and New York Harbor, which cleared Washington out of Long Island at the end of August. In early September, he still held Manhattan, but he expected the British to attack him again, and he wanted to know when and how. "Everything . . . depends on intelligence of the enemy's motions," he wrote. "I was never more uneasy than on account of my want of knowledge on this score."

Nathan Hale, a twenty-one-year-old captain from Connecticut, volunteered to supply that knowledge. Hale was idealistic and handsome; no picture of him survives, but three detailed descriptions do, which agree that he was light-haired, blue-eyed, and well built. Although he was "fully sensible of the consequences of discovery"—spies were hanged—he thought he "owed to his country the accomplishment of an object . . . so much desired by the commander of her armies." Hale was to go to occupied Long Island disguised as a schoolteacher, observe the enemy's positions, then make his way back to American lines. His orderly didn't like the mission. "He was too good-looking. . . . He could not deceive. Some scrubby fellows ought to have gone." The orderly was right. Hale went to Long Island on a Monday, was arrested Saturday, and was executed Sunday, without making any reports. Hale failed as a spy, but his bravery made him the first hero of American intelligence, with statues at Yale, where he went to college, New York City, where he was hanged, and the headquarters of the CIA.

Washington approved the Hale mission because he had performed a similar one when he was the same age. In 1753, the colony of Virginia sent Major Washington, of the militia, to a fort that the French had just built in the upper Ohio Valley, in wilderness that Virginia claimed. He was to assert Virginia's title, and incidentally see what the French were up to. Because it was peacetime, Washington did not disguise himself and ran no risk of being hanged. But his hosts knew as well as he did that intelligence gathering was one of the goals of his visit. (The French, who were in a strong position, were not unwilling to be inspected.)

Two decades and one war later, as Alexander Rose, the modern expert on Washington's spies, writes, Washington had a simple view of intelligence, based on his youthful experience: when information is needed, send someone to get it and bring it back. But Hale's mission failed, as did others: brave young officers went into enemy territory, without learning very much, or died trying. These experiences led Washington to change his view.

The British conquered Manhattan shortly after they executed Hale, and held it for the rest of the war. It became their main base in occupied America, and a hub of military activity. Any moves they might make, by land or sea, would be planned there and launched from there. In 1778, Washington still wanted to spy on them—but his methods had changed. "Get some intelligent person into the city," he wrote, "and others of his choice to be messengers . . . for the purpose of conveying such information as he shall be able to obtain." What Washington now had in mind was a network of agents in place.

The officer who set it up for him was a college classmate of Hale's (Yale class of 1773), Benjamin Tallmadge. Tallmadge, a major in the dragoons, was from Setauket, a Long Island town fifty miles from New York. He recruited a cell of agents, mostly from his hometown— a quiet farmer, a daredevil whaler, a depressed merchant—who could learn things while doing legitimate business in the city, then convey it to Tallmadge. These were different men from Nathan Hale and the young George Washington. They were brave—they lived with incredible tension—and the "messengers" among them relished action: all their intel had to be smuggled from occupied Setauket across Long Island Sound. But they were secretive by nature, able to lead double lives as a matter of course.

Washington took a keen interest in the operation. He gave it its code name, Culper—an echo of Culpeper, a Virginia county he had surveyed as a teenager. He supplied his agents with state-of-the-art invisible ink, code-named "medicine," and told them how to use it: "[Write on] the blank leaves . . . of registers, almanacs, or any new publication. [Be guided by] the goodness of the blank paper, as the ink is not easily legible, unless it is on paper of a good quality." He authorized their expenses—five hundred pounds, by war's end—and advised them on maintaining their covers: "He will be able to carry on," he wrote of the merchant, "with greater security to himself and greater advantages to us, under cover of his usual business, than if he were to dedicate himself wholly to the giving of information." Clearly, Washington's own nature had secret chambers he was able to access.

In return, the Culper ring kept Washington informed of everything from British troop movements to the counterfeiting of American money. Their greatest coup came in July 1780, when they warned that the British were preparing to ambush a friendly French fleet that was on its way to Rhode Island. "Let not an hour pass," wrote the excited farmer, "for this day must not be lost you have news of the greatest consequence perhaps that ever happened to your country." In the event, bad weather kept the British surprise party from sailing. But Washington had been forewarned.

The British knew about the French fleet in the first place, thanks to a spy of their own: Major General Benedict Arnold, whose treason would be revealed two months later. If your organization competes with other organizations, they will be trying to learn to do everything that you are learning.

Washington became a skillful spymaster—a talent that commanders in chief, and even some civilians, must have. But he did it only by unlearning the experience of his youth, and ignoring what seemed so obvious to him, and to brave young officers like Nathan Hale.

THE POWER OF RULES

A start-up can be smoothed by rules or guidelines, provided by the relevant governing body: owners, directors, Congress.

The rules for the presidency had been written by the Constitutional Convention. Not everybody was happy with them. One of the delegates thought the president was too strong: "[His] powers are full great, and greater than I was disposed to make them." Another delegate thought he was too weak: "We are acting a very strange part. We first form a strong man to protect us, and at the same time wish to tie his hands behind him." The first reaction of Thomas Jefferson, who was not a delegate, was that the president would be "a bad edition of a Polish king." Since the kings of Poland in the late eighteenth century were both impotent and corrupt, this was quite a harsh judgment. Whatever the flaws of the job, eleven of the thirteen states approved it and the rest of the Constitution by the summer of 1788, and Washington took office the following April.

One of Washington's powers as president concerned foreign affairs. The president, says Article II, Section 2, of the Constitution, "shall have Power, by and with the Advice and Consent of the Senate, to make Treaties." The consent of the Senate is a straightforward concept, and the Constitution spells it out in the very next phrase: "two thirds of the Senators present" had to "concur." But how was Washington supposed to get the Senate's "advice"?

The first treaties Washington had to negotiate were with the "southern Indians"—Cherokees, Chickasaws, Chocktaws, and Creeks, who lived in the backcountry of Georgia and the Carolinas. These tribes could throw hundreds of warriors into battle if they chose and had their own relations with Britain and Spain; it was essential to be on their good side. One Saturday in August, Washington arrived at the Senate with Henry Knox, his secretary of war. We know what happened thanks to William Maclay, a senator who kept a diary. Washington "was introduced and took our president's chair." (The presiding officer of the Senate was—and is—the vice president of the United States.) Knox sat at Washington's left, Vice President John Adams to his right. Washington then "rose and told us bluntly that he had called on us for our advice and consent to some propositions respecting the treaties to be [made] with the southern Indians," and "said he had brought Gen. Knox with him who was well acquainted with the business." (Indian affairs were then handled by the War Department.) "Gen. Knox handed him a paper which he handed" to Adams to read.

Then came the first glitch. The Senate met on the second floor of Federal Hall, a building at the intersection of Wall and Broad Streets in New York City. New York, then the nation's capital, was one of the biggest cities in the country, and Wall and Broad was one of its busiest intersections. "Carriages were driving past," wrote Maclay, "and such a noise. I could tell it was something about Indians, but was not master of one sentence of it. Signs were made to the door keepers to shut down the sashes" of the windows. Adams read seven action items, and asked the Senate to vote up or down on the first one. Then came the second glitch. Robert Morris, another senator, "said the noise of carriages had been so great that he really could not say that he had heard the body of the paper which was read and prayed it might be read again. It was so." Adams asked the first question a second time. Third glitch. Maclay rose. "The paper you have read to us appears to have for its basis [older] treaties and public transactions. . . . The business is new to the Senate, it is of importance, it is our duty to inform ourselves as well as possible on the subject. I therefore call for the reading of the [other] treaties and . . . documents alluded to." As Maclay finished, he "cast an eye" at Washington, and "saw he wore an aspect of stern displeasure."

The session spun slowly and unstoppably out of control. ("The business labored" was how Maclay put it.) After much discussion, Adams asked once again for a vote, whereupon Morris moved that all the papers be "referred to a committee of five, to report as soon as might be on them." Pierce Butler, another senator, objected. "Committees were an improper mode of doing business, it threw business out of the hands of the many into the hands of the few, etc., etc." Maclay objected to the objection. "Committees were used in all public deliberative bodies, etc., etc. I thought I did the subject justice."

Now Washington objected. "The President of the United States started up in a violent fret. *This defeats every purpose of my coming here*, were the first words that he said. . . . He cooled however by degrees, [and] said he had no objections to putting the matter off."

On Sunday the Senate rested. Everyone was back in place on Monday, but the mood had changed. Washington, Maclay noted, now "wore a different aspect. . . . He was placid and serene, and manifested a spirit of accommodation." The mood had changed, but not the ways of the Senate. "A tedious debate took place." Even Maclay admitted that, by the time the Senate had finished giving its advice, "it was late." Washington rose and withdrew, having fulfilled his constitutional functions. But as he left the Senate chamber, the doorkeeper overheard him say he would "be damned if he ever went there again!"

He never went there again to seek the Senate's advice on a prospective treaty, nor has any president. Some presidents have asked in writing for the Senate's advice, while wise ones sound out powerful senators informally (Woodrow Wilson's failure to do so before negotiating the Versailles Treaty after World War I doomed the treaty when it came before the Senate). But although the Senate retains its power to reject treaties, in whole or part, the model of formal, personal consultation with the president fell by the wayside after the first trial.

Rules are useful in start-ups, but every rule needs a road test.

CHAPTER 2

STRATEGY

ALL LEADERS, in business or government, war or peace, have goals. General Washington's goal, as stated by Congress the day they picked him, was "the defence of American liberty." President Washington's goal, according to his oath of office, was to "preserve, protect and defend" the Constitution of the United States of America. The goal of the master of Mount Vernon was to make enough money to live in the style to which he expected to become accustomed.

Strategy is the leader's plan for achieving his goals, based on the resources at hand, the obstacles in his path, and the likely strategies of enemies or competitors.

EVERY STRATEGY IS GOOD

Every ambitious, self-confident person around a leader—including the leader himself—has a plan. And since every such person has some degree of talent or intelligence (otherwise they wouldn't be so close to the top), every one of their plans looks good, or at least reasonable. Picking a strategy is a trek among plausible options. It sometimes happens that they are all desperate options, because the underlying situation is dire. But even then, any strategy that floats to the surface has something to be said for it. Every strategy is good.

Historians, who live after the fact, know that multiplicity and uncertainty—multiplicity of choice, uncertainty of result—are the hardest features of any story to recover. We, who know what happened next, see, or think we see, what should have been done. But a leader in the moment cannot see; or, rather, he sees so clearly that he is dazzled. Everything should be done—because every strategy is good.

Our best access to the minds of leaders in history is today's news—not the accounts of what has just happened, which are already history's first draft, but everyone's attempts to predict or control tomorrow: the clamor of speeches, press conferences, reports, quotes, leaks, op-eds, talk-show chat. Soon it will all be history, but now it is all advice, and though everyone has his own favorites and rejects, it is surprising how few of these many plans are utterly senseless.

George Washington and his colleagues and comrades in the political and military elites of America had a half-dozen possible strategies for defending their liberty in the early years of the American Revolution. The fate of their country depended on making the right choice, but choosing was difficult, because every strategy was good.

The First Continental Congress, which met in Philadelphia in 1774 (Washington was a delegate from Virginia), hoped to change British policies by economic pressure, vowing not to import British goods and threatening to stop exporting American goods to Britain. Alexander Hamilton, a bright young man (he was still in college) who did not yet know Washington, though he would soon know him very well, wrote a glowing defense of economic warfare. "It is notorious that [Britain] is oppressed with a heavy national debt. . . . Her subjects are loaded with the most enormous taxes. . . . [A] suspension of [our trade] for any time must introduce beggary and wretchedness in an eminent degree." The nonimportation agreement didn't work—

Congress could not enforce compliance—but once real warfare began in the spring of 1775, trade ceased, except for smuggling, and patriots hoped for devastating economic effects. England's "strength," wrote the immigrant journalist Thomas Paine in 1777, was based on economic clout. "But as her finances and her credit are now low, her sinews in that line begin to fail fast. . . . [W]ere the whole kingdom and all that is in it to be put up to sale, like the estate of a bankrupt, it would not fetch as much as she owes."

Two of Washington's senior officers recommended a strategy of evasion and harassment. Horatio Gates was a veteran of the British army—he had fought in the French and Indian War—who resigned once he hit the glass ceiling of the class system (his mother had been housekeeper, perhaps mistress, to a duke). He settled in Virginia, and took the American side in the Revolution. He was a shrewd, cautious officer—his nickname was "Granny"—who believed in avoiding major encounters whenever possible. "Our business," he wrote, "is to defend the main chance; to attack only by detail, and when a precious advantage offers." A second Brit-turned-patriot filled in the outlines of Gates's strategy. Charles Lee, another French and Indian War veteran, had also freelanced for the king of Poland when that country was racked by virtual civil war (the fighting there, he recalled, was "about as gentle as ours was in America with the Shawnees and the Delawares"). Lee's rough-and-ready experiences led him to disdain what he called "Hyde Park tactics," the formalized movements of eighteenth-century armies that, he believed, were better suited to parade grounds than battlefields. He proclaimed his ideas in numerous letters, endless talk, and a report to Congress in 1778. "If the Americans are servilely kept to the European plan"—that is, drilled like a regular army—"they will make an awkward figure, be laughed at as a bad army by their enemy, and defeated in every *rencontre* [encounter] which depends on maneuvers." The idea that "a decisive action in fair ground may be risked is talking nonsense. . . . [H]arassing and impeding can alone succeed." Washington had fought alongside both men in the French and Indian War; he was a neighbor of Gates's, and, like everyone else, he was impressed with Lee's passionate seriousness. Both men, finally, had a credit on their résumés that few native-born Americans ever got (Washington never had it)—a commission in the British army.

One of the first battles of the war suggested a third strategy. In June 1775, two and a half weeks before Washington arrived to take command of the troops besieging Boston, the British attacked an American position on a hilltop overlooking Charlestown, northwest of the city. The British marched uphill, without artillery cover—the ships that were supposed to provide it could not come in close enough to shore—toward men who were dug in behind fences. They took the position, but only on the third try and after losing nine hundred men killed or wounded (American losses were about a third as heavy). The Battle of Bunker Hill suggested a strategy of defending strong points—a war of posts. Washington acknowledged the popularity of this strategy when he reminded Congress, in a 1776 letter, "I have never spared the spade and pickax."

Another popular strategy was perimeter defense—guarding the borders wherever they were threatened. For a magic moment after the British evacuated Boston in the spring of 1776, there was not one of His Majesty's soldiers in all of the thirteen colonies. Why not keep it that way? Of all the strategies that made their way to Washington, this came closest to being utterly senseless—he had barely enough resources to defend anyplace, much less everyplace—but it was repeatedly recommended to him by political expediency. How could Americans be asked to support a cause that would abandon them to the enemy? So, in September 1776, as the British were preparing to attack New York, and Washington's young general Nathanael Greene advised him to burn it and leave it, though Washington may have known that Greene was militarily right (since Manhattan, an island surrounded by navigable rivers, was indefensible), he also knew that in republics, what is politically right must be heeded.

Washington's own instinct was always to attack. He never read the *Aeneid*, Virgil's epic about the founding of Rome, but he didn't have to to believe that *audentis fortuna iuvat*—fortune favors the bold. In 1754, when he was twenty-two years old, he started the French and Indian War by firing on a party of Frenchmen in the wilderness. That clash was soon followed by his first drubbing, which began a long education in prudence. But two decades later he still yearned for the fight, the showdown, that would settle it all. At one point, during the siege of Boston, he considered sending his soldiers into the city on ice skates.

If the war went badly, there was a final course to consider. As part of the harassment strategy, Charles Lee suggested pulling the army beyond the Susquehanna River, to central Pennsylvania. In case of disaster, Washington considered retreating even farther, beyond the Alleghenies to western Virginia. "In the worst event," he wrote his brother-in-law early in 1776, it would be "an asylum." Like the Indians, Washington would go west, fighting all the way.

Faced with this array of strategies, Washington displayed an aspect of his leadership that was as deeply ingrained as the urge to fight: a disposition to consider his options. Years later, Thomas Jefferson wrote that this was "perhaps the strongest feature in his character . . . never acting until every circumstance, every consideration was maturely weighed." While the weighing was going on, bystanders could mistake it for hesitation. "The General does want [for] decision," Nathanael Greene once remarked. "For my part," he added pertly, "I decide in a moment." With the fate of the army, and the country, on his shoulders, Washington was willing to take an extra moment.

In the search for the proper strategy, he took years, trying most of the available options, or aspects of them, looking for the right mix. Economic warfare was a fact of life, mostly beyond his control, though he did, somewhat counterintuitively, tolerate a fair amount of smuggling between British-occupied cities and the patriotic country-side, not least because it was a way to introduce spies. He never ac-cepted the conclusions that Charles Lee drew from the harassment strategy—Washington always wanted professional, well-trained troops—though he was as mindful as Lee and Gates of the need for caution in going head-to-head with the British. Some of his experi-ence with posts and perimeter defense was disastrous, particularly his failed attempt to defend New York City in 1776. Once Manhattan fell, however, he made good use of the highlands of northern New Jersey and southern New York—nature's posts, from which he could keep an eye on the enemy and keep him pinned down; much of his time during the last half of the war was spent in feints and maneuvers designed to draw the British out of position, or to prevent himself from being drawn. Always he looked for possible attacks. Some never happened: he could not find the knockout blow that would retake New York. One was brilliant. In October 1781 the golden opportunity presented itself. A British army under Lord Cornwallis had marched to the Virginia coast, awaiting resupply by sea. Two French fleets, one French army, and two American armies converged, from as far away as Rhode Island and the West Indies, in a miracle of timing and logis-tics, and scooped the British up. It had taken only six years. Fortune favors the bold, and the patient. Washington would not have to con-sider option six, the flight to West Virginia.

Many leaders do not have a long time scale. Shareholders, analysts, or constituents may demand quick results. Some leaders may not feel the need to take time, believing they have the right strategy from the beginning. Whatever the case, a leader must know that he will encounter a variety of choices; he should realize that the people who advocate them, although they may be wrong, are not necessarily stupid, and he should expect, if they are malicious—*We would have won if we had followed my plan*—that they can make a plausible case. Fortune favors the bold, the patient, and the well prepared.

WHEN THE WORLD CHANGES, CHANGE THE WORLD

Finding the right strategy depends on your character and needs, and the needs of those around you. But it also depends on the world in which you operate. Two great environmental changes, as drastic as the arrival of an ice age, happened during Washington's life, one when he was a planter, the other when he was a retired postwar hero. In each case he responded to a change in the world by changing his strategy.

Washington inherited Mount Vernon in 1761, after the last of his elder half brother's family died (he had been renting it for six years before that). Retired from the militia and newly married to a rich widow, the master of Mount Vernon threw himself into cultivating tobacco. Virginians had been growing quality tobacco since 1612, when they imported from South America the seeds of *Nicotiana tabacum*, which produces a milder leaf than *Nicotiana rusticam*, the local weed. People liked what Virginians were smoking. By 1700, Virginia and Maryland were exporting twenty-eight million pounds of tobacco to England every year.

Tobacco was a demanding crop, requiring tender, loving care at every stage from planting to packing. Seeds went in the ground, in small beds of enriched soil, in late December or early January (twelve days after Christmas was the traditional planting date). The seedlings were transplanted to the main fields, each into its own little hill of dirt, when the leaves were the size of a silver dollar, around April. As the plants filled out, they were topped, to prevent them from flowering. In

September they were harvested. Then they had to be dried, or cured, in barns (not too dry, or they would crumble; not too damp, or they would rot). Cured leaves were stripped from the plant and their stems removed, then pressed or prized together in hogsheads weighing half a ton. By then, the new seeds were going into the ground. Planters oversaw all these operations, since the quality of their crops and their own reputations depended on it. Successful planters were awarded titles redolent of feudalism, almost of myth—crop masters, lords of the soil. T. H. Breen, the modern scholar of Virginia tobacco planting, compares it to wine-making: "The quality of a man's tobacco" was "the measure of the man."

Washington bought more land to grow more tobacco to make more money, and to increase his measure. From 1760 to 1772, he acquired 3,700 tidewater acres, more than doubling his plantation holdings. More land meant more slaves to work it: over the same period, his adult slaves at Mount Vernon more than doubled, from forty-three to ninety-five.

But there was trouble for the crop master of Mount Vernon. One problem was that his tobacco did not quite make the grade. The soil of Mount Vernon, on the Potomac River, was thinner and poorer than the soil of plantations on the Rappahannock, York, and James Rivers farther south. Drought baked it; storms washed it away. "Our plants," he wrote in 1762, "in spite of all our efforts to the contrary are just destroyed." When his plants survived, their leaves were not valued as highly as he wished. "I am at a loss to conceive the reason," he wrote his British middleman, "why . . . some other gentlemen's tobaccos should sell at 12 pence last year and mine . . . only fetch $11\,{}^{1}/_{2}$."

Another factor weighing on Washington was a credit crunch that hit all Virginia tobacco planters hard. Until the middle of the eighteenth century, British merchants offered their Virginia suppliers easy terms, and their own services as personal shoppers (the merchants would take orders for luxury goods, and charge them to the planters' accounts). When the merchants felt squeezed, they passed the pain on to the planters, who were by now their debtors.

There was a third factor dragging Washington down as a planter, and that was his spending. He could not stop ordering carriages, china, clothes (the catchphrase that he and other Virginians used to describe what they wanted, not knowing exactly the latest trends across the Atlantic, was "neat and fashionable"). But this was expected of a man in his station in life. In 1764 Washington owed merchant Robert Cary almost 2,000 pounds, a large sum for a colonial who was land rich but cash poor.

All his peers bought the same goods at the same prices. All suffered alike from the credit crunch. But some made more from their tobacco. Washington was never an economist; the workings of international markets were mysterious to him, as they were to all Virginians. But, unlike many Virginians, Washington could look at his own balance sheets without blinking. In 1766 he decided to stop growing tobacco at Mount Vernon.

There followed a burst of diversification, which continued for the rest of his life. He planted alfalfa, buckwheat, corn, flax, hemp. ("I GREW HEMP" says the slogan that potheads stencil over Washington's head on dollar bills. So he did, though these plants were not for smoking.) He grew wheat, an easy and lucrative crop, which he sold locally and shipped to Europe and the West Indies. He fished the Potomac, and sent his catches to Antigua. He even kept growing tobacco on York River properties owned by his wife, which had better soil. But it was only one crop among many.

Successful businessmen often change their business in midcareer. In the early nineteenth century John Jacob Astor, America's first millionaire, switched from fur trading to New York City real estate; in midcentury, Cornelius Vanderbilt moved from shipping, which had given him the title Commodore, to railroads. Washington's switch was tougher, because it risked his prestige. By abandoning the cultivation of tobacco, he stepped outside the tobacco culture, surrendering his status as planter, crop master, and lord of the soil and becoming instead a farmer—a rich farmer, to be sure, though the term had, to older Virginian ears, a humbler sound. But the new regime at Mount Vernon kept him, for at least a decade, from sliding deeper into the hole of debt. "Many families," he observed in 1769, "are reduced, almost, if not quite, to penury and want, from the low ebb of their fortunes." Among those families, as the years passed, would be Thomas Jefferson's and James Monroe's. Washington could have kept banging his head against a wall, trying to wring new perfections out of an already perfected process. Instead, he tried a new world.

A second transformation of Washington's environment occurred after the Revolution. It was a public matter, concerning the political structure of the country, and Washington's status as its hero.

Everyone knew, as the Revolution ended, that they had witnessed something remarkable, almost unprecedented—not just the overthrow of an old government but also the refusal to overthrow the new one. The almost universal experience of great generals and the republics they served was that the generals replaced the republics. Julius Caesar tried it in ancient times; Oliver Cromwell had done it in England a century earlier. General George Washington hadn't, and everyone, at home and abroad, was impressed. The Marquis de Chastellux, a French officer and political scientist, made Washington's self-discipline and service the high points of a book he wrote about the new country, *Travels in North America*, in 1782: "This is the seventh year that he has commanded the army, and he has obeyed Congress: more need not be said." But what if Congress failed?

Washington offered his parting thoughts on the future of America in June 1783. (He would resign his commission after the peace treaty was signed, and the last British troops evacuated, in December.) A few things had to happen to make the United States "respectable and prosperous." There had to be a "supreme power" to regulate the common business of the republic. The main item of common business was "public justice," or paying the country's debts. This elementary task of government had fallen by the wayside. America owed money to investors who had bought its bonds; more important to Washington, it owed money to the men who had given it their time and blood—the army. As recently as March, Washington had talked his unpaid officers out of mutinying. He had held them to their duty; now he was calling on the government to do its.

The form of government under which Washington had fought and won the Revolution was Congress, a one-house legislature without an executive or a judiciary. Typically, countries ruled by such lonely bodies are prone to mood swings and power grabs (a few years later, revolutionary France, ruled by the one-house National Assembly, would suffer from both disorders). Congress, by contrast, suffered from impotence and paralysis—because it was not in fact lonely at the top but was actually beholden to the legislatures of the thirteen states. The state legislatures picked the delegates to Congress, and the state legislatures collected, or refused to collect, the taxes that Congress requested. On paper (and occasionally in reality) Congress could do many things: declare war, make peace, run post offices, deal with Indians, commission George Washington. But its members and its money came from the state legislatures—which had shown themselves to be self-interested, and tightfisted. What is more, any change to that fundamental power structure required the unanimous approval of those very legislatures. In his parting words, Washington was suggesting that this state of affairs had to be modified.

Fighting a war had allowed everyone to postpone the ultimate reckoning to peacetime. Perhaps Congress and the state legislatures could now put their houses in order. But as the years passed, it became clear that this would not happen. The United States was not paying the interest on its debts; American paper was junk, trading at a quarter to a third of its face value in European money markets. Congress asked the state legislatures to allow it to collect tariffs, and thus raise some money on its own; two states vetoed the plan. One state's efforts to haul itself out of debt caused a conflagration: in 1786 Daniel Shays, a former army captain, led an uprising of Massachusetts farmers crushed by a state land tax. Washington followed events from Mount Vernon with dismay. "Thirteen sovereignties pulling against each other, and all tugging at the federal head, will bring ruin on the whole."

Washington was not the only American leader who thought so; a cadre of politicians, especially younger ones whose careers began during the Revolution, agreed. They had been trying for months, first to give Congress a revenue stream, then, failing that, to call a convention of the states, approved by but independent of their legislatures, to propose reform. One of the most energetic was James Madison, a young Virginia politician, wily and tireless, who was the recipient of Washington's letter about the thirteen tugging sovereignties. Madison was both a member of the Virginia legislature and a delegate to Congress, and wearing both hats he, and like-minded politicians in other states, engineered a call for a convention to meet in Philadelphia in May 1787.

Washington spent much of the late winter and early spring of 1786–1787 deciding whether he would go. He raised a number of objections—he was retired, he wasn't feeling well—which, in cold black and white, seem fussy, or, as Nathanael Greene had said, wanting for decision. Certainly, he was concerned about his own image. Four years earlier he had retired from public life, to the applause of the world; what would the world think if he came back? But beneath these considerations was a larger one: he wanted to be sure that Madison and all the other reformers were truly on board, and that there was a prospect of success. If everyone was going to Philadelphia to talk, he might as well stay home. "Like a house on fire," he wrote another friend in February 1787, "whilst the most regular mode of extinguishing it is contending for, the building is reduced to ashes." Once he moved, he would move. By March, partly because Madison had been supplying him with likely vote counts of all the delegations to the convention picked so far, Washington was convinced that Philadelphia would be for real. He arrived in May, ahead of the official starting day, and waited impatiently for his fellow delegates to show up.

The paper trail of Washington's decision to attend the Constitutional Convention foreshadows the making of another famous decision—Dwight Eisenhower's to launch the Normandy invasion in June 1944. The armada was assembled; Eisenhower watched the tides and the weather. Though the conditions were not perfect, on June 5 he gave the word: "O.K., let's go." It was a command so laconic it seems almost inaudible. Washington's private correspondence is more wordy, but his style is so lacking in flourishes, or uses such conventional ones, that it too resists calling attention to itself. Both leaders kept their eye on the moment of action—because acting was a serious thing. Jefferson described Washington's decision making well: "Refraining if he saw a doubt, but, when once decided, going through with his purpose, whatever obstacles opposed." Going to Philadelphia in 1787 would fill up Washington's life for the next decade—because once the convention met, a new constitution would have to be written, and once it was written, it would have to be ratified, and once it was ratified, the office of executive would have to be filled. When Washington changed his strategy and the world, he did not shrink from the consequences of his choice.

Finding the right strategy for changing conditions always takes a major investment of thought and action, and often the new strategy changes the conditions yet more. A leader must be flexible enough to leave old worlds, and tough enough to survive in new ones.

CHAPTER 3

The Future

WASHINGTON TENDED to look on the dark side of things, especially things that might lie in the future, and indeed the future often brought dark things to pass. There were four world wars in his lifetime: one of his half brothers fought in the first; he fought in the next two, and prepared to fight in the last.

His favorite philosopher, the Roman Seneca, assured him that nothing bad can happen to a wise man, because he already expects and accepts every possible loss. Fortune may take his "servants, possessions, dignity; assault his body, put out his eyes, cut off his hands. . . . But what does all this amount to, more than the recalling of a trust, which he has received, with condition to deliver it up again upon demand?" Such thoughts may give strength to the wise man, in his dealings between himself and fate. But leaders have responsibilities, to shareholders, troops, constituents. Before telling them to cheer up, all is lost, a leader is obliged to prepare for bad contingencies.

Anticipation

There were some problems Washington could see coming, and take steps to avoid. One problem was his, and America's, greatest opportunity—western land.

Washington's first view of the West came when he made a two-month trip, age sixteen, over the Blue Ridge Mountains into the Shenandoah Valley, to survey property that belonged to his rich in-laws, the Fairfaxes. Now the Shenandoah Valley is a tourist destination and a beauty spot. In the 1740s it was frontier, the edge of the West, a strange-enough place that the teenager from the tidewater flatlands kept a journal of his trip. He slept under a verminous blanket and on straw that caught fire, saw wild turkeys and a rattlesnake, waited by a river swollen with snowmelt. From the moment he crossed the mountains, he took note of the land. "We went through the most beautiful groves of sugar trees [sugar maples] and spent the best part of the day in admiring the trees and richness of the land." This was not the reaction of an aesthete or a nature lover, though Washington had elements of both in his makeup. It was the judgment of an aspiring landowner.

American history is the history of a land rush (which continues in the real estate market today). In Washington's lifetime Americans moved from the East Coast over the first mountain barriers. The passage was difficult, but land-hungry Americans were insatiable. British efforts to control this migration helped cause the Revolution; one of the Declaration of Independence's complaints against George III was that he "rais[ed] the conditions" for "new appropriations of lands." Americans won their freedom, including the freedom to move. The long march to the Pacific was well under way.

The engine of this land rush was economic. Poor Americans wanted a stake of their own; rich ones wanted to become richer by acquiring large tracts and selling or renting them off in pieces to the hopeful poor. (Washington became one of those rich ones himself.) But the movement of so many people beyond the mountains raised political questions that could not be ignored. In 1785, Washington addressed them in a letter to a fellow easterner. "New states," he predicted, "are rising to our view in the regions back of us." Though people could cross the Alleghenies, crops or goods could not, easily or cheaply; anything westerners grew or made would have to go "to the Spaniards southwardly" (down the Mississippi to New Orleans) "or the British northwardly" (through the Great Lakes and the St. Lawrence to Montreal) in order to reach consumers. In that case, westerners would identify with their middlemen, not their country of origin, becoming "quite a distinct people." In time, they "may be very troublesome neighbours to us." This might happen, Washington added, "merely" because they were "a hardy race [people]." Though he had no natural sympathy for frontiersmen—he called the squatters he met in the Shenandoah Valley "ignorant"—he had, through long experience, learned to know their qualities, bad and good, and he knew that tractability was not one of them. "How much more" troublesome would they be "if linked with either of those powers"—Spain or Britain—"in politics and commerce?"

Washington's solution was inland navigation. "Interest," he wrote, is "the only cement that will bind." The interest of westerners would be served "by opening such communications as will make it easier and cheaper for them to bring the product of their labour to our markets." That could be done by making Virginia's longest rivers, the James and the Potomac, navigable all the way to their sources in the Alleghenies, then linking them with rivers that flowed west and south. A farmer in Kentucky or Ohio could then ship his crops to Alexandria, Virginia, rather than New Orleans or Montreal. In the 1780s Washington became a zealot on the subject, talking it up to anyone who visited Mount Vernon. "The General sent the bottle about pretty freely after dinner," one guest wrote, "and gave success to the navigation of the Potomac for his toast." He also cemented his own interest to the project, buying stock in companies that planned to improve the rivers, and looking forward, if the Potomac became an inland waterway, to seeing the value of Mount Vernon skyrocket. Washington expected his fellow Americans to be hardheaded because he was hardheaded himself. But the national interest, and the political problem that threatened it, was never far from his mind.

His worries for the nation's unity were not idle. Throughout the 1790s Kentuckians threatened to attack the Spaniards or work for them; they weren't sure which. When western Pennsylvanians became unhappy with their taxes, they sent feelers to the governor-general of Canada. One of Washington's comrades in the Revolution, General James Wilkinson, moved to Kentucky and became a secret agent of the king of Spain, earning $2,000 a year for twenty years to keep watch on the American West.

Washington was wrong about the James and the Potomac, which were simply too hard to tame, but he was right about inland navigation and its effects. The passage to the West was actually made in upstate New York, by digging a canal from the Hudson River to Lake Erie, which opened the heart of the continent to the world, and bound the Midwest, the Great Lakes, and New York City together. (The leaders of that effort would be Washington's friend Gouverneur Morris and New York governor DeWitt Clinton.) In time, the United States would split apart, but it would not be west from east, and it would not be for lack of infrastructure. Intelligent forethought, based on human nature and the natural environment, helped to head off some problems before they arrived.

Another problem Washington saw coming, related to western land, was the people who already lived on it.

On his teenage trip to the Shenandoah Valley he met a party of thirty Indians. The white men he was traveling with gave them some liquor, "which put them in the humor of dancing," and he wrote a long description of their performance in his journal, in which condescension (their jumping was "comical") and appreciation (their gourd rattle had a horse's tail tied to it "to make it look fine") are inextricably mixed. He also noted that the Indians were a war party, and carried "only one scalp."

He would meet many more Indian war parties during his life, fighting alongside him or firing at him, and would learn that Indian wars were long, expensive, and deadly. They became likely for the same reason that made inland navigation necessary—the flow of Americans west. Preventing Indian wars whenever possible was one of the goals of Washington's presidency.

He believed that it was better to buy land than fight for it. "That it is the cheapest as well as the least distressing way of dealing with them, none who are acquainted with the nature of Indian warfare . . . will hesitate to acknowledge." This is what brought him to the Senate in August 1789 to discuss possible treaties with the southern Indians. As a result of his efforts, a delegation of Creek Indians came from Georgia to New York City in July 1790 to sign a treaty.

The chief was Alexander McGillivray. His father was a Scottish merchant, and his mother's father a French officer, but his mother's mother belonged to a powerful Creek clan, which gave McGillivray his entrée to leadership in a matrilineal culture. He had served as a British colonel during the Revolution, and took money from Spain after the war. Getting him to New York required almost a year of preliminary negotiations and false starts. When he finally arrived, Washington and Secretary of War Henry Knox then offered him $10,000 plus an annual payment for a contested 3 million–acre parcel, a guarantee of other Creek lands, and a private subsidy to McGillivray personally, along with the rank of brigadier general. The chief agreed. By means of such arrangements, Washington tried to split the difference between white land hunger and Indian independence.

Such methods did not always work. Washington was able to negotiate a treaty with the Seneca Indians in upstate New York. But the Indians of Ohio ("bad Indians," Washington called them in a proclamation addressed to the Senecas) were not amenable, especially since the British in nearby Canada egged them on. America had to fight an Indian war after all, and Washington had to go through three generals before it was successful. Of Josiah Harmar, the first general, he wrote: "I expected *little* from the moment I heard he was *a drunkard*. I expected *less* as soon as I heard that *on this account* no confidence was reposed in him by the people of the western country. And I gave up *all hope* of success, as soon as I heard that there were disputes with *him* about command." Arthur St. Clair, Harmar's successor, was no better. Finally, Washington turned to Anthony Wayne, nicknamed Mad Anthony. "More active," Washington noted, ". . . than judicious and cautious. No economist, it is feared. Open to flattery, vain, easily imposed upon, and liable to be drawn into scrapes. . . . Whether sober or a little addicted to the bottle I know not." Whatever his flaws, Wayne was a fighter. After the Battle of Fallen Timbers, near present-day Toledo, the Indians of Ohio finally signed a treaty of their own.

The treaty with McGillivray finally fell apart when the Spaniards offered him better terms, though no major war followed, because he died in 1793 of alcoholism and syphilis.

Avoiding Indian wars was harder than digging canals. Trying to balance the interests of settlers and Indians always ran the risk of thwarting either side. It also left later presidents to make their own calculations of interest, which would be less generous than Washington's. He did the best he could for the years that he served.

Sometimes a leader can see far ahead and act accordingly; sometimes dealing with the day after tomorrow is all the anticipation that a leader can manage. Whatever he does, a leader has to be interested in the future—because the future is interested in him.

SURPRISE

Some problems are extrapolations of present trends, reappearances of familiar events. We see them approaching miles off and months ahead of time, like comets. Others come with the speed of a crank call. Men who make revolutions expect to fight enemies, not smallpox, but in 1775 Washington found himself doing both.

There had been an outbreak of smallpox in eastern Massachusetts in February 1774. Boston was suffering from it when it was besieged by American militias in the spring of 1775; one refugee from the occupied city reported ten to thirty funerals a day.

The British army knew how to deal with smallpox. Because England was a small, populous country with numerous cities and towns, many Englishmen had been exposed to the disease; if you caught it and lived, you were immune for life. When smallpox appeared in the British army, regimental surgeons pulled aside all men who had not been exposed, and inoculated them. Inoculation involved deliberately inducing the disease and keeping the patients quarantined until they lived or died; the mortality rate from inoculation was much lower than from catching smallpox naturally. (Vaccination—infecting with non-lethal cowpox—had not yet been invented.) Survivors of inoculation were fit for duty, and safe from further attacks.

America had experience with inoculation—Cotton Mather, the Puritan minister, had introduced it to Boston in the 1720s—but it was never popular. Since America was large, sparsely populated, and rural, people bet that they would never be exposed, and preferred not to take the risk of inoculation, however slight. That meant that when smallpox appeared, however, its ravages would be greater, and greater still in an army of soldiers drawn from thousands of farms, in several states.

Washington had experience with smallpox, for he had caught it on his youthful trip to Barbados in 1751. Because Barbados was as strange to him as the Shenandoah Valley, he had kept a journal of this trip, too, in which he noted, after two days on the island, that he and his half brother accepted a dinner invitation "with some reluctance" because the host's family was suffering from smallpox. Two weeks later he was "strongly attacked" by the disease, and made no more entries for a month until he recovered. Young Washington's case of smallpox had given him light scars on his nose that he carried for the rest of his life, as well as immunity. But now he was responsible for the health of thousands of men, in a country where organized prevention was unknown.

In his first General Orders, July 2, 1775, Washington instituted a quarantine: poxed soldiers were sent to a hospital at Fresh Pond in Cambridge; no one else was allowed to go there, for "fishing or on any other occasion." Refugees from Boston were not allowed in camp; letters from Boston were dipped in vinegar to disinfect them.

In the static situation of a siege—eight and a half months from Washington's arrival to the British departure—the quarantine worked. When the Americans were on the move, however, smallpox had its chance. Late in 1775, Washington approved a two-pronged invasion of Canada. One army under Richard Montgomery went along Lake Champlain to Montreal, then down the St. Lawrence; another under Benedict Arnold struggled up the Kennebec River in Maine, then down the Chaudière. The two armies met before Quebec, which they failed to take in a desperate attack on New Year's Eve. Whether advancing or retreating, they were ravaged by smallpox. Panicky soldiers tried inoculating themselves and only spread the disease faster. "It is a very dying time," wrote one American. "The lice and maggots" on the sick "seem to vie with each other," wrote another.

Washington spent 1776 leading the main American army from Boston to New York to the Delaware River, before it finally went into winter quarters in Morristown in northern New Jersey. It fought five battles; shrank from death, desertion, and expiring enlistments; and swelled again with new recruits. In January 1777 Washington noticed that smallpox had reappeared in camp. "I find it impossible to keep it spreading through the whole army in the natural way [that is, by quarantine]," he wrote in February. He therefore ordered inoculations at Morristown, and at recruiting centers in the mid-Atlantic states. "Inoculate your men as fast as they are enlisted."

Washington spent the next winter at Valley Forge, outside Philadelphia. By now, the army was changing from ever-new recruits serving short terms to veterans signed up for the long haul. Nevertheless, Washington found that thousands of his men had not been exposed to smallpox, and "the disorder began to make its appearance." Even though the troops suffered from bad food and a host of other ailments, he ordered more inoculations. By spring, he told recruiters to send their new men to Valley Forge immediately, to be inoculated there: that way, he got his reinforcements as soon as possible, and spared them from making a long march after their bouts of smallpox.

The whole program had to be carried out secretly, lest the British attack while sick Americans waited their illness out. (In one month, March 1778, one-third of the troops at Valley Forge were inoculated, or sick from other diseases.) Henry Lee, one of Washington's cavalry officers, guessed they were half done before the British learned what was going on.

Washington had accomplished what historian Elizabeth Fenn calls "the first large-scale, state-sponsored immunization campaign in American history." He reaped the benefits over the years of active fighting that lay ahead. As the fortunes of war shifted south, units of the American army crisscrossed hundreds of miles in four states. Smallpox erupted among civilians, militias, and escaped slaves. The slaves ran for freedom from patriot masters to the British army. But if they had smallpox, the British turned them into delivery systems for biological warfare. "About 700 Negroes are come down the river in the small pox," General Alexander Leslie wrote Lord Cornwallis in July 1781. "I shall distribute them about the rebel plantations." In all this turmoil and unexpected death, American soldiers, inoculated by their commander in chief, maintained their effectiveness. When a new problem sat down beside him, Washington improvised new solutions, through trial and error, and saved his men and the cause.

No leader ever knows exactly what is coming, or all the things he should prepare for. He can, however, know that he doesn't know, and prepare mentally for that. Be light on your feet, because you will be moving a lot.

CHAPTER 4

SMALL STUFF

EVERYONE KNOWS the feeling of drowning in minutiae. *What is all this junk? Why can't we just get the job done? Why can't we all get along?* The impulse to cut through can feel volcanic. It has produced a myth: the story of Alexander the Great slashing, instead of trying to untie, the Gordian knot. Slashing is often the right thing to do; so is leaving the details to others. Thomas Jefferson served with George Washington in the Virginia House of Burgesses, the colonial legislature, and remembered that, as a lawmaker, he laid his shoulder "to the great points, knowing that the little ones would follow of themselves." The alternative, Jefferson wrote, was to get swept up in "the morbid rage of debate."

No one likes morbid rage, especially other people's. But there are times when the little points are in fact great ones, and a leader must lay his shoulder to them.

RESPECT

In July 1776 dozens of man-hours of the British and American general staffs were consumed by the address on a letter.

Washington had the Declaration of Independence read to his troops, then in New York, on July 9. Three days later an enormous British expeditionary force sailed into New York Harbor and began disembarking on Staten Island.

The British were commanded by two brothers, General Sir William and Admiral Lord Richard Howe. Through a grandmother who had been a royal mistress, the Howes were cousins of George III. After fighting in the French and Indian War, they were elected to Parliament, where they took a liberal, pro-American line. Lord Richard once chewed out the king for his "invincible obstinacy" on the American question, while William wrote his constituents that the colonies would return to obedience once they were "relieved from the grievance" of taxation. In 1775, however, George III asked the Howes to join the war effort, and they agreed. They arrived in America with military commands, to which was added a commission to negotiate peace, if possible.

Two days after the British landed on Staten Island, Admiral Lord Howe sent a boat under a flag of truce toward Manhattan. It was stopped halfway across the harbor, and three American officers went aboard. The British boat carried a letter to Washington, hoping for "peace and lasting union between Great Britain and America," and proposing further discussions. The Americans didn't know that, however, because they never opened the letter. When they saw that it was addressed to "George Washington Esq. &c. &c. &c.," they said "there was no such person among them," since their commander was General George Washington. A second letter from General Howe two days later, similarly addressed, met the same fate.

Finally, on July 20, a British barge flying a flag of truce delivered Lieutenant Colonel James Patterson, adjutant general of the army, to Manhattan, where he met with Washington, whose own adjutant general wrote a report of the occasion. Colonel Patterson said that

General Howe "much regretted the difficulties which had arisen respecting the address of the letters. . . . Lord Howe and Gen. Howe [had] not mean[t] to derogate from the respect or rank of Gen. Washington." They could speak of Washington as a general, apparently, but they couldn't write it down. "The addition of &c. &c. &c. implied everything that ought to follow." Patterson then laid the same letter, addressed in the same way, on the table. Washington declined to take it, saying that "a letter directed to a person in a public character should have some description or indication of it, otherwise it would be a mere private letter," and that he would "absolutely decline any letter directed to him as a private person when it related to his public station." He agreed that the etceteras "implied every thing," but suggested that was not good enough: "they also implied any thing."

Patterson, giving up, delivered the contents of General Howe's letter orally. Most of it concerned the treatment and exchange of prisoners, though he ended with the point that Admiral Howe had tried to make in the first letter: the king had appointed the Howe brothers "to accommodate this unhappy dispute." Washington answered that he himself "was not vested with any powers on this subject by those from whom he derived his authority" (meaning Congress). He understood that the Howes had the power to grant pardons, but "those who had committed no fault wanted to pardon. . . . [W]e were only defending what we deemed our indisputable rights." Patterson observed, "That would open a very wide field for argument." Washington offered the colonel a snack, which the colonel refused, and "with a great deal of marked attention and civility" (Patterson's words), the meeting ended.

Washington and the Howe brothers had more than protocol on their minds. Five weeks after the meeting with Colonel Patterson, the two armies met on the eastern end of Long Island, in what is now Brooklyn, in the first battle of American independence, and the largest encounter of the war so far. Twenty-two thousand British and

Hessian troops engaged 11,000 Americans in the Battle of Long Island, and administered a crushing defeat. Washington lost 300 killed and 1,100 captured, as opposed to 63 killed and none captured on the enemy side. "The Hessians and our brave Highlanders gave no quarter," wrote a British officer afterward, "and it was a fine thing to see with what alacrity they despatched the rebels with their bayonets." If Washington had paid a little less attention to etceteras, could he have paid a little more attention to the task at hand?

Washington made a number of mistakes before the battle, shuffling units and commanders confusingly, since he could not decide whether Long Island was a feint or the main show, and ignoring the importance of cavalry as an early warning system, thus allowing the British to slip around his flank and attack his forward line from behind. All the attention in the world could not have improved the underlying situation, since the British outnumbered him in total forces by more than three to two, and their soldiers were all professionals, while most of his were still amateurs. As summer turned to fall, Washington would be driven out of New York City, and New York State entirely.

But the words on the flap of a letter were also important, because they defined the terms of the contest. For all their liberalism and their willingness to negotiate, the Howe brothers were ex officio incapable of treating Washington as anything other than a gentleman outlaw. He might be an esquire, but he could not be a general, at least on paper. That meant that his soldiers were common outlaws, and his civilian superiors in Congress were outlaw politicians. Washington took the view that if you cannot call me by my right name, we cannot talk. Respect for him was respect for his cause, and for "those from whom he derived his authority." Americans knew what he meant. The adjutant's account of the meeting was printed in the newspapers, and Congress directed all other commanders to emulate Washington, who had "acted with a dignity becoming his station."

After the Battle of Long Island, the Howes tried another negotiation. This time they sent a messenger (a paroled American prisoner) to Congress, which sent Benjamin Franklin, John Adams, and Edward Rutledge to Staten Island to meet General Howe. He had nothing substantive to offer, however, and the conference ended after a few hours. Americans would talk to their enemies throughout the war, mostly about prisoners, until the final talks in Paris that ratified independence.

By attending to details, a leader can make clear who is talking and what he is talking about—essential preliminaries for planning, and action.

AUTHORITY

In his polite wrangle with the Howes in 1776, Washington explained that he served Congress. In 1793, when he was president, he had to consider where to put Congress when the capital was uninhabitable.

Yellow fever is a disease of the tropics, first observed in the West Indies in the seventeenth century, but it occasionally appeared in North America. In August 1793 it struck Philadelphia, which had replaced New York as the capital. Refugees from the Haitian revolution arrived that summer bearing the disease, and mosquitoes, thick after a rainy spring, spread it. But no one at the time understood yellow fever's causes or transmission. The death rate in Philadelphia, normally three to five a day, rose to a dozen, then two dozen. Alexander Hamilton, the treasury secretary, and his wife, Eliza, came down with the fever, but lived. Polly Lear, wife of the president's personal secretary, died of it.

Washington was not one of the heroes of the epidemic. He left town, along with almost all national, state, and local officials. Mayor Mathew Clarkson bravely stayed on, keeping order and caring for the sick, with the help of a grocer, a barrel maker, and two black ministers. He was not helped by the medical establishment. Benjamin Rush, the city's leading physician, prescribed a regimen of ferocious bloodletting, widely imitated, that slaughtered hundreds. Only a handful of doctors, including Edward Stevens, a childhood friend of Hamilton's from the Virgin Islands, prescribed milder treatments that did less harm. The final death toll reached 5,000—10 percent of the population.

A new session of Congress was due to meet the first Monday of December. As fall arrived, Washington wondered where. Hardly any information was coming out of Philadelphia, and what came suggested that the fever was growing worse, not better. He decided that he and the cabinet would assemble on November 1 in Germantown, a suburb northwest of the city, and he asked Edmund Randolph, the attorney general, to rent him a house. But what about Congress? He posed a series of questions to Randolph. Suppose the infection spread to Germantown. Wilmington, Delaware, and Trenton, New Jersey, were farther away, but since they were on the main north-south road, they seemed equally vulnerable. Annapolis, Maryland, was out, because it was too close to Mount Vernon: picking it would smack of favoritism. "What sort of a town," he wondered, "is Reading?"

There was a problem harder than location, which was Washington's role in choosing the place. "What, with propriety," he asked, "can the president do . . . ?" The Constitution gave Congress the power to choose the seat of government (they had decided that it would be in Philadelphia until 1800, and on the Potomac thereafter) and to pick the time that Congress met. English history and colonial experience had taught Americans to fear legislatures that could be capriciously summoned or dismissed by the executive. Even so, the president had the power to "convene both Houses, or either of them . . . on extraordinary Occasions" (Article II, Section 3). Did this count? Washington solicited the opinions of other advisers besides Randolph. Representative James Madison, a prominent congressman, thought not. The word *Occasions* in the Constitution referred only to the timing of special sessions of Congress, not the place. Besides, the law that made Philadelphia the capital until 1800 could not be waived. Alexander Hamilton, by now recovered from his fever, thought the president's power to convene Congress "extends to *place* as well as *time*. . . . The usual seat of the government may be in possession of an enemy; it may be swallowed up by an earthquake. . . . I know of no law," he added, "that could abridge a constitutional discretion of either branch." But since there were "respectable" doubts in the present case—for example, Madison's—he advised Washington not to use his power. Instead, he might "recommend" that Congress meet informally in Germantown to discuss what should be done. Questioning Madison and Hamilton was not like consulting modern constitutional experts, since they had signed the Constitution only six years earlier (as had Washington himself). Their views could make a powerful claim to be authoritative—if only they had agreed.

Washington presented options to Randolph. Summoning Congress to meet before the first Monday in December might be illegal. Asking it to meet to decide when and where to meet would be "a novel proceeding. Either would be food for scribblers." Four and a half years into the job, Washington was beginning to feel chewed over by critics and did not relish the sensation. Yet if Philadelphia continued to be a pesthole, "something preliminary seems necessary.—I wish you to think seriously of this matter."

Randolph thought, and Washington ended up agreeing with him: Do nothing until Congress was scheduled to meet. If it failed to assemble, that would be an unignorable "extraordinary Occasion," about which he would be expected to act. Washington was kicking the can down the road, but the road seemed to require it.

The president arrived in Germantown on November 1, as planned, and took rooms at the house of a German teacher in the local school. Thomas Jefferson, the secretary of state, found nothing better than a bed in the public room of an inn—"the only alternative," he wrote, "being to sleep on the floor in my cloak by the fire."

On November 10 Washington rode into Philadelphia. Randolph had asked him not to: he might risk his health, and encourage people to return too soon, risking theirs. But Washington wanted to see for himself. The city was like a ghost town. There was no welcome; he was alone; he bowed to a few stray pedestrians. The air was cool; in fact, it was healthier, for the first frost had killed the mosquitoes. Washington did not know the importance of that, but he did know that the daily death rate had been slipping, from a ghastly eighty-two on October 22 to two on October 28. The president returned to Germantown. By the first Monday in December, Congress, and some semblance of normality, returned to Philadelphia.

During the Revolution, Washington was commander in chief. But this was a position assigned him by Congress. He was the CEO, answerable to them. During his presidency, he had his own authority, derived from his independent election. But he also had to consider the authority of Congress over itself, and carefully weigh the conditions that might change their interactions—even in the middle of a raging epidemic.

There is nothing small about lines of authority, because even little changes shift the balance of power, and considering change will make the powerful feel threatened. Catastrophes may happen—Hamilton's earthquakes—in which all bets are off. But even then a leader should remember what it is he is ignoring. When the dust settles, others will remind him.

CHAPTER 5

Management Style

————

PROBLEMS ARE PROTEAN, but over time a leader develops a characteristic style of dealing with them. In decades of public service and private business, Washington learned a lot, but his management style showed broad continuities. It flowed in one channel, like a river, past battles and politics alike.

Hub and Wheel

When Thomas Jefferson became president, he reminded the members of his cabinet that he had served in George Washington's. Washington's role as president, Jefferson explained, was to be the hub of the wheel. "He formed a central point for the different branches" of government, "preserv[ing] a unity of object and action among them."

There are different ways of arranging the people who present problems to a leader and then execute the decisions he has made. They can be arrayed in a pyramid, passing questions and answers up or down ever-narrowing or -widening channels of communication. Or they can be made to deal with a chief of staff or prime minister, who then deals with the leader (and sometimes, like the shoguns of imperial Japan, becomes the leader).

Washington, as commander in chief and president, solicited the views of a team of associates, either individually or collectively, in councils of war or cabinet meetings. To pursue the image of the wheel, dealing with his associates as individuals emphasized the spokes; dealing with them in a group emphasized the rim. Sometimes he reached outside his official team to get the input of people lower down in the organization, or outside it altogether. At all times, he remained the central point—even if he allowed himself to be overruled.

Early in the Revolution, his councils of war took binding votes. In October 1775 Washington suggested to his generals that the army surrounding Boston attack the city. He had 20,000 men, who were reasonably healthy; the British had 8,000, who were rather sick and cooped up. Aggression suited Washington's temperament, and he knew besides that his men's enlistments would end by the first of the year and that they had no winter clothing. On the other hand, the Americans were raw militia, while the British were professionals, and, since Boston, in those days before the Back Bay was filled in, was a tadpole of land connected to the mainland by a slender tail, any assault on it would have to be complex and partly amphibious. Considering these factors, the only general who supported Washington was Nathanael Greene, who, at that point, had never fought a battle. All the others were negative: five generals opposed the plan; one opposed it for the present, while another suggested waiting until winter. Washington submitted to the vote of no confidence. He would propose attacking Boston again, and once again abandon the idea when most of his generals nixed it. Even so, the exercise may not have been futile, if he noted that young General Greene's temper was like his own.

At the end of 1776, he offered another aggressive move to a council of war. Four months of loss and retreat, beginning with the Battle of Long Island in August, had just ended, when 2,400 Americans crossed the Delaware River on Christmas night and overwhelmed

1,500 Hessians in a surprise attack on Trenton the next morning. The Americans lost 2 killed, the Hessians 22 killed and 900 captured. This day-after-Christmas present came so unexpectedly, in such desperate circumstances, that it fully deserves its place in the honor roll of American heroism, just as Emanuel Leutze's painting *Washington Crossing the Delaware* belongs in the gallery of American icons. But the victory was a glorious one-shot. If the year's fighting ended there, the British would remain in possession of most of New Jersey, with Philadelphia, the capital, temptingly close to their garrisons. Washington wanted a second stroke. "If we could happily beat up the rest of their quarters . . . on or near the [Delaware] river, it would be attended with the most valuable consequences." Some militia units that had pushed themselves ahead of the main army reported encouraging signs of disarray among the enemy. On the other hand, most of Washington's troops were exhausted from the Battle of Trenton, sick, or about to go home.

Washington called a council of war on December 27. No minutes have survived, but we have a secondhand account. "Some doubts, it is said, arose in the general council on this occasion." No doubt they did. "Some of the members who disapproved the enterprise advised . . . sending orders to the [advanced parties of] militia to return. But the General and some others declared that, though they would not have advised the movement [of the militia in the first place], yet being done it ought to be supported." This compressed report does not describe opinions followed by a vote but the seesaw of a discussion. Those (Washington and "some others") who favored seizing the opportunity the militia had discovered (especially since it was the opportunity that Washington wanted in the first place) prevailed. The commander in chief had gotten better at presenting his ideas in a group format; he had also come up with better ideas. Desperation, and a taste of victory, focused everyone's mind. Much more work had to be done besides discussing; Washington had to persuade his troops to serve for six more weeks, and get money to pay them from a friend, Philadelphia merchant Robert Morris, since Congress had none. His reward for pouring it on was the Battle of Princeton on January 3, in which 4,500 Americans surprised 1,200 British, the Americans losing about 35 killed, the British 100 killed and 260 captured. The one-two punch of Trenton and Princeton drove the enemy out of central New Jersey, and lifted up a falling cause.

In 1794 President Washington faced a different threat, possibly military, from angry Americans. At the suggestion of Treasury Secretary Alexander Hamilton, Congress had levied an excise tax on distilled spirits. Distillers in the Alleghenies and beyond hated the tax, and taxes generally. In July the collector of excise in western Pennsylvania fought two gun battles with the local militia, in which 4 people were killed. The frontier blossomed with revolutionary flags, and rhetoric. "Should an attempt be made to suppress these people," wrote one of their leaders to the capital, "I am afraid the question will not be, whether you will march to Pittsburgh, but whether they will march to Philadelphia. . . . There can be no equality of contest, between the rage of a forest, and the abundance, indolence and opulence of a city." A tax dispute had turned into a rebellion.

Or was it a second Revolution? The Whiskey Rebellion recapitulated the Revolution's rhetoric. That struggle had begun with protests of taxes on stamps and tea. This struggle began with protests of taxes on whiskey. Weren't the spirit of '76 and the spirit of '94 the same? If the rebels were not confronted politically or even militarily, they might set the frontier aflame. If they were not answered intellectually, they might hijack the legacy of the Revolution.

Washington did not need any advice on the intellectual issues involved; he was crystal clear about them. The taxes that provoked the colonies had been passed in London, by Parliament; the taxes that provoked the West had been passed in Philadelphia, by Congress, in which the West was represented. The earlier taxes were British laws, passed for the empire; the whiskey excise was an American law, passed for America. "If the laws," Washington wrote, "are to be so trampled upon, with impunity, and a minority (a small one too) is to dictate to the majority, there is an end put, at one stroke, to republican government." He was the guardian of the spirit of '76, not the whiskey rebels.

But how could he get the country, and as many rebels as possible, to agree with him? As he had during the Revolution, he asked his team for advice. Hamilton told him to call out the militia and send it west. "The very existence of government demands this course." He volunteered to go along since, as the proximate cause of the problem, he had responsibility for fixing it. Secretary of War Henry Knox told him a "super abundant force" could be raised from the militias of Pennsylvania, New Jersey, Maryland, and Virginia (the regular army was in the wilderness, fighting Indians). William Bradford, the new attorney general, wanted a call-up too, but cautioned that "the public mind [must] be satisfied that all other means in the power of the executive have failed." Edmund Randolph, who was now secretary of state, argued that calling up the militia would be threatening "terror." He wanted to send a commission to meet with the rebels: if that failed, then they could be prosecuted; if the courts could not function, "then let the militia be called." The governor of Pennsylvania, Thomas Mifflin, was also consulted. He advised that the excise was so unpopular in Pennsylvania that the militia might not appear when called.

Washington's cabinet, like many of his councils of war, was all over the lot, but this was no bad reflection of the country itself (except for the rebels, whose views were not represented). He decided to blend all their advice, calling up the militia of four states, but not sending them until a three-man commission had reported from the West. Mifflin's gloomy advice about the Pennsylvania militia had a backstory. During the Revolution, he had schemed to get Washington demoted, but had finally given up and gone along ungraciously. Perhaps he was not sorry to be telling such an inconvenient truth now, but in time he would probably follow if the nation did. There were also, as Knox pointed out, three other states' militias to rely on.

The commission, which included two Pennsylvanians (not Mifflin) and Bradford, went out the first week of August, as did a call to the four states for troops. The last week of September, the commissioners returned to Philadelphia and made their final report (most westerners were now willing to obey the law, but special force was still necessary to execute it), and almost 13,000 militia set off the next day. Washington reviewed them at the staging areas in October, and sent them on.

Together, the delay and the show of force did their work. Most westerners cooled off; some fled. There was no fighting; one hundred people were arrested; two (both small fry) were convicted of treason, and pardoned by the president. The combination of patience and power showed the country and most rebels what was at stake, and gave them time to think about it. Washington found the formula for action in sifting the advice of his team.

Managing by the hub-and-wheel system has built-in advantages. Information and advice come directly to the leader; even more comes when he looks beyond his team. After the council of war on December 27, 1776, Washington heard from New Jersey locals about back roads that might take his army from Trenton to Princeton; their knowledge was confirmed by his adjutant, who was from the area. Some opinions are unhelpful, or even malicious, as with the advice of Governor Mifflin during the Whiskey Rebellion. But hearing bad advice can be important too, in terms of knowing where you stand with key players.

The system can be good for the spokes as well as the hub. Everyone knows he has been heard. People fail to prevail because they have lost an argument, not because they have been ignored. This in turn builds unity of purpose. Since everyone played a role, everyone can support the result. The leader can expect that everyone is on board, more or less.

But sometimes everyone is not really on board; when a problem is ongoing, as almost every problem is, people often keep their original view of it, regardless of what decisions were reached along the way. Consensus is superficial and vanishes at the first setback. Military discipline holds (mostly) after defeats, but politicians, mindful of the next election, soon look out for number one.

Another bad consequence of hub-and-wheel management is decisions that don't truly decide, lazily splitting the difference. They can get a leader and his team through a calm patch, or a small problem, but what happens if the problem suddenly swells? In the summer of 1778, halfway measures almost lost a battle. Despite the Trenton-Princeton campaign, the British had captured Philadelphia after a major effort in 1777. Yet when the world learned, next spring, that France had agreed to enter the war on America's side, the British decided to concentrate their forces in New York, evacuating Philadelphia in June 1778. The question for Washington then was whether his army should engage them as they marched across New Jersey.

He called a council of war in Hopewell, a dozen miles north of Trenton, on June 24. The retreating British were perhaps 10,000 strong; the Americans, including militia, numbered 13,000. The council voted narrowly not to fight a major battle, but to send a force of 1,500 to shadow the enemy's rear guard, and "act as occasion may serve." Hamilton, then a colonel on Washington's staff, was contemptuous of the plan: he thought it "would have done honor to the most honorable society of midwives, and to them only." But that evening, some of the generals who had been outvoted, including Greene and a young French volunteer, the Marquis de Lafayette, urged Washington to double the shadowing force, and launch a "partial attack" on the rear guard. The command was given, after some hesitation, to Charles Lee, who asked for it as a matter of seniority, even though he had opposed making an attack in the first place. "To speak as an officer," he told Washington, "I do not think that this detachment ought to march at all."

Lee met the enemy at Monmouth Court House, now Freehold, on June 28, and found that he was engaged not with the rear guard but with the main British army. The ensuing battle confused most of the participants, and has confused historians ever since. Only in the past ten years, by digging up musket balls and other ordnance on the field, have historians and archaeologists begun to understand exactly who fired on whom and from where. Everything about the battle was made worse by 100-degree heat, baking into sandy soil. Years later, Billy Lee, Washington's slave and personal servant, remembered the punishment. "Was it not cold enough at Valley Forge? Yes, was it; and I am sure you remember it was hot enough at Monmouth." Washington blamed the confusion on Charles Lee, riding up to him in mid-battle and chewing him out. "I was disconcerted, astonished and confounded by the words and the manner in which His Excellency accosted me" was how Lee later described the scene. Washington then took command himself, and by personal force and skillful deployments fought the battle to a draw, each side losing perhaps 350 men to bullets, artillery, and heat. "His coolness and firmness were admirable . . . " wrote Hamilton. "He directed the whole with the skill of a master workman."

The original planning, however, had not been very workmanlike. Half a plan almost led to total defeat, hub-and-wheel management at its worst.

If you depend on your team for special insights and initiative, then the advantages of Washington's style of management outweigh the disadvantages. It is worth putting up with the occasional free-for-all, and the occasional deadlock, in return for energy and creativity. But management style is a tool, and like other tools, it breaks. Then the hub has to become the whole wheel; the leader has to plunge in and pull it out however he can.

Delegate to Innovate

When does a leader need the insights and creativity of others? Only if he doesn't know everything. Leaders who have access to systems of universal explanatory power, or who are guided by an overriding force of destiny, are not in this position. The Communist Party of the Soviet Union, led by Stalin, issued binding directives for literature, theater, music, biology, and the circus: "Only by full unmasking of the cosmopolite-theoreticians and formalistic directors who have planted in the arenas of Soviet circuses alien bourgeois tendencies can Soviet circus art achieve a new renaissance and become a genuine expression of the spiritual strength of the peoples inhabiting our great fatherland." But leaders who are not so favored realize that they must often look elsewhere for help. For them, farming out decisions can lead to better decisions. They delegate to innovate.

In 1775, as Washington besieged Boston, he was impressed with the skills of Henry Knox, whom he asked Congress to make commander of artillery. One of Knox's earliest assignments was a labor of Hercules: Washington asked him to go from Boston to upstate New York and retrieve whatever artillery the American forces there had managed to capture from the British. Knox moved fifty-eight cannons, mortars, and howitzers, weighing sixty tons, three hundred miles over lakes, rivers, and mountains, in the dead of winter. Later in the war, Congress unwisely proposed installing a French artillerist over Knox; the problem passed when the Frenchman, spurring his horse onto a ferry, rode off the other side and drowned. Knox warmed to Washington, writing that he "dispenses happiness around him"—partly a reflection on Washington, partly a reflection of Knox's own "jubilant personality."

Knox was creative, as well as energetic and good-tempered. He added a company of artillery to every brigade of infantry, thus increasing its firepower. Integrated artillery also made infantry units all-weather. Muskets often became unusable in heavy rain or snow, which dampened the gunpowder in their exposed firing pans. The business apertures of cannon were easier to keep dry with tampions (muzzle plugs) and touchhole covers. At the wintry battles at Trenton and Princeton, the American tyros were better served by their artillery than the British and Hessian professionals.

When he became president, Washington turned to another artillerist to take over the nation's finances. Robert Morris had been chief of finance during the waning days of the war, but he did not want to become the first treasury secretary, a job that promised to be both frustrating and unremunerative. He told Washington that Alexander Hamilton, a thirty-two-year-old lawyer in New York, was "damned sharp." Washington already knew that—during the war, Hamilton, after a stint as an artillery captain, had been a colonel on his staff. Hamilton was the youngest and hardest-working member of the cabinet (Thomas Jefferson at state and Knox at war were his peers). With a combination of brilliant planning and political hardball, Hamilton lifted the burden of debt and insolvency that had threatened to crush the young republic. He consolidated the debts of the nation and the thirteen states into one sum (almost $80 million); he devised a system of tariffs and taxes to fund it, and a schedule of repayment to satisfy creditors; and he founded a national bank to expand and regulate the money supply of the country. The proof of his handiwork was the approval of the moneymen of Amsterdam and Antwerp, the international bankers and de facto credit raters of the late eighteenth century. When Hamilton took office in September 1789, they were trading American paper at a quarter to a third of its face value; when he stepped down, in January 1795, they were trading it at 110 percent of its face value. The gnomes of the Netherlands were paying a premium to hold it; it was more than worth its weight in gold.

In each case, Washington turned to an autodidact. Knox had dropped out of school at age twelve to support his family by working for a bookseller, and ultimately opened his own shop, in which he studied the military books, especially those having to do with artillery. He never fired a gun in combat until the Battle of Bunker Hill. Hamilton was an even odder choice than Knox. He had learned business by going to work as a clerk in a merchant house in the Virgin Islands at the age of nine. But all his theoretical knowledge was ad hoc, snatched from treatises and almanacs in his spare time in the army, and jotted down in his artillery company's pay book. He had written a few letters of financial advice to his elders and betters, lecturing them on what ought to be done; as a lawyer, he had helped set up the Bank of New York. But he was by far the least-experienced man in the cabinet—Jefferson had been a diplomat, Knox a general.

Washington trusted these men because he sensed their abilities. He also backed them when they came under attack. When Knox's French rival appeared on the scene, Washington could not flout the direction of Congress. Yet he always did his best to stick up for his homegrown veterans against overbearing foreigners. Hamilton's policies as treasury secretary raised a domestic storm. To many of the farmers and lawyers in the founding elite, they seemed like black arts; Hamilton's cabinet colleague Jefferson became a bitter enemy.

Hamilton's "history," Jefferson wrote President Washington, "from the moment at which history can stoop to notice him, is a tissue of machinations against the liberty of the country." Not "his country" or "Hamilton's country": in Jefferson's mind, Hamilton was un-American, a rootless cosmopolite. But Washington stood by his man. Jefferson could not put America in the black; Hamilton could, and had. Hamilton stayed in the cabinet a year longer than Jefferson did.

Most important, Washington counted on these men and let them count on him because he knew his own lack of ability. Washington's pre-Revolutionary experience, in the French and Indian War, had been commanding light infantry, and giving advice as a staff officer to British higher-ups, who sometimes took it, sometimes didn't. He needed a Knox directing his cannon. As president, he could have been his own secretary of state or war—he had been fighting and negotiating with Indians, British, and Frenchmen since his twenties—but he could not have been his own treasury secretary. Finance struck him, as it did most of the founders, as a mysterious, if not sinister, subject. He knew, from his own experience as commander of a shivering, starving, unpaid army, that credit was important and that debts had to be paid. But he did not know how to do this. Few of his great peers did. Happily, one of that small number had been a colonel on his staff.

When a leader cannot generate important ideas himself, he must look elsewhere. Washington had the good luck and the good judgment to spot those who could, and the strength of purpose to let them do their work.

HANDS-ON

Some tasks cannot be delegated. A leader has to do them himself, or be there while they are being done.

This is especially true on farms. "Our forefathers," wrote Pliny the Elder, a Roman writer who lived 2,000 years ago, used to say that "on a farm the best fertizlier is a master's eye." Writers and farmers have kept saying it ever since. Even as tobacco requires intense oversight, so do humans.

We have a vignette of Washington watching men at work on his farm, from his own diary. In February 1760 he noticed that four of his carpenters at Mount Vernon, Tom, Mike, George, and Billy, had spent one day hewing 120 feet of wood into square-cut timber. He decided to do a time-motion study. "Sat down therefore and observed . . . letting them proceed their own way." In an hour and a quarter, Tom and Mike cleared brush away from a poplar tree they had felled earlier, fetched a crosscut saw, cut the tree into sections, put the sections on blocks, and squared them off, each producing 20 feet of timber. Washington calculated that, at that rate, each man should produce 125 feet of timber per day "while the days are at their present length, and more in proportion as they increase" (he allowed two hours for meals). In other words, they could be four times as productive as they had been the day before. Each species of tree, he added, has it own density: "What may be the difference therefore between the working of [poplar] wood and other, some future observations must make known."

Washington's own work habits ran to method and effort—he organized his time, and he filled it with exertion—and as a boss he expected others to do the same. He was an exacting employer, with his managers as well as his workers, even when the managers were friends or relatives of his. "As you are now receiving my money," he wrote one manager, "your time is not your own; [since] every hour or day misapplied is a loss to me, do not therefore [be] under a belief that, as a friendship has long subsisted between us, many things may be overlooked in you."

Washington's inclinations and expectations kept running up against the fact that almost all of his farm labor in Virginia was done by slaves. How could they be motivated? Washington could sit watching Tom and Mike; even if he was silent, his mere presence meant that he was hardly letting them "proceed their own way," but once he left, they had no incentive not to go back to their usual rate of one-quarter full speed. By constant travel about his plantations, Washington could keep everything under his eye, but the effects were short-lived; when he was with the Continental army, or in New York or Philadelphia as president, he could not do even that. His surrogates, his overseers and managers, could threaten punishment, and deliver it ("I . . . has whipped them when I could see a fault," one overseer wrote of the slaves he managed in 1758). In extreme cases, incorrigible slaves could be sold; in 1766 Washington gave "a rogue and a runaway" named Tom (not the carpenter) to a skipper bound for St. Kitts, where he was to be sold for rum, molasses, limes, and "one pot of tamarinds." But such extreme measures ran counter to a master's desire, not entirely hypocritical, to see himself as a patriarch, presiding beneficently over his bondmen, rather than an owner, maximizing the returns on his chattel. As the years passed, punishment also became harder to square with Washington's evolving image, national and international. So where his slaves were concerned, he could watch, and he could order, and he would be lucky if one-quarter of what he wanted got done.

The case was different with freemen. Between the Battles of Trenton and Princeton in the winter of 1776–1777 there was another conflict, indistinct in historical memory, though David Hackett Fischer has written about it recently as the Second Battle of Trenton. The decision to give the enemy another blow after the first Battle of Trenton had been made on December 27, 1776. The enemy did not wait to receive it. On January 2, 8,000 British and Hessians marched on Trenton from their garrison in Princeton; 1,000 Americans were assigned to delay their advance down the Post Road. Almost 6,000 more Americans were stationed outside town, across Assunpink Creek, on a height from which their artillery could fire. The Americans on the Post Road were supposed to harry the British as much as possible, then, when they had fallen back on Trenton, retreat across a single bridge to safety on the other side of the creek.

The American delaying force was in sporadic contact with the enemy all afternoon. They reached Trenton about four o'clock; night would fall at a quarter to five. The flashing of the muzzles of muskets was visible in the dusk. We know what the retreat over the bridge felt like from the recollections of John Howland, a private in a Rhode Island regiment. "The bridge was narrow, and our platoons in passing it were crowded into a dense and solid mass, in the rear of which the enemy were making their best efforts." *Narrow, crowded, dense*: he is not saying that he panicked, but clearly it was an option. On the far side of the creek, "the noble horse of General Washington stood with his breast pressed close against" the bridge rail. Washington was watching. But Howland was watching too. "The firm, composed and majestic countenance of the General inspired confidence and assurance." Almost at the moment of safety, the soldier had an even closer contact. "At the end of the bridge, I pressed against the shoulder of the General's horse and in contact with the boot of the General. The horse stood as firm as the rider, and seemed to understand that he was not to quit his post and station." So, in that moment, did the retreating teenager. General Washington was there; Private Howland would do what he must. The commander in chief could have delegated some other officer to oversee the retreat, but a leader had to do it himself. It was a hands-on—or eyes-on—job.

The enemy tried to force Assunpink Creek, with no success. Altogether the day's fighting was bloody, killing or wounding perhaps 365 British and Hessians, and 100 Americans. But the Americans' work was scarcely begun—for the council of war that evening decided on a night march, twenty miles over frozen back roads, to Princeton. The sudden, surprising victory there would end that year's campaigning.

But there would be seven more years—five of fighting, two of sitting around. Washington's command of his men would be tested again and again, in battles, mutinies, bad weather, and boredom. (Washington would even be tested in his command of men of color, since there were both Indians and free black men in the American army.) Washington and his troops passed all these tests, in part, because of their confidence in him, and his contact with them.

Slavery is a rocky foundation for a farm, to say nothing of a country; happily, America is free of it (though the world, as the news from Darfur tells us, is not). Freedom produces better results when men are inspired to make the most of it. There are times when a leader has to supply that inspiration himself.

Woody Allen famously said that 80 percent of success is showing up. One hundred percent of leadership is showing up—at the necessary moments.

CHAPTER 6

COMMUNICATION

IF A LEADER LEADS in the forest, and no one hears him, is he really leading? A great part of any leader's time is spent in making himself known, by communicating to others: to his organization, to his public. He tells the organization what to do, and the public how to think about what was done. Both target audiences, of course, are at liberty to ignore what they are told, which obliges the leader to be skillful.

Our notions of those who lived before the invention of photography and recording are formed almost entirely by the written words they have left us—a fact that favors the literary. As a result, Washington, whose writing was clear and solid but rarely sparkling, has faded a bit. If it were not for his image on Mount Rushmore and the money in our pockets, he might have faded a bit more. But in his lifetime he was very present, and a master of communication.

WRITING

Thomas Jefferson, the greatest writer among the founders, said that Washington "wrote readily, rather diffusely, in an easy and correct style." *Easy* and *correct* are the compliments of an eighteenth-century stylist. *Diffusely* undermines them, especially coming from Jefferson, who could be banal or even nonsensical, but was always crisp; at his best—the opening of the Declaration of Independence—the phrases and the consonants roll like drum taps.

The most important quality for Washington in Jefferson's little list, though, is *readily*. He had to be able to write readily because he had a mass of writing to do: as commander in chief, ceaseless orders to his officers; correspondence with Congress; correspondence with state governors, who, since they had more real power than Congress, were the men who could make things, such as this month's supplies, happen; letters to Mount Vernon, his refuge, visited only once during the eight and a half years he served, but visited in his thoughts constantly; after the war, correspondence with everyone who wanted to write to the most famous man in America; correspondence with bright, anxious men—James Madison, Alexander Hamilton—who were telling him how the government should be changed, and that he must do it; as president, replies to letters of congratulation, all of them routine, some of them immortal (to the Hebrew Congregation at Newport a gentle correction: religious liberty is not a blessing, but "the exercise of . . . inherent natural rights"); once more, the business of office.

Of course, he could not produce it all by himself. During the war, Washington was served by a staff of young officers—Robert Hanson Harrison, thirty years old in 1775, was the oldest—who acted as executive assistants. Washington called them his family; their job was to understand him better than family members often understand each other. "Those about me," he wrote, will be "confined from morning to eve, hearing and answering . . . applications and letters." He expected them "to possess the soul of the general; and from a single idea given to them, to convey his meaning in the clearest and fullest manner." The thought had to be Washington's; the expression was the aide's, though, from long familiarity, it became Washington's too.

He used similar help during his presidency. James Madison wrote Washington's first inaugural address in 1789. Then, since Madison was a member of the new House of Representatives, he wrote the House's response. He finished by writing Washington's response to the response.

In 1796 at the end of his second term, which Washington decided would be the end of his presidency (there was no two-term limit then), he turned to Alexander Hamilton for help with his Farewell Address. He had an old draft by Madison, which had been written four years earlier when he had considered stepping down after only one term. Washington now sent Hamilton a draft of his own, which began with eight paragraphs from Madison's. Hamilton wrote yet another draft, keeping Madison's opening, then going on with Washington's thoughts, Hamilton's voice. Washington preferred Hamilton's version, but edited it carefully. He may also have shown it to John Jay, which would make the Farewell Address the last collaboration of the three authors who wrote *The Federalist Papers*. When Washington gave it to the *American Daily Advertizer* of Philadelphia for publication, he was, the editor remembered, "very minute" in editing the punctuation.

Now speechwriters are commonplace for presidents and CEOs alike. The details have changed—press conferences, board meetings, PowerPoint presentations—but the principles of collaboration have not. The leader has to look over the shoulders of his writers, and tinker with their prose; they have to know his mind, and his rhythms. The process works only if the leader has (as Washington had) firm beliefs, clear ideas, and a strong personality.

PERFORMING

Words aren't the only medium of communication. Washington gave his first inaugural address in New York City on April 30, 1789. Fisher

Ames, a congressman from Massachusetts, described the occasion in a letter to a friend back home as a pageant, almost a play. "It was a very touching scene, and quite of the solemn kind." He supplied details: Washington shook from modesty; he was "grave, almost to sadness," his voice "so low as to call for close attention." He moved his audience, "overwhelming it, producing emotions of the most affecting kind." Ames mentioned no words, only actions, appearances, and emotions. "It seemed to me," he concluded, "an allegory in which virtue was personified, and addressing those whom she would make her votaries. Her power over the heart was never greater." Washington and his listeners were acting a drama. Ames highlighted the theatricality of the occasion by turning Washington, the six-foot-three war hero, into Virtue, a female character.

Washington's taste in fiction was conventional for a gentleman of his day—he owned *Don Quixote*, and a collection of the best-loved bits of Laurence Sterne—even restricted, for he knew no foreign languages. But he loved plays, from Shakespeare to costume dramas to light comedies to weepers. There wasn't much theater in America, and Puritan prejudice against playacting still lingered (during the Revolution, Congress urged the states to ban plays as sources of "idleness" and "dissipation"). But Washington watched them whenever he could, even in the face of Congress's displeasure. There was something in his nature that responded to the presentation and the emotion, and to the reactions of the audience. By temperament and physique, he was made for stardom, and leadership called on his theatrical qualities. Ronald Reagan is thought of as the first actor-president, but as biographer Noemie Emery points out, he was only the first to have acted on camera for money. Every effective leader is a performer, and the first performer president was Washington.

The play of the first inaugural was one in which everybody knew his part ahead of time. Washington had been personifying virtue on the national stage since 1775, and the country had applauded every appearance. The first inaugural was an encore—the hundredth? the thousandth? Sometimes, though, the play was unfinished. Different cast members had different stories in mind, with very different scripts.

In the spring of 1783, the army was camped at Newburgh, New York, fifty miles up the Hudson from New York City. Major fighting had ended with the Battle of Yorktown in October 1781, but it took the diplomats a long time to negotiate peace; the British still occupied New York City, and the Americans had to be in Newburgh in case something went wrong. One thing had gone wrong already—had, in fact, been going wrong for the whole war: the officers of the army had not been paid. With peace at hand, they feared they would be sent home with worthless IOUs. "The temper of the army," Washington warned a friendly congressman, "is much soured." In March the sourness took mutinous form. An anonymous letter, from "a fellow soldier," circulated through camp, calling for action. The officers should demand their due from Congress, or worse would follow. We now know who "a fellow soldier" was—a young major named John Armstrong; we aren't clear who exactly was behind him, though suspicion falls on a number of senior officers and too-clever-by-half politicians. Whoever conceived the anonymous letter, it followed a well-known script, which had been played throughout history by ambitious or impatient military men, from Caesar to Cromwell.

Washington called a meeting of officers on March 15. Samuel Shaw, a captain, is our witness to this scene, recounting it, like Ames, in a letter to a friend. Washington had ordered "the senior officer in rank present" to preside, implying that he would not be there himself. Yet he appeared "unexpected[ly]," explaining that the anonymous address required him to "give his sentiments to the army." He then read "his brother officers" a speech. "It is needless for me to say anything" of it, Shaw wrote; *it speaks for itself.*" To prove Congress's good intentions, Washington also read a letter from a "worthy" lawmaker, which was "exceedingly sensible." But "one circumstance in reading this letter," Shaw added, "must not be omitted." Soon after he began, Washington "made a short pause, took out his spectacles, and begged the indulgence of his audience while he put them on, observing at the same time, that he had grown gray in their service, and now found himself growing blind."

Like Ames after the first inaugural, Shaw said hardly anything about Washington's speech. He knew it had been written up in the newspapers, but he wanted to talk about something else: the gesture, which he called "superior to the most studied oratory," and the feelings it induced—"it forced its way to the heart." Washington and the army had been through a lot together; he was showing it in his own head, his eyes and hair, and asking them to take one step more.

Had he planned the gesture with the glasses? Or was it the second nature of a man used to being on the public stage? We cannot know, but it had its effect. Washington left the meeting as soon as he finished speaking, and the officers agreed to do as he directed. Shaw understood exactly what had happened. "For a dreadful moment the interests of the army and its general seemed to be in competition! He spoke . . . and the tide of patriotism rolled again in its wonted course." Washington had taken up arms to lead a free people to independence; that couldn't be done by bullying their lawfully elected representatives. He rewrote the play of Newburgh in midperformance.

We can feel suspicious of actor-leaders; where are they taking us? Parson Weems, Washington's first biographer, insisted on his transparent honesty, from his very boyhood: "I can't tell a lie, Pa; you know I can't tell a lie," six-year-old George supposedly told his father, admitting that he had accidentally chopped a prize cherry tree with his hatchet. Washington played on our suspicion of acting in his own speech at Newburgh, when he called the anonymous address a piece of "great Art" and "secret Artifice." Yet he himself used the arts of the stage to argue the anonymous address down.

Performance is manipulation when a leader uses it to display emotions he does not feel and advance causes he does not believe in. If, after years of obeying Congress, Washington had told the army in Newburgh to go get 'em, or if, after years of grumbling and intrigue he had suddenly urged them to fly right, he might well have failed, offering such unexpected advice, however well he performed. Acting works for a leader only if you play yourself, or the self you have tried to become. It works only if you are a character actor.

SILENCE

In August 1789 Senator William Maclay was invited to dine at President Washington's. It was, as he told his diary, "the most solemn dinner I ever ate at." After the dishes were cleared, the president "with great formality drank the health of every individual by name round the table. Everybody imitated him . . . and such a buzz of 'Health, sir,' and 'Health, madam,' and 'Thank you, sir,' and 'Thank you, madam' never had I heard before." This was followed by "a dead silence." After Mrs. Washington and the ladies retired, Maclay "expected the men would now begin" to talk, "but the same stillness remained." Washington broke it to tell a story about a clergyman who lost his hat and wig crossing the Bronx River. "He smiled and everybody else laughed." John Jay told a joke. The president had "kept a fork in his hand . . . I thought for the purpose of picking nuts. He ate no nuts but played with the fork, striking on the edge of the table with it." Maclay was as censorious as he was observant, yet there is enough other testimony of the public functions of the Washington administration (the president, besides giving dinners, held weekly receptions) to suggest that they were all rather stiff affairs, thanks in great part to Washington's reserve as a host.

Thomas Jefferson thought Washington was just a bad talker. "His colloquial talents were not above mediocrity, possessing neither copiousness of ideas, nor fluency of words." (Jefferson, by contrast, shone in conversation; Maclay said "he scattered information wherever he went.") But Washington had good reason to keep his own counsel. Even in the first peaceful days of his presidency, when the nation soaked in a bath of good feeling, he was surrounded by quarrels and contending ambitions. His inauguration had been followed by a debate in Congress over what he should be called: plain "President of the United States," as the House of Representatives wanted, or "His Highness, the President of the United States of America, and Protector of the Rights of the Same," Vice President John Adams's choice? This was a question on which Washington wished to express no opinion. Hordes of people were willing to serve him and the United States. Not a bad problem to have, but Washington could not satisfy them all. One of his guests at the dinner Maclay described, John Jay, would become the first chief justice. Mrs. Jay, the former Sarah Livingston, was the cousin of another prominent patriot, Robert Livingston, who as one of New York State's highest judges had sworn Washington in as president. But he would not be getting a seat on the Supreme Court, or any other job—yet another topic to be avoided.

As time passed, the land mines multiplied. Everyone knew everyone. Everyone had an opinion of everyone, and everything. With the years, these opinions became more acrid. On many of the issues of the day, Washington had to have a policy. If he had not yet formed one, he needed to keep his options open. If he had formed one, he had to avoid picking needless fights (there were enough unavoidable fights already). He understood that when it was not necessary to speak, it was necessary not to speak. Washington adopted a strategy of keeping his mouth shut.

The men who followed him as president had their own strategies for navigating their thoughts through a treacherous world. Jefferson was as good as Washington at keeping his thoughts to himself. But since he had an almost morbid dislike of confrontation, he tended to overcompensate, appearing to agree with whomever he was with. Jefferson thought he was being polite; when his interlocutors discovered his true opinions, they accused him of being two-faced. Unlike Washington or Jefferson, John Adams was a great public speaker. He was far more learned than Washington, perhaps even more learned than Jefferson. But he could never keep his knowledge or his tongue to himself. His comments on what the president should be called had been offered in his capacity as presiding officer of the Senate. He went on and on from the chair, and buttonholed senators after adjournment ("He got on the subject of checks to government and the balances of power," Maclay wrote. "His tale was long"). His role in the controversy over titles would follow him for the rest of his political career, like a tin can.

Better that your dinner guests feel uncomfortable than that you prepare discomfort for yourself. When Adams was in retirement, and Washington was in the grave, he wrote a long, quirky, thoughtful letter about the leadership qualities of the first president. Adams listed several—looks, grace, wealth. But the most interesting quality on Adams's list, especially considering the source, was this: Washington "possessed the gift of silence. This I esteem as one of the most precious talents."

CHAPTER 7

TIMING

YOU CAN READ about Washington's problems in an airport, or on a beach; you can listen to them while you commute. If you are busy, you can put this book aside; if you are bored, you can forget about it. But the problems themselves came to Washington when they came, sometimes in a steady (and relentless) procession, like the walking brooms of the sorcerer's apprentice in *Fantasia;* sometimes all together, in a cluster bomb. Washington did not get to choose them, and he did not, in most cases, get to choose when they appeared. They chose him.

Consider the specific problems in this section, in chronological order.

He began growing tobacco in 1755. He decided to stop growing it, at all but his wife's York River plantation, in 1766. He began considering strategies for securing American rights at the First Continental Congress in 1774—a process that would continue until the Battle of Yorktown in 1781. The year 1775 was a busy one. Smallpox and latrines presented themselves to him simultaneously, when he took command of America's troops outside Boston in July; he would be actively involved with smallpox until 1778, with latrines until 1779. In October his council of war debated attacking Boston. In November he sent Henry Knox to get British artillery. The year 1776 was another busy one. He dealt with General Howe's and Admiral Howe's letters in July, and began thinking seriously about spies in September (his concern with spies would last for the rest of the war). The Battle of Trenton was fought on December 26. The council of war that decided on further action was the next day. The year 1777 began with the Second Battle of Trenton (January 2) and the Battle of Princeton (January 3). The bungled Battle of Monmouth was fought in June 1778.

The Newburgh near-mutiny came to a head in March 1783. Washington wrote his thoughts on governmental reform in June, revisiting them with increasing frequency until March 1787, when he decided to attend the Constitutional Convention. In between, he gave his warning about restive westerners in October 1785 (he would send the army against some restive westerners in October 1794). He was inaugurated president at the end of April 1789; in August, he gave his silent dinner, attended by Senator Maclay, and sought the Senate's advice on Indian treaties, also described by Senator Maclay. In September Alexander Hamilton began his work at the Treasury Department, which increasingly involved Washington in controversies until Hamilton retired in January 1795.

In July 1790 Washington met with Alexander McGillivray, one of the Indian chiefs he had proposed negotiating with. Other negotiations did not go well, and Indian wars continued until August 1794. In 1792, he asked James Madison to write a Farewell Address, but was persuaded not to bid farewell. In the summer and fall of 1793 he had to deal with yellow fever and its impact on the nation's capital. From July to October 1794, he had to discuss, plan, and execute a strategy for dealing with the Whiskey Rebellion. In June 1796 he and Hamilton began preparing his actual Farewell Address.

This chronology omits his perennial problems—writing or editing the rest of the ninety volumes of his letters and speeches, mainly during his years as commander in chief (1775–1783) and president (1789–1797), and the constant struggle of being hands-on at Mount

Vernon (December 1755 until the day he died, in December 1799). It also omits the tens of thousands of other problems, great and small, that landed in his life.

The fecundity of problems has two positive consequences for a leader. Over time, problems reveal their patterns (but don't rely too heavily on the patterns, because sometimes they change). They develop a leader's abilities and his temperament. Young Washington could have learned that from Seneca: "He that has lost one battle, hazards another." He certainly learned it from the many battles he lost, and hazarded.

When a problem comes, you better look at it, because, while you may decide not to deal with it just yet, here comes another.

Part Two

PEOPLE

———————

John Guare's play *Six Degrees of Separation* takes its title
from the belief that anyone can be linked to anyone else
by a chain of acquaintance consisting of only five intervening people. How many degrees of separation lay between anyone in late-eighteenth-century America and
George Washington? Fewer than six. True, it was a smaller
country, but travel was harder, which made it large again.
Even so, Washington got around, fighting in five states
during the Revolution, visiting all thirteen during his
presidency. When he wasn't on the move, people came to
him. One evening he noted in his diary, with some surprise, that he and Martha had dined alone for the first
time in twenty years. From the masses he met he picked
(or Congress picked for him) his assistants and associates,
the men he led most intimately.

Problems, and a leader's solutions to them, consist of
ideas, forces, facts of life. But they are always accompanied by, or incarnated in, people. Judging people accu-
rately and managing them well can make the difference
between success and failure.

CHAPTER 8

Unusual People

───────

IT IS NATURAL to be wary of people who are unusual, whether because of their talents or their peculiarities. Since they are unlike us, we may not be able to understand them, or control them.

No one can ever be rid of this wariness, but a leader must also discern the qualities of the unusual person who has appeared in his government, in his army, or on his doorstep.

Smart People

An expert may be defined as someone who knows more than you do about a particular thing, and the world is full of such people. (Do you fix your own computer, or grow your own food?) A smart person is someone who knows more than you do about many things, and although there may be fewer of those in the world, depending on how smart you are, a leader will meet his share.

The first smart person Washington knew well and worked with closely was George Mason, a fellow planter who lived on Dogue's Neck, just down the Potomac from Mount Vernon. George Mason IV, six years older than his neighbor, was a conventional man, immersed in family and private business, who happened to be a genius.

He never went to college, and never studied law, but men who had done both were impressed by his knowledge of political and legal theory, and a little afraid of his sharp tongue; his language, wrote Thomas Jefferson, "was strengthened by a dash of biting cynicism, when provocation made it seasonable." Mason wrote the Virginia Declaration of Rights, his state's severance of ties with Britain, which influenced both the Declaration of Independence and the Bill of Rights, not a bad twofer.

He and Washington were enmeshed in all the ways, great and little, that Virginia gentlemen living a few miles apart could be. They served on the vestry of the same Anglican parish; they were interested in improving the navigation of the Potomac and speculating in Ohio Valley land; they hunted deer together on Dogue's Neck.

As the relationship of the colonies and the mother country came to a crisis, the two neighbors worked together to assert America's rights. They brought complementary skills to the task. Mason once defined himself as "a man who spends most of his time in retirement, and has seldom meddled in public affairs." Mason was the intellectual, versed in colonial charters and English law, and in the theoretical works of John Locke and Algernon Sidney. Washington was the man who put his friend's ideas, which he shared, before the public. Mason was the formulator, Washington the effectuator.

The Fairfax Resolves showed how the partnership worked. In the spring of 1774, Parliament closed the Port of Boston, as punishment for local tax protests. The Virginia House of Burgesses proclaimed a day of sympathetic fasting and prayer, whereupon the royal governor of the colony sent the burgesses home. Instead, they called for an extralegal convention of delegates from all Virginia's counties to meet in Williamsburg in August. The voters of Fairfax County met in Alexandria on July 18 to instruct their representatives; Washington chaired the meeting. A committee, dominated by Mason, had prepared a set of resolutions, denying that Parliament had any right to tax the colonies without their consent, and calling for a continental congress to coordinate a response. Mason's resolutions were approved, and Washington took them to Williamsburg, as a delegate from their county, and then on to the First Continental Congress in Philadelphia as a delegate from Virginia.

Mason was happy to let Washington present his ideas; Washington was happy to present them, because he knew his own mind. "Much abler heads than my own," Washington wrote at the time, "convinced me" that Parliament's policies were contrary to the British constitution. But "an innate spirit of freedom first told me" that they were "repugnant to every principle of natural justice." Washington willingly let Mason keep tabs on the innards of the British constitution; he and Mason were equally capable of understanding justice.

Washington met an even more brilliant man in 1777. Alexander Hamilton, twenty-five years his junior, was as remote from his world as Mason was integral to it. Hamilton grew up on the sugar islands of the Caribbean. His mother, a divorcée, and his father, a failed businessman, were not married. Hamilton won the attention of local patrons by hard work as a merchant's clerk, and by precocious journalism: his first published article in a lifetime of many was a description of a hurricane that he wrote at age fifteen. He was sent to New York to be trained as a doctor, but dropped out of college after two years to become captain of an artillery company. Late in 1776, as the army retreated across New Jersey, an officer noticed "a youth, a mere stripling, small, slender, almost delicate in frame, marching beside a piece of artillery with a cocked hat pulled down over his eyes, apparently lost in thought, with his hand resting on the cannon and every now and then patting it as he mused, as if it were a favorite horse or a pet plaything." After the Battle of Princeton, he became a lieutenant colonel on Washington's staff, a position he held for four years.

Hamilton had several dozen peers as a young aide, but none in the freedom with which he offered economic advice to acquaintances and strangers, drawing on his ground-floor experience of commerce and trade and his hit-and-run reading of contemporary economists. A new financial world had been born in Holland and Britain, with a modern understanding of banking and debt, and by a combination of energy and effrontery, he made himself one of a half-dozen people in America who understood it. He had a knack for law as well as economics, nourished by a similar feeding frenzy of irregular study. "There is no skimming over the surface of a subject with him," an acquaintance wrote. "He must sink to the bottom to see what foundation it rests on." When he resurfaced, he had to have his hands on all the details. In the postwar years Hamilton became a lawyer, a politician, and an advocate for political reform.

In September 1787, after he had signed the Constitution, he wrote a memo to himself on the pros and cons of the new document. If it was ratified, he thought it "probable" that Washington would be president (that was a very conservative estimate). "This," he added, "will insure a wise choice of men to administer the government." One of the wisest choices Washington made, two years later, was Hamilton as treasury secretary.

In the winter of 1781–1782 Washington was in Philadelphia to consult with Congress, where he met a third smart man. James Madison was a thirty-year-old congressman from Virginia who had been doing the best he could for the army. The eldest son of a planter, he was a reserved young man, concerned with his health (though he would live to be eighty-five). A friend called him "sedentary and studious. . . . His ordinary manner was simple, modest, bland and unostentatious, retiring from the throng and cautiously refraining from doing or saying anything to make [himself] conspicuous. . . . [H]is form, features and manner were not commanding, but his conversation exceedingly so." His conversation commanded attention because he was intelligent, well educated (he burned through Princeton in two years), and able to express himself clearly, carefully, and (in private) with charm.

After the war, he became a delegate to the Virginia Assembly, which brought him together with Washington again, when he served on a committee to commission a statue of the hero. The two men also began to discuss inland navigation and other political problems, Madison consistently pushing the envelope—or urging, as a contemporary put it, "measures of relief to a greater extent than was generally contemplated." (Madison's reforming zeal cemented his new friendship with fellow politician Alexander Hamilton.) Madison's activities over the next five years as a polemicist, wire-puller, debater, and compromiser entitle him to be known as the Father of the Constitution. One of his many tasks, before and after the Constitutional Convention, was serving Washington, as a trainer handles a prizefighter, briefing him and strategizing with him. Madison knew the Constitution needed Washington's blessing if the country was to accept it; Washington needed to know it would be a serious effort before he would give it his blessing. By 1788, Madison was spending so much time with Washington that when his friends wrote letters to him, they sent them to Mount Vernon.

When Washington arrived in New York in April 1789 to be inaugurated, Madison was already there, as a representative from Virginia. A fellow member of the House called him "our first man." He was also the first man in Washington's inner circle, advising him on matters ranging from presidential etiquette to a bill of rights to how to induce Thomas Jefferson to become secretary of state.

Washington worked well with these smart people. If the United States had been a basketball team, it would have had a great first string, and a deep bench. But smart people have a characteristic shortcoming—pride. If they disagree with you, their very talents can make them harder to disagree with.

Washington's break with Mason was sudden and sharp. Mason emerged from his customary retirement to attend the Constitutional Convention, as part of a powerful Virginia delegation that included Washington and Madison. Yet at the end of the convention, he refused to sign. He had his reasons: he wanted a bill of rights, which the Constitution as originally written lacked (why, went the reasoning, forbid the federal government to do things it has no power to do?); he also wanted sumptuary laws, to regulate luxury and conspicuous consumption. He assailed the Constitution at the convention itself, where he said "it would end either in monarchy, or a tyrannical aristocracy; which, he was in doubt, but one or the other, he was sure," and back home in Virginia, where it took all Madison's tenacity and Washington's silent influence to overcome his opposition. Washington saw motives beyond reason in Mason's objections: "Pride on the one hand, and want of manly candor on the other, will not . . . let him acknowledge an error in his opinions." The political fight ended their friendship.

Washington's break with Madison came later and developed more slowly. By the middle of Washington's first term, Madison had come to the conclusion that Mason was partly right: though the Constitution was not dangerous, Hamilton at the Treasury Department was laying the foundations of monarchy and aristocracy, by creating a new elite of bankers and merchants (Washington thought Hamilton was digging America out of a debt hole). Foreign policy became another field of disagreement: Madison was enthralled by the French Revolution; Washington, disturbed by French meddling in American affairs, was not. Madison retained his respect for the president only by imagining that he had been bewitched by Hamilton; he could not conceive that his hero honestly disagreed with him. The final clash involved a

treaty with Britain that Washington sent to the Senate for confirma-
tion in 1796. Madison, anxious not to offend France by signing a
treaty with its enemy, claimed that the House too had a role in ratifying treaties. Washington denied it ("absolute absurdity," he wrote in
private). The congressman and the president both appealed to the
Constitution, which they had both signed. Washington's interpreta-
tion prevailed. The two men were strangers thereafter.

The smart man Washington worked with longest was Hamilton—
surprisingly, considering what a touchy know-it-all Hamilton could
be. He even resigned from Washington's staff once, in 1781, after a
small, meaningless quarrel. The commander in chief told his colonel
that he was ten minutes late for a meeting. "I am not conscious of it,
Sir," Hamilton answered, "but since you have thought it necessary to
tell me so we part." Officers are typically conscious of rights and
slights; young officers more so; young, self-made, illegitimate officers
most of all. After a half hour had passed, Washington sent another
aide to ask Hamilton to reconsider his resignation, but he would not.
Hamilton was not done with his boss, however; after he left headquarters, he bombarded him with requests for combat duty. Washington looked past the impudence and the inconsistency, and let him
command an infantry charge at Yorktown, which he did gallantly.

Hamilton continued to give Washington headaches as treasury
secretary—he insisted on slugging it out with his critics in the press.
But Washington kept turning to him because of his willingness to
give copious advice on all problems, because of the high quality of the
advice he gave, and because other intimates, chiefly Madison and Jefferson, gave him even greater headaches. Washington turned to
Hamilton a last time in 1798, when he came out of retirement to
command the army in case of a French attack. He insisted that
Hamilton be second in command, and wrote an eloquent tribute:
"That he is ambitious I shall readily grant, but it is of that laudable

kind which prompts a man to excel in whatever he takes in hand."
Washington valued the excellence, despite the heartburn.

A leader cannot afford to be intimidated by smart people, and he
must not be controlled by them. He can avoid both problems by being
confident of his own abilities and clear about his beliefs. Then he will
be able to draw on their talents, overlooking personal clashes, though
not disagreements about fundamentals.

WEIRD PEOPLE

Sometimes it is hard to tell whether a person is smart—or anything
else about him—because he moves through life in a dense cloud of
oddity.

At the beginning of the Revolution, America was desperate for experienced officers. Only a few native-born veterans of the French and
Indian Wars fit the bill, and some of them were not ideal: Israel Putnam was fifty-eight years old; Artemas Ward suffered from kidney
stones. Of necessity we turned to foreigners.

Put yourself in Washington's shoes, and consider two foreign officers who came his way.

Officer A has been a major in the English army. For the past few
years he has lived in America; politically, he identifies with his new
homeland, and warmly embraces the patriot cause. Though he is witty
and learned, his people skills are zero. His best friends are a pack of
dogs, his favorite among them a huge Pomeranian, which he calls Mr.
Spada. When he first meets Abigail Adams, he asks her to shake Mr.
Spada's paw. He lived for a time with the Mohawk Indians, who
called him "Boiling Water" on account of his temper.

Officer B says he is a baron (many Europeans acquire titles in mid-
Atlantic). He has served in the army of Frederick the Great, an excellent credential. He is fluent in German and French; unfortunately, he

speaks no English, so his orders, and his curses, have to be translated by aides. Two years after he arrives, Washington gets a letter charging that he is a pedophile: back in Europe, he had "taken familiarities with young boys."

Officer A was Charles Lee; Officer B was Friedrich Wilhelm von Steuben. Washington had to deal with both of them since they came to him via Congress: Lee was one of the four original major generals commissioned in 1775; Steuben, newly arrived from Europe, had presented himself to Congress early in 1778, carrying a letter of recommendation from Benjamin Franklin. But organizational charts are one thing, spirit another; the tenor of a leader's relations with those who are formally his comrades can range from enthusiasm to mere tolerance, or worse. Washington embraced both men, seeing past their peculiarities traits that he and the army needed. Lee had fought as a British officer and a soldier of fortune on two continents, and had military theory and history at the tip of his tongue. Steuben had personal experience of what was still, in the 1770s, the most efficient and effective army in Europe. In order to access their expertise, Washington was willing to put up with courteous dogs and unintelligible swearing.

With Steuben he struck gold. The German knew Prussian military habits, and understood their purpose: drilling led to cohesion and speed on the battlefield; organization made for health and order in camp (see Chapter 1, "Start-ups"). Far more valuable was his ability to modify old rules for a new situation. He stripped down the Prussian drill so that soldiers who were not military lifers could learn it easily. He told his new charges what they were doing and why. "You say to [a European] soldier," he wrote, "'Do this,' and he doeth it, but here I am obliged to say, 'This is the reason why you ought to do that' and then he does it." His explanations might have to be translated, but they were appreciated; his flamboyant profanity made them intriguing. He understood, finally, the importance of the quasi-paternal bond between officers and men. The "first object" of a captain, he wrote, "should be to gain the love of his men by treating them with every possible kindness and humanity, enquiring into their complaints, and when well founded, seeing them redressed. . . . He should often visit those who are sick [and] speak tenderly to them. . . . The attachment that arises from this kind of attention to the sick and wounded is almost inconceivable."

What about the charge of pedophilia? Washington ignored it. Historians wonder about Steuben's sexual orientation: he was a lifelong bachelor, cared for in his old age by devoted younger aides. If he was gay, he had reason to conceal it, for homosexual acts were crimes in the army, then as now. But no accusations of pedophilia arose in America; Washington dismissed the accusation he received as European backbiting. His policy was, "Don't ask, don't tell, and don't listen to gossip."

Charles Lee, on the other hand, developed into a problem that got worse over time. He helped repel an attack on Charleston, South Carolina, in the summer of 1776. But after the British successfully attacked New York that fall, he began to snipe at Washington behind his back. "A certain great man," he wrote General Horatio Gates, "is most damnably deficient." His criticisms ended only when he was captured by a party of British dragoons in December.

Did he turn traitor in prison? He gave the British advice as to how they might win. Was he trying to save his own skin from a British prosecution for treason (he was, after all, a Briton and a veteran)? Or was he trying to plant disinformation? This is a historians' debate that does not concern Washington as a leader, since he and other Americans were unaware of what was going on. They could only judge Lee by what he did after he was released in a prisoner exchange in April 1778. Lee was unimpressed by the reforms that Steuben had instituted. His performance at the Battle of Monmouth Court House is described above (see Chapter 5, "Management Style"). Washington's explosion of anger was in part the pent-up rage of a leader who senses that he has been badly served for a long time, but who hasn't been able to let himself know it until the evidence stares him in the face. Ignoring the increasingly obvious was Washington's fault; Lee's bad behavior and bungling were his own. Lee was court-martialed, and died four years later, with his dogs at his bedside.

Oddity is not just an individual trait. Entire subcultures can seem weird to strangers—their accents and their diets, obviously, but also their mind-sets.

Washington had been to New England once before the Revolutionary War, on a visit to Boston in 1756, but he had never dealt with New Englanders as soldiers. Shortly after he returned as commander in chief in 1775, he wrote his cousin Lund Washington that he did not much like them. The embattled Yankees for whom all America had rallied "have obtained a character [reputation] which they by no means deserved. Their officers generally speaking are the most indifferent kind of people I ever saw. . . . I daresay the men would fight very well (if properly officered) although they are an exceeding dirty & nasty people." Something must have told him that writing this down might be unwise, for he added, "I need not make myself enemies among them by this declaration, though it is consistent with the truth." Cousin Lund did not rat him out, though Washington shared similar thoughts with a Virginia congressman who did. One of his aides, who happened to be in Philadelphia at the time, heard the resulting gossip and warned Washington to keep quiet. He thanked his aide for the tip. "I can bear to hear of imputed or real errors. The man who wishes to stand well in the opinion of others must do this, because he is thereby enabled to correct his faults."

Washington wasn't the only outsider who found New Englanders strange. That winter a Virginia regiment crossed paths with the

Fourteenth Massachusetts Continentals, a regiment recruited in Marblehead from the sailors of the north shore, some of them Indian or black. Jeers led to snowballs, then to biting and gouging. Soon there was a regular hoedown. The commander in chief rode to the spot and, in the words of one soldier, "leaped from his saddle . . . rushed into the thickest of the melees, with an iron grip seiz[ing] two tall, brawny, athletic, savage-looking riflemen by the throat, keeping them at arm's length, alternately shaking and talking to them." Evidently, the riflemen were persuaded by what he said, for they, and the other rioters, dispersed.

Regional difference often excites derision, and eighteenth-century America's regions were at least as different as red and blue states now. New Englanders were both pious and shrewd, which could make them seem canting. They did not believe in display, or in being ordered around (hence they looked "dirty & nasty," in Washington's eyes). Eastern Virginia, in turn, was a society of deference, whose leaders aspired to be gentlemen. They could seem like blowhards ("Virginian geese are all swans," complained John Adams). Washington learned, first, to keep his thoughts about these differences to himself, then to change his thoughts as experience showed him the fighting qualities of individuals and units. Henry Knox of Massachusetts and Nathanael Greene of Rhode Island turned out to be two of the best generals in his army, and the Fourteenth Massachusetts, whose fight he broke up, would row his army across the Delaware before the Battle of Trenton.

The lesson for a leader is never to judge a book by its cover. When you read the book, it may turn out to be bad, as in the case of Charles Lee. But you may be pleasantly surprised.

CHAPTER 9

Troublemakers

TROUBLE HAPPENS, all the time, everywhere; if there were no troubles, we might not need leaders. You expect enemies and competitors to cause it; troublemakers are people, on your own team or nominal allies, who fill the day with unpleasant surprises. They specialize in friendly fire and own goals. Eliminating or diverting troublemakers can take a fair portion of a leader's time.

How Do You Get Rid of Troublemakers?

Washington was rid of Charles Lee only after working with him for years, and putting him in a position where he almost lost a major battle. Are there better ways to get rid of troublemakers?

One of the many foreign officers commissioned by Congress was Thomas Conway, an Irishman who had grown up in France and risen to the rank of colonel in the French army. Congress made him a brigadier general in 1777, and he fought at the Battles of Brandywine and Germantown, after which he requested a promotion to major general—the highest rank in the army, below commander in chief. Washington disliked him almost instantly. "General Conway's merit as an officer and his importance in this army exist more in his own imagination than in reality. For it is a maxim with him to leave no service of his own untold, nor to [lack] anything that is to be obtained by importunity." Washington knew many ambitious men who thought highly of themselves (Lee, Alexander Hamilton), but Conway struck him as unusually self-seeking.

Self-seeking and hostile, for Conway allied himself with Washington's critics. The end of 1777 was a bad patch for Washington. America won a great victory over Britain, but he did not win it: in October, Horatio Gates defeated a British army outside Saratoga in upstate New York. At the same time, Washington failed to prevent another British army from capturing Philadelphia (Brandywine and Germantown were the battles he fought, unsuccessfully, in defense of the capital). Philadelphia politicians, like Thomas Mifflin, resented the loss of their city. New Englanders, who liked Gates, remembered and resented Washington's dismissive comments from two years before. As a foreigner, Conway did not understand all these currents, but he thought he understood what was good for him. He wrote Gates saying that "a weak general" had almost "ruined" America. In December, Congress promoted Conway to major general, as he had asked, and made him inspector general of the army to boot, reporting directly to a congressional committee.

Criticism of leaders is inevitable; it is necessary, for checks and balances. The movement against Washington, known as the Conway Cabal, was precriticism, the hostility that dare not speak its name, and that is, consequently, even more effective in the early stages of any political maneuver. In all such plots, one observer wrote, "there are prompters and actors . . . candle snuffers, shifters of scenes, and mutes."

One of the first, and most telling, of Washington's responses was to expose Conway's friends, and their interrelations. He forced the mutes to speak. He was aided by a lucky break when one of Gates's aides,

Colonel James Wilkinson, told another officer in a tavern about Con-
way's "weak general" line. That officer told his superior, a friend of
Washington's, who wrote the commander in chief. Washington sent
Conway a little note:

Sir,

*A letter which I received last night contained the following
paragraph: "In a letter from General Conway to General Gates,
he says, '. . . a weak general . . . would have ruined [America].'"*

I am, Sir, Your humble obedient Servant,

George Washington

Washington accomplished several things in this countermaneuver.
He let Conway know that he knew what was going on, without telling
him how he had found out, or what else he knew. Once Conway's
friends learned of Washington's note, they would know that their
quarry was aware of them. They would also be filled with doubt (how
much had Washington learned?) and suspicion (who told him?).

Conway was too dense to understand what had happened; he let
three weeks pass before he showed Washington's letter to Mifflin. But
as soon as Mifflin read it, he understood. He wrote Gates immediately, and both men panicked. Gates protested that someone must
have rifled his papers (not a convincing defense, if what the mystery
thief had found was damning). When Washington told Gates the
whole story of how he had learned of the letter, Gates and Wilkinson
almost fought a duel.

The second thing Washington did was rally his own friends. One
of the most energetic was another French newcomer, the Marquis de

Lafayette, a nineteen-year-old nobleman who had arrived in America about the same time as Conway but whose attitude could not have been more different. When Washington, at their first interview, made some apology for the condition of the American army, Lafayette answered, "I am here, sir, to learn and not to teach." The young man defended his new commander in chief, and father figure, in passionate franglais. "Yes, Sir, [Washington's campaigns] would do one of the finest part of the life of Caesar, Condé, Turenne, and those men whose any soldier cannot pronounce the name without an entousiastik adoration." Caesar had conquered ancient France, Condé and Turenne were France's greatest generals, but Lafayette unhesitatingly put his hero in the pantheon beside them. When Congress offered Lafayette the chance of leading an invasion of Canada, with Conway as second in command, Lafayette refused unless Conway was bucked down to third.

These developments, plus time and the plotters' mistakes—the invasion of Canada was so badly planned that it never got off the ground—caused the plot against Washington to unravel. The intention had been to provoke him into resigning, by making him serve alongside Conway; in the end, Conway, frustrated by Washington's hostility, grandly submitted his own resignation, which Congress, to his surprise, accepted. Washington's critics had been happy to gripe behind his back, and Conway had been happy to be their ally, but they could not risk an open confrontation. As Alexander Hamilton put it, in an artillery man's metaphor, they had unmasked their batteries too soon.

Sometimes troublemakers have to be outwitted and outwaited, because they are (or seem) powerful and promising, and the leader is (perhaps temporarily) weakened. Dealing with troublemakers in this fashion assumes that a leader has friends of his own to fall back on, and that his reputation can outlast a time of trial.

In 1793 Washington had to deal with another provocative French-man, this one a diplomat accredited to the United States.

France supported America's War of Independence out of calcula-tions of realpolitik, to damage its ancient enemy England. But many Frenchmen who served the cause, Lafayette most flamboyantly, did so out of idealism, and wished to see reform in their own country. This impulse, blending with purely domestic discontent, produced a French revolution in July 1789, three months after Washington's first inauguration. The country seemed headed for a liberal constitutional monarchy, with Lafayette playing a leading role. The Revolution, however, ran on under its own momentum: the king was executed, Lafayette fled, and France went to war with its neighbors, including England. Though the United States maintained relations with France, Washington was determined to stay out of the new world war.

In 1793 Edmond Charles Genet was named minister to America. A handsome thirty year old from a family of diplomats, Genet be-longed to the Gironde, the radical faction then leading the Revolu-tion. Like the Trotskyites of the Soviet Union, the Girondists were idealistic, bloodthirsty, and dedicated to spreading their principles worldwide. (The Jacobins who succeeded, and killed, them were the Stalinists: idealistic, bloodthirsty, and dedicated to securing the revo-lution in one country.) Before he sailed, Genet dined with America's minister to France, Gouverneur Morris, who sent a description of him to Washington: "He has I think more of genius than of ability"—more flair than competence—"and you will see in him at the first blush the manner and look of an upstart." Morris warned, prophetically, that Genet would talk too much. After Genet had left the country, Morris learned that he was carrying three hundred blank commissions for privateers—Americans who would volunteer to attack the shipping of France's enemies, from American ports: "a detestable project," thought Morris, for a diplomat posted to a neutral nation.

Genet headed for Philadelphia to present his credentials, but his ship, blown off course, landed in Charleston, South Carolina, in April. He made the trip north in a leisurely twenty-eight days, in the style of a rock star. The French Revolution was still popular in America, with all but a few conservatives, and Citizen Genet—for so all good revolutionaries addressed him—basked in goodwill and ignited more. "It is beyond the power of figures or words to express the hugs and kisses that were lavished on him," one journalist reported. ". . . [V]ery few parts, if any, of the Citizen's body escaped a salute." "I live here in the midst of perpetual fetes," Genet himself wrote. Genet met the president in May, who received him cautiously, without "too much warmth or cordiality."

Genet had concrete actions to perform, and proposals to make. He began issuing his commissions to privateers, and instructing French consuls to set up admiralty courts in American ports, to sell captured ships at a profit to the combatants, and to France. He also wanted to recruit volunteers in the West for an attack on Spanish territory (Spain was one of France's many enemies). Finally, he addressed America's debt to France, left over from the Revolution, which America had been paying off in regular increments. He now suggested that America pay the debt in one swoop to him, so that he could fund his various projects. After all, he pointed out, the money would be spent in America.

Washington instructed Thomas Jefferson, his secretary of state, to tell Genet he could not do any of these things; the United States was not to become a staging area and banker for French foreign policy. Genet couldn't understand it. These were the "diplomatic subtleties" of "ancient politics." The people supported Genet—he had heard them himself. He commissioned a privateer in Philadelphia, under the federal government's nose, and told a state official that if Washington didn't like it, he would "appeal from the President to the people." With that threat, Genet went from waging war on American soil to meddling in American politics. "What must the world think of such conduct," Washington asked angrily, "and of the government of the United States in submitting to it?" In July he decided to stop submitting; France would be asked to recall its troublesome ambassador.

Washington wanted it all done officially, that is, confidentially. Genet was not Conway, the tool of a domestic faction that had to be brought to light. He was the representative of a foreign power—a superpower, in fact—which should be given the chance to set matters right by bringing him home. An account of Genet's threat to appeal to the people was leaked to the newspapers in August, which caused a public backlash in Washington's favor. But that is not the course that Washington himself chose. Pursuing a steady foreign policy was more important to him than the passing ups and downs of his reputation.

Across the ocean, Genet's patrons, the Girondists, went to the guillotine in October, and the Jacobins who replaced them were all too happy to subject Genet to the same fate. He wisely asked to be allowed to stay in America as a private citizen, which Washington approved. "As long as we were in danger from his intrigues," wrote one senator, "we wished him ill—[now] we felt compassion and were anxious he should not be sacrificed."

Many troublemakers will hang themselves, given time and rope. A wise leader lets them do that, rather than go to the additional trouble of fighting with them.

How Do You Work with Troublemakers?

Some troublemakers are not just formal colleagues or allies, but talented, valuable people, even personal friends. They are human artichokes—spiky and time-consuming, but sweet inside. A leader has to find a way—and with each troublemaker of this kind, it will be a different way—of drawing on the good qualities, without getting pricked.

Gouverneur Morris was a New York aristocrat twenty years younger than Washington—tall, attractive, smart, funny, and sexy (even a scarred arm and an amputated leg, souvenirs of various accidents, did not deter unhappily married women from parading through his bedroom). He was sufficiently fluent in French and German to write poems in both languages; he was one of a half-dozen Americans, along with Alexander Hamilton, who understood modern economics; he massaged the Constitution into its final draft, writing the Preamble out of his head.

Despite all these abilities and accomplishments, he could be a pain in the neck. He did not suffer fools, and he placed half the world in that category. If he had a better idea than you did, he said so; if your incompetence or discomfiture amused him, he joked about it. The best-known story about him is a little drama of impertinence. At the Constitutional Convention, Hamilton offered Morris dinner with a dozen friends if he would go up to Washington, slap him on the back, and say, "My dear general, how happy I am to see you look so well." Morris won the bet, but said that the look Washington gave him made it the worst moment of his life. The story is almost certainly not true, but like many tall tales, it captures a truth: if anyone in the founding generation would pull such a stunt, it would be Morris.

Early in 1792, Washington nominated Morris to be America's ambassador to France. Morris had been living in Paris and London for three years, as an international businessman; he was intimate with the main players in both countries (very intimate with some: his girlfriend was the mistress of a French politician); he had been sending Washington letters filled with political briefings that were sharp and shrewd. He did not have a typical diplomat's personality, however, and the Senate grumbled about it, confirming him only narrowly. Washington decided the time had come to read him the riot act:

You were charged . . . with levity and imprudence of conversation and conduct. It was urged that your habits of expression indicated a *hauteur* disgusting to those who happen to differ from you in sentiment. . . . [T]he promptitude with which your lively and brilliant imagination is displayed allows too little time for deliberation and correction, and is the primary cause of those sallies, which too often offend, and of that ridicule of characters which begets enmity not easy to be forgotten, but which might easily be avoided, if it was under the control of more caution and prudence. . . .

I have the fullest confidence (supposing the allegations to be founded in whole or part) that you would find no difficulty . . . to effect a change, and thereby silence, in the most unequivocal and satisfactory manner, your political opponents.

This is a mixture of reporting and command. Washington begins in the third person, recording what was said in the Senate—"You were charged," "it was urged"—but he ends in his own voice, expecting Morris to change. He also mixes praise and criticism—your very brilliance makes you offensive. He asks Morris to silence "political opponents" by behaving differently; implicitly, he wants Morris to silence his own reservations as well.

Morris replied that he would mend his ways. "*I now promise you* that circumspection of conduct which has hitherto, I acknowledge, formed no part of my character. And I make the *promise* [so] that my sense of integrity may enforce what my sense of propriety dictates."

Any promise that has to be written twice, in italics, will probably be hard to keep, and Morris did some undiplomatic things as minister to France (he schemed with the king, in a vain plot to save his life). But he served well in an exceptional time. The king and queen were executed, as were several of Morris's friends. Every nation, except the United States, pulled its diplomats out of Paris; Morris's house was searched, and he was harassed in the street by mobs. He stayed at his post through the Reign of Terror, like a character in an eighteenth-century Alan Furst novel, until France asked for his recall, as tit-for-tat when America demanded the recall of Genet. Washington was pleased with his choice. "He pursued steadily the honor and interest of his country with zest and ability, and with respectful firmness asserted its rights."

More talented and more troublesome was the Virginia aristocrat who was Morris's immediate boss as secretary of state, Thomas Jefferson.

Jefferson was happiest when he was dealing with peas and philosophy—with homely details and immortal insights. He sometimes left the middle ground of policy in the care of his prejudices—an inattention that, though it hampered him as an executive, made him very effective as a politician, for he could express people's ideals and fears with clarity and force, and without thinking.

Washington had known Jefferson longer than anyone else in his administration—since 1769, when they met in the Virginia House of Burgesses. Washington had Jefferson's masterpiece, the Declaration of Independence, read to his troops in New York on July 9, 1776; six weeks later hundreds of them died in defense of it. From 1785 to 1789 Jefferson was America's ambassador to France. When John Jay refused to become the first secretary of state, preferring instead to be chief justice, Washington tapped his fellow Virginian.

All went well for many months. While the capital was still in New York, Washington took Jefferson and Treasury Secretary Alexander Hamilton out beyond Sandy Hook to catch bluefish. But Hamilton's financial program drove the two administration heavyweights apart. Jefferson thought Hamilton intended to increase the government's power, corrupt the legislature with Treasury Department favors, then subvert the Constitution. Washington, who remembered starving troops and unpaid officers, thought Hamilton was giving him a functioning revenue stream and a good credit rating. During the summer of 1792 the rivalry of the two men went public, in a flurry of angry opinion pieces in the newspapers. At the end of August, Washington asked them to cool it, urging "mutual forbearances and temporizing yieldings *on all sides*." Hamilton admitted that he had "some instrumentality" in the newspaper war, which was true, for he had written a number of essays himself under pseudonyms. Jefferson replied that "not a syllable . . . has ever proceeded from me," which was false: the chief pro-Jefferson journalist worked as a translator at the State Department.

The French Revolution drove another wedge into the administration. Hamilton's financial system depended on tariffs, which depended on continued trade with England (*"We think in English,"* he assured an Englishman early in the administration). Jefferson saw France's struggles as the fulfillment of our own. "The liberty of the whole earth was depending on the issue of the contest," he wrote in January 1793. ". . . [R]ather than it should have failed, I would have seen half the earth desolated."

Jefferson was not only a brilliant man who detested one colleague and was unhappy with the direction of things (for Washington had backed Hamilton's fiscal program). Jefferson was also a party leader, with followers across the country, including fellow Virginians James Madison and James Monroe, as well as his State Department journalist. Lyndon Johnson's remark about the best position for J. Edgar Hoover—"I would rather have him inside the tent pissing out than outside the tent pissing in"—lay far in the future. But Washington sensed that it was better to have Jefferson, even unhappy, inside his administration, rather than Jefferson, openly unhappy, outside.

These conflicts came to a head with the arrival in April of Citizen Genet. Jefferson did both what he was told and what he liked. At Washington's direction, the secretary of state forbade Genet from commissioning privateers. "For our citizens . . . to commit murders and depredations on the members of nations at peace with us, or to combine to do it," was "as much against the laws of the land, as to murder or rob, or combine to murder and rob, its own citizens." At the same time, he gushed privately over how "affectionate" Genet was, and gave him briefings on who the good guys (Jefferson) and bad guys (Hamilton) in American politics were.

Early in July, Genet raised the ante, outfitting a privateer in Philadelphia itself. Washington was vacationing at Mount Vernon, so the cabinet conferred. Hamilton wanted the ship blown out of the water by artillery (we had no navy to stop it); Jefferson felt assured, by Genet's "look and gesture," if not his words, that it would not sail away. It sailed. When Washington returned to town in the second week in July, he found a bundle of papers from Jefferson marked "Instant attention," relating all these events.

But Jefferson himself was not to be found, having gone to his house in the suburbs. Washington was not pleased. "After I had read the papers put into my hands by you, requiring 'instant attention,' and before a messenger could reach your office, you had left town. . . . Circumstances press for decision, and, as you have had time to consider them (upon me they come unexpected), I wish to know your opinion upon them."

He got a note in response: "T.J. has had a fever the last two nights. . . . [B]ut nothing but absolute inability will *prevent* his *being in town* early tomorrow morning." Historians have taken Jefferson's excuse of sickness at face value, but perhaps Washington did not: Jefferson had said all the right things to Genet, at least officially, yet Genet had fooled him, and put the government in an awkward position. Jefferson's credulity had made him the instrument of Genet's troublemaking. No doubt Jefferson was reluctant to face the music.

Over the next six weeks, Washington had to decide how to handle both the Frenchman and his secretary of state. Everyone in the cabinet agreed that America should ask France to recall Genet; they disagreed over whether to reveal his indiscretions to the public. Hamilton was all for full exposure; he was almost certainly the source of the leak of Genet's threat to "appeal from the President to the people." Jefferson wanted our unhappiness confined to diplomatic protests.

Washington sided with Jefferson, because he did not want to provoke France. He also sided with him because he did not want to provoke Jefferson. At the end of July the secretary of state wrote that he expected to retire soon, to "scenes of greater tranquility." Washington rode out to Jefferson's suburban retreat for a heart-to-heart talk, which, like many such discussions, was thick with double-talk. Jefferson denied having "any communication" with any political party; Washington said he believed the motives of Jefferson's party were "perfectly pure." In the end Jefferson agreed to stay on until December.

If the secretary of state had quit while the Genet affair was still up in the air, it would have inflamed domestic politics even further. In return for Jefferson's fidelity, Washington agreed to rebuke Genet only through official channels, which was his inclination anyway. (Jefferson would write the demand for Genet's recall.) At the cost of some blundering—Genet's privateer had gotten away—Washington avoided both an international incident and a domestic incident.

Sometimes a troublemaker can be put to good use, as Washington put Morris; sometimes he can be kept on, still useful, as long as possible, and prevented from doing greater trouble, as Washington did with Jefferson. Open troublemakers can be dealt with openly; conflicted, secretive ones often have to be met on their own turf. There is always a lot to put up with, but the gains can be worth it.

CHAPTER 10

SUPERIORS AND SUBORDINATES

A HERMIT'S CELL has no hierarchy because it is inhabited by only one person. A mob has no hierarchy because it has no order. Every other human organization has rank, even those that say that all men and women are brothers and sisters.

Dealing properly with superiors and subordinates is a perpetual task of leaders.

SUPERIORS

Unless you are at the pinnacle of a very top-down organization, you have superiors to whom you must answer, or peers who in special cases become your superiors—boards of directors, trustees, executive committees, legislatures. A leader must keep them in mind, since they are keeping him in their minds.

Washington did not always play well with superiors. When he was a twentysomething militia officer during the French and Indian War, he went behind their backs to even more exalted superiors, carping at decisions that had already been made ("Nothing now but a *miracle* can bring this campaign to a happy issue"; "behold! How the golden opportunity is lost") or angling for promotion for himself, in language that creeps like a creeping vine ("Don't think my Lord I am going to flatter. . . . My nature is honest, and free from guile"). But age and confidence bred this behavior out of him before it became habit, and by the time Congress picked him to be commander in chief in 1775, he had achieved maturity in his dealings with higher-ups.

The speech he made in Congress on June 16, 1775, accepting the appointment, signaled his acknowledgment of his new status, and of the obligations he would thenceforth be under. Up to that moment, he had been a member of Congress from Virginia, one among equals. When he made a passing reference to "every gentleman in the room," he used the language of parliamentary politeness, in which peers address each other. But when he promised to "exert every power I possess in [Congress's] service," he was showing that his new responsibilities, however great, made him their subordinate.

Over time, General Washington learned that some congressmen were his friends, while others were not. Some moved from one column to the other. Richard Henry Lee of Virginia (no relation to Charles Lee) was an old acquaintance of Washington's, and the two men wrote with freedom and intimacy during the early days of the war. But Lee repaid Washington's confidence by leaking his tart comments on New Englanders, then by playing with the Conway Cabal. Henry Laurens of South Carolina went the other way, from fence-sitting to support, in part under the influence of his son John, a colonel on Washington's staff. As the Conway Cabal unraveled, Washington wrote Laurens senior with real thankfulness: "I have a grateful sense of the favourable disposition you have manifested to me in this affair." Politics happens within and around every formal structure, like mice chewing behind a baseboard. But Washington remembered the formal structure, and where he stood in it, even at moments of desperation.

One such came at the beginning of 1781. By then the war had been going on for almost six years. French help had given America a shot in the arm, and Baron von Steuben had professionalized the troops. But somehow the winning combination eluded the allies, while problems of payment and supply never went away. On New Year's Day 2,000 Pennsylvania soldiers mutinied in their winter quarters in Morristown, New Jersey, and threatened to march to Philadelphia to demand better treatment by Congress. The commanding officer they disobeyed, General Anthony Wayne, almost sympathized: "not having received a paper dollar for near twelve months; exposed to winter's piercing cold, to drifting snows and chilling blasts, with no protection but old worn-out clothes, tattered linen overalls and but one blanket between three men." While the mutineers were still en route, Washington decided to go over Congress's head, by writing directly to the governors of the New England states.

Necessity drove him. New England was the cupboard of the Revolution, providing the army with food and supplies. When Congress asked the states for the wherewithal to keep the army going, the states that answered most readily were the New England states. By writing their governors himself, Washington was taking a shortcut through the chain of command.

Or was he? "It is not within the sphere of my duty," he admitted, "to make requisitions, without the authority of Congress, from individual states; but at such a crisis, and circumstanced as we are, my own heart will acquit me; and Congress . . . I am persuaded will excuse me, when once for all I give it decidedly as my opinion." Two thousand men have mutinied, and he still stops at his opinion "that it is in vain to think an army can be kept together much longer . . . unless some immediate and spirited measures are adopted." He mentions two measures—more regular supplies of food and clothes, three months' pay—but who does he expect will adopt them? "I have transmitted Congress a copy of this letter, and have in the most pressing manner requested them to adopt the measure which I have above recommended." His most pressing manner is to make a request. "And as I will not doubt of their compliance, I have thought proper to give you this previous notice, that you may be prepared to answer the requisition." The only word that might carry a whiff of compulsion in all this is *compliance*, but it is so wrapped in deferential assumptions ("as I will not doubt") that even a dog would not smell it.

The crisis of discipline was real. The Pennsylvania mutineers were talked down, but two weeks after Washington's letter to the governors, troops from New Jersey marched out of their barracks; their ringleaders had to be shot. The state of the army was a matter of life and death, yet the hardest Washington pushed the envelope of congressional authority was to send a heads-up to some governors.

But maybe the best measure of Washington's view of his relationship to Congress is how he reacted when someone proposed changing it.

Congress scraped together the funds for a last campaign in 1781, which ended in victory at Yorktown. The army had to stay mobilized until peace was concluded, however, and the situation returned to normal disarray. On May 22, 1782, Washington got a letter from Colonel Lewis Nicola, commander of the Invalid Corps, injured veterans assigned to garrison duty. Nicola was getting on (sixty-five), foreign born (Irish), learned, and meticulous. He brought the last two qualities to bear on a long essay he sent the commander in chief.

He began by reviewing what everyone knew, the problems of the army, then what every literate person knew, the hypothetical advantages and disadvantages of different forms of government. A "mixed government," Nicola argued, combining republican and royal elements, might enjoy the advantages of both. The British government, for example, though "far . . . from perfect," was "no despicable basis" for a "good" system. Then he made his pitch. The war itself had made the case for mixed government in America, since it had shown both "the weakness of republics, and the exertions the army has been able to make by being under a proper head." Congress had almost lost the war, but Washington had won it. Congress should be part of a postwar mixed government, but it should work in tandem with a king, and Nicola had a potential sovereign in mind. "The same abilities which have led us . . . to victory and glory . . . would be most likely to conduct and direct us in the smoother paths of peace."

Washington answered the same day. Nicola's proposal had filled seven closely written pages; Washington demolished it in two paragraphs. The colonel's ideas, he wrote, filled him with "surprise," "astonishment," "painful sensations," and "abhorrence." In return, he urged Nicola to "banish these thoughts from your mind." He had his copy of the answer witnessed by two aides, so that there should be no doubt about what he had written. A flustered Nicola sent him three apologies over the next six days.

As commander in chief, Washington reached out to friendly congressmen, and offered his opinions to Congress as a whole. After the war ended and he had returned to private life, he joined a movement to change the form of government. But so long as he worked for Congress, he never forgot who his bosses were, and wanted no one else to forget it either.

Washington made the template for American military leaders and their civilian superiors. Although some former commanders would make trouble for the politicians who cashiered them—George Mc-Clellan for Abraham Lincoln in the Civil War, Douglas MacArthur for Harry Truman in the Korean War—they accepted their dismissals, and made their trouble as civilians, peers of the men they disagreed with. CEOs who enter into improper relations with their directors do not risk upheaval in the state, though if they collude with them to defraud shareholders, they risk jail. A leader watches his back, defends his turf, sticks by what he believes—and knows his place.

SUBORDINATES

Rudyard Kipling's poem of life coaching, "If," says we should be able to "walk with kings—nor lose the common touch." But don't kings, and other leaders, need the common touch—at least a touch of it?

Joseph White enlisted in a Massachusetts artillery regiment in the spring of 1775, age nineteen. Because he could spell, the adjutant, or the colonel's assistant, took him on as his own assistant (a made-up rank). Young White bought himself a used uniform trimmed with gold lace. The following December, the colonel sent White with a message to the commander in chief. When he presented himself at headquarters in Cambridge, Washington asked, "Pray sir, what officer are you?" Assistant Adjutant White gave his rank. "Indeed," said Washington, "you are very young to do that duty." White answered smartly: he was young, but growing older every day. Washington turned to his wife, who had joined him in camp, and smiled.

William Lloyd began serving in the New Jersey militia in the summer of 1776, also age nineteen. During the winter of 1778–1779, the army camped at Middlebrook, now Bound Brook, in central New Jersey. Lloyd's unit made an all-night march to Middlebrook to counter a movement of the British (along the way, Lloyd and a few friends snatched some sleep under the porch of a house). For a few days, nothing happened; then as now, hurry up and wait was a fact of military life. Finally, the British withdrew. Lloyd "saw General Washington view them striking their tents, and by his permission I looked at them through his spyglass." Lloyd was not as obviously cheeky as White, but he had some spunk nonetheless. Why would Washington have given him permission to look through his spyglass, unless he asked?

White and Lloyd wrote these stories when they were old men, in order to get veterans' pensions. But they had served when they were young. Other young men—Alexander Hamilton, the Marquis de Lafayette—started in high ranks, or earned them, and won fame and glory. White and Lloyd were typical of the thousands who served and fought and died, or lived to live out ordinary lives. A great proportion of these men saw their commander in chief, and a number of them met him, if only for a moment. Without surrendering a bit of rank or dignity, Washington knew how to appreciate a joke, which was partly on the teller of it, and when to loan his spyglass.

The name for a leader who never does these things is martinet; he does everything by the book. Such a man can accomplish a lot, though he is limited, for his inferiors will obey him by the book. He never breaks the glass ceiling of his own rigidity.

CHAPTER 11

FAILURE AND BETRAYAL

HOW DO YOU respond to the bad things people do? The seriously bad things, not workaday blunders and cross-purposes, but failure and betrayal? Washington's favorite play, Joseph Addison's *Cato*, an eighteenth-century hit about ancient Rome, gave him a model to emulate. "Thy steady temper," says one Roman admiringly to another in the very first scene, "can look on guilt, rebellion, fraud . . . in the calm lights of mild philosophy."

Easy to say on stage. Is that how it works in real life?

FAILURE

In October 1776 America suffered the worst defeat of the Revolution so far thanks to the advice of a thirty-four-year-old major general who had been in only one battle in his life.

Nathanael Greene had a rapid rise through the ranks. He enlisted as a private in the Rhode Island militia in 1774; profiting from political connections, he was promoted to general the following year. In the spring of 1776, Congress bucked him up to major general. The qualities that sped Greene along in the world, besides helpful friends, were optimism, a capacity for organization and hard work, decisiveness, and a willingness to proclaim his decisions. (As Washington considered how to defend New York against superior British forces that summer and fall, Greene told him not to try: since two-thirds of the property belonged to Tories anyway, "I would burn the city and suburbs.") For these reasons, Greene and the commander in chief hit it off. But his combat experience was almost nil, restricted to a skirmish on Harlem Heights in September (a fever had kept him out of the Battle of Long Island in August).

Greene was assigned to prepare the defense of New Jersey, and to oversee two forts that faced each other across the lower Hudson River—Fort Lee on the Jersey side, and Fort Washington in northern Manhattan (the George Washington Bridge connects these two points today). In October Washington took most of his army off Manhattan to the north. But he left 2,000 troops in Fort Washington, to keep British ships out of the river, and to keep an American presence on the island.

Washington was away from the immediate New York area for four weeks, playing a game of ring-around-the-Hudson with the pursuing British. He felt some doubts about the fort named after him when he learned that three British ships managed to sail up the river at the beginning of November, despite a bombardment from the fort's guns. "What valuable purpose can it answer," he wrote Greene, "to attempt to hold a post [from] which the expected benefit cannot be had"? But he ceded the decision to stay or go to the new major general. "As you are on the spot, [I] leave it to you to give such orders as to evacuating . . . as you judge best." Greene, meanwhile, remained confident—"I cannot conceive the garrison to be in any great danger"—and even reinforced it with a thousand more men.

Washington appeared back on the scene, on the Jersey side, on November 13, Greene assuring him once more that Fort Washington could be maintained. His judgment was tested very soon. On the fifteenth, the British massed thousands of troops around the fort, and demanded its surrender. Washington and Greene rowed across the Hudson the next morning to assess the situation. The British attack began as they sailed. When they arrived, they concluded that it was too late to change anything for the better. Greene urged Washington to return to New Jersey, and volunteered to stay behind to lead the defense, but the commander in chief brought him back, leaving the garrison in the command of its colonel. In a few hours, he surrendered; some 2,800 men were taken prisoner, many of them destined to die in filthy confinement.

Years later, writer Washington Irving was told by an old veteran that when the fort fell, Washington wept "with the tenderness of a child." Greene's reaction survives in a letter to Henry Knox. "I feel mad, vexed, sick and sorry. . . . This is a most terrible event. Its consequences are justly to be dreaded." Dreaded certainly by Greene, on whom many were willing to pin the blame. "Oh, general!" one critic wrote Washington, "why would you be over-persuaded by men of inferior judgment to your own?"

Greene's judgment had been warped by several factors. Other problems distracted him. In the big picture, the fort was a piece on a military chessboard; even if it no longer guarded the river effectively, it could be worth holding, since that would force other British pieces to stay nearby to check it. But what if the British made it the focus of their attack? In that case, Greene was still swayed by the Battle of Bunker Hill a year earlier, when the British took an entrenched hilltop at the cost of 1,000 casualties. Give them a tough nut to crack, and let them bleed trying. But Fort Washington—not a single building, but an immense tract of fortified ground—had many liabilities as a defensive position. If the British controlled the water (as they did), it could be approached from several directions. The perimeter was too large to be defended by even 3,000 men, yet the redoubt in the middle too small to hold them if they had to retreat.

Washington, reporting to Congress the day after the debacle, divided the blame between himself and his major general, admitting that he had "determined . . . to risk something" to defend the fort, but adding that Greene, "direct[ed] . . . to govern himself by circumstances," had dug in even deeper. Does this blame Greene too much, since it was Washington, after all, who had directed him to use his judgment? Or does it avoid the peculiarly modern vice of leaders who "take full responsibility" for the failures of subordinates, when they mean to do no such thing? (Since you aren't going to replace me, if I say that I take full responsibility, then nobody has to take any.)

Washington had little time to consider the matter, since the fall of his namesake was followed by six weeks of retreat, from the Hudson to the Delaware. Washington kept Greene by him during this grim time, still relying on the qualities he saw in him, despite his great mistake. Greene's optimism returned very soon. "Fortune seems to frown upon the cause of freedom," he wrote his wife in mid-December. "However, I hope this is the dark part of the night, which generally is just before day." He showed his mettle at the end of the year, in the Battles of Trenton and Princeton, over the next three years, and finally in 1780, when he was sent to retrieve an even greater failure than his own, Horatio Gates's defeat at the Battle of Camden, South Carolina, which left the entire Deep South at the mercy of the British. In six months of nerve and brilliance, Greene won it all back, reclaiming one-quarter of America.

Would the men who were taken prisoner at Fort Washington have appreciated Greene's redemption? Probably not, but they would have appreciated his redemption of the cause.

A leader must face failure squarely, including the failures of people he likes. But life is not a reality show, with an elimination after every round. If a leader believes there is ability and solidity in a man, he should be given the opportunity to show it. Good men are rarer than good days, and more valuable.

BETRAYAL

In ordinary competition, the other side fights yours: In the case of failure, your side lets you down; in the case of betrayal, your side becomes the other side. Your plans become your competitors' reading material, your men become your enemies' men, your efforts are made to serve another cause—all unbeknownst to you. For these reasons, betrayal must be roughly dealt with. Ordinary business or political backstabs deserve firing or shunning; betrayal of the state deserves prison or death (in Washington's time, many countries threw in torture).

Because the offense is serious, proving it must also be serious. Because traitors are hateful, there is always a temptation to hang the label on miscellaneous enemies. Most of the discussion of treason that Washington heard at the Constitutional Convention consisted of defining very strictly what treason was, since, as Benjamin Franklin put it, prosecutions for treason were typically "virulent." The cure could be as contagious as the disease.

The complaints of the officers at Newburgh, New York, in the spring of 1783 (see Chapter 6, "Communication") were not treasonous—no one was proposing to switch sides and fight for England—but they were certainly mutinous. The unpaid officers thought they were standing up for their rights, which had been ignored by a feckless Congress. Major John Armstrong, who wrote their rallying cry, warned his comrades that they were on "the very verge" of "sinking into cowardice, or plunging into credulity"—too scared to defend themselves, or too dumb to see that they were being cheated. "Another step would ruin you forever." Washington thought they were on a different verge, "the precipice of despair," where another step would "lead to an abyss of misery," filled with disobedience, commotion, and bloodshed.

Time for drastic measures then. But what sort? Who were the mutinous officers? Armstrong worked for Horatio Gates, who had several blots on his record: dabbling with the Conway Cabal, losing the Battle of Camden, trying now, perhaps, through his aide, to regain his luster as the army's champion. But Gates had served his country loyally, and at least once (Saratoga) very well; he was vain and grumbling, not wicked. Armstrong himself, then twenty-four years old, would go on to a long political career, ending as James Madison's secretary of war. And who else was complaining, if not endorsing Armstrong's appeal outright? Washington's favorite aide, Alexander Hamilton, now a congressman, thought pressure from the military might get Congress moving, and advised the commander in chief "to guide the torrent." Washington's favorite gadfly, Gouverneur Morris, was telling one of his favorite officers, Henry Knox, that Congress "will see you starve rather than pay you a six-penny tax." Many of the men in and around the plot were friends; all of them were patriots. Washington wanted to bring them to their senses, not punish them.

So Washington called for the officers to meet, and made his dramatic appeal. His gestures fitted his argument. I have grown gray in your service, and now find myself growing blind, he told the officers when he put on his reading glasses; in his prepared remarks he reminded them, "I have never left your side one moment. . . . I have been the constant companion and witness of your distresses, and not the last to feel and acknowledge your merits." They had served together for nearly eight years; they should go on together, in obedience to the laws (and to him). With an emotional preemptive strike, he kept potential mutineers from committing themselves irreparably. "It is easier," he wrote, "to divert from a wrong to a right path, than it is to recall the hasty and fatal steps which have already been taken."

At Newburgh, years of neglect almost led good men wrong. Another temptation to act badly was the quick rewards of corruption. Eighteenth-century armies allowed those who supplied them to take percentages as commissions, which virtually invited insider trading and kickbacks. It happened all the time, and all the time people complained about it. Silas Deane, America's first minister to France, entangled himself in the military supply racket, and so did Major General Benedict Arnold, when he was military governor of Philadelphia.

Arnold got the Philadelphia posting in 1778 because he was crippled in battle. A Connecticut merchant who had enlisted at the start of the war, he swiftly became the best fighting leader on the American side. In a series of campaigns in Canada and upstate New York, he was creative, active, and bold to the point of recklessness. The height of his efforts were the twin battles of Saratoga in 1777, Freeman's Farm and Bemis Heights, in which he helped crush a British invasion, fighting with "the fury of a demon," as one of his men put it. Horatio Gates, his commanding officer, shared the effort and took all the credit. At Bemis Heights, Arnold was shot in the leg; the Philadelphia posting would give him a chance to recuperate.

He used it as a chance to recoup some of his prewar fortune, requisitioning military transport for private business, and doing official favors for ventures in which he had an interest. He also picked needless quarrels with the Pennsylvania state government, which gave it all the more incentive to prosecute him for graft. Arnold's case went before Congress, and finally a court-martial. Many of his comrades thought he was being harshly judged. "I wish America may not become famous for ingratitude," wrote Nathanael Greene. In the end, Washington was directed to reprimand him, which he did, early in 1780, more in sorrow than in anger. "In proportion as you have rendered yourself formidable to our enemies, you should have been guarded and temperate in your deportment towards your fellow-citizens. Exhibit anew those noble qualities which have placed you on the list of our most valued commanders [and] I will myself furnish you . . . with opportunities for regaining the esteem of your country." Be a hero again, Washington was saying, and I will give you a new command. Arnold asked to be sent to West Point, a second Fort Washington overlooking the Hudson River.

But Arnold already had new commanders, for he had been negotiating with the enemy since the previous spring, spurred by his travails, and encouraged by his wife, a pretty young Philadelphia Tory. Arnold's grand stroke for his new masters would be to hand over West Point, and George Washington himself. His reward would be 10,000 pounds (he had asked for 20,000) and a major general's commission, to replace his American major general's commission. The plot, which was supposed to be sprung in September 1780, when Washington and his staff arrived for an inspection, was revealed when the Americans captured Arnold's British handler, and a sheaf of incriminating documents. When Washington first read them, he exclaimed, "Whom can we trust now?"

Arnold had managed to get away, leaving his wife, and her newborn, behind. She put on a first-class act, which Alexander Hamilton described in a letter. "[Washington] went up to see her and she upbraided him with being in a plot to murder her child; one moment she raved; another she melted into tears; sometimes she pressed her infant to her bosom and lamented its fate. . . . All the sweetness of beauty, all the loveliness of innocence, all the tenderness of a wife and all the fondness of a mother showed themselves in her appearance." Loveliness, maybe, but no innocence, which the Americans soon figured out.

Mrs. Arnold was finally allowed to rejoin her husband in Britishoccupied New York. In every other way, Washington was implacable.

He hanged Arnold's captured handler, a British major, as a common spy, despite the protests of his officers, who admired the young man's manner, and hoped he might be shot instead, the honorable way to go. Washington took a strict view: the major had been captured, out of uniform, behind American lines, which made him a spy, and the penalty for spying was the gallows. Washington approved a plot to have Arnold kidnapped from New York: an American sergeant "defected" to the British, ingratiated himself with the traitor, and planned to mug him at night in his garden and hustle him to a waiting rowboat. The plot misfired due to a last-minute change in Arnold's schedule. (He died, underpaid—after all, he hadn't delivered West Point—and unmourned by his new compatriots, in 1801.)

Washington reacted sternly to Arnold's treason. Should he have detected him sooner? Mrs. Arnold, assisted by her tears, her infant, and her bosom, fooled Washington for a few days. Benedict Arnold schemed, unsuspected, for a year and a half.

But how could Washington have found him out? They were not in regular contact; Washington had no system of informers to keep tabs on his officers. It would be nice, sometimes, to know everything. Failing that, Washington made the same judgment of Arnold that he made of the Newburgh conspirators—they were all good men in need of correction. Wrong in one case, right in the other.

The consequences of not presuming good faith can be seen in a leadership failure that Washington committed as president in 1795. When he discovered gross indiscretion in a trusted aide, he did the right thing, in the wrong way.

He had gone to Mount Vernon in midsummer to clear his head, which needed it—America's relations with Britain and France, and the quarrels of pro-British and pro-French Americans at home, were still inflamed, two years after Citizen Genet (they would stay inflamed for twenty years more). But Washington came back to

Philadelphia earlier than he had planned, because of a request from the new secretary of war, Timothy Pickering, who mentioned "a *special reason*" that could be explained "only in person." Washington was dining with his secretary of state, Edmund Randolph, when Pickering appeared. The president took him aside to ask what he meant. Pickering pointed to the dining room where Randolph remained, and said, "That man is a traitor." His proof of this charge was a document that he and Oliver Wolcott, now treasury secretary, laid before Washington later that night.

This was a French diplomat's report, seized at sea by the British the previous fall. The seizure was straight out of Patrick O'Brian: a British frigate encountered a French corvette in mid-Atlantic; the French ship, as it fled, threw something overboard, which, when the British retrieved it, turned out to be a diplomatic pouch. The follow-up was straight out of John le Carré: the foreign minister sent the report to his ambassador in Philadelphia, with instructions to show it to "well disposed [that is, pro-British] persons." The ambassador gave it to Wolcott.

In the report, the Frenchman boasted that he had learned the "secret views" of the American government from private conversations with the secretary of state. True patriots considered America's taxes "immoral and impolitic," and its policy toward Britain "imbecil[e]." The Whiskey Rebellion of 1794 may have been a put-up job, deliberately provoked "to introduce absolute power." Washington was not responsible for these nefarious measures, but he was misled, and would be misled still more if it were not for "the influence of Mr. Randolph."

Diplomats not only tell lies for their country but also tell lies to their country, to show off who they know and how much they have learned. But if even a portion of what the Frenchman wrote was true, then Randolph had stepped out of line. In a meeting a week later, with Pickering and Wolcott present, Washington handed the report to Randolph, and asked him to "make such explanations as you choose."

Washington staged the little scene to see if Randolph would react guiltily. Instead, he reacted angrily, reading the report, answering a few questions, and then shouting that he could not stay in office "one second after such treatment."

Anyone would be bitter about being put on the spot, as if for a public urine test, but Randolph had special reasons. His father, John Randolph, Virginia's colonial attorney general, had gone to Britain at the beginning of the Revolution rather than break his oath of office. George Washington then took on twenty-two-year-old Edmund as an aide for three months. Now the man who had saved him from the taint of his father's conflicted loyalties was questioning his own loyalty.

Washington had his own reasons to be suspicious. The last trusted associate whose dealings with a foreign power he had learned of from captured papers had been Benedict Arnold fifteen years earlier. He must have wondered, all over again, "Whom can we trust now?" Still he owed it to his secretary of state to have first challenged him privately. Pickering and Wolcott wouldn't have liked it; they didn't like Randolph, and already knew he had acted suspiciously. Too bad.

After resigning, Randolph explained his conduct in a pamphlet of more than a hundred pages, which has convinced almost nobody, then or since, that he had not been indiscreet. Randolph talked to the French ambassador the way he did because he was torn between his personal loyalty to Washington and his growing disenchantment with Washington's policies. Randolph, like most Virginians, was a Francophile and an agrarian, if less zealous than Thomas Jefferson. If he felt that bad about the direction of the administration, he ought to have quit; he certainly should not have shared his unhappiness with foreign powers. But the bungle of his exit was not only his fault.

Randolph was also not the only man hurt by it. His departure left Washington, for the first time in six years, with a politically monochromatic cabinet. Although Washington had been annoyed by in-house skeptics (see Chapter 9, "Troublemakers"), he had also profited from their input (see Chapter 5, "Management Style"). To replace Randolph, Washington turned to one of his accusers, Secretary of War Timothy Pickering, called by a recent historian a "glowering hack." Six other men were offered the job, but turned it down, unwilling to serve in the noxious political climate. Washington was not trading up.

A leader should coax the wavering back from destruction, especially if they are good men otherwise, but once they commit themselves to betrayal they must be cast out. Betrayal is serious; so is the search for it. Leaders who are slow to judge leave themselves vulnerable to the machinations of the soulless, but leaders who rush to judgment may damage their colleagues, disrupt their organizations, and demoralize themselves.

CHAPTER 12

ENEMIES

ENEMIES HAVE to be beaten—killed or impoverished in war, defeated in politics, outsold in business. Everyone understands this, from the earliest childhood game with winners and losers. But as we grow older, we learn there are other things we have to do with enemies, during and after the contest.

LIVING WITH ENEMIES

Washington played to win. He went to the Constitutional Convention only when he was sure that most of the delegates were as serious about change as he was; once the Constitution was written, he did everything in his power to ensure that his state ratified it. "Be assured," wrote James Monroe, a Virginian who opposed the Constitution, "his influence carried this government."

When, as a private citizen, assigned to survey land claims for French and Indian War veterans, he was accused of shortchanging a fellow veteran (and benefiting himself), he reacted with wrath, telling the complainant in a letter that he was impertinent, drunk, rude, stupid, and sottish. He stepped so far outside the bounds of normal discourse between gentlemen because his honesty and honor had been questioned: that demanded a nuclear response. In real war, he could show a stern face, hanging Benedict Arnold's spymaster.

He went to great lengths to secure specific goals, or to respond to particular offenses. Yet his behavior toward enemies was usually modified by his awareness of time. He looked beyond the moment he was in to the time that was to come. Some enemies would survive the struggle; perhaps the struggle was over, and they had already survived it. They might be fellow citizens; even if they lived on different continents, they would still be sharing the same world. That thought influenced how he treated them as he was beating them.

The Revolution had some of the characteristics of civil war, and the internecine strife of city-states. As rival armies came and went, many ordinary people sat on the sidelines, while others, more zealous in the cause, recommended harsh measures for timeservers. When the British left Philadelphia in 1778, after an exceedingly pleasant occupation, Gouverneur Morris suggested that the city be fined for collaborating. At their worst, grudges morphed into vendettas. In 1780 Nathanael Greene reported that patriot and loyalist guerrillas in the Deep South "pursue[d] each other" like "beasts of prey." After the war, survivors longed to settle accounts; New York, which had suffered a long occupation, encouraged patriots to sue loyalists for doing business under British rule. Washington set his face against reprisals, monetary or violent. Morris's plan to punish Philadelphia, he wrote, "widely differs from mine." Like Greene, whom he had sent to run the southern theater, he wanted a war conducted by disciplined troops, not partisans settling scores. When New York's courts interpreted the state's punitive laws in a humane spirit, Washington, observing from out of state, gave his "hearty assent."

Washington dealt coolly with enemy nations. Many of his colleagues, including three future presidents—Thomas Jefferson, James Madison, and James Monroe—were frozen by the Revolutionary War, becoming diehard Anglophobes and Francophiles, especially after France's revolution made her a sister republic. Washington was guided by the longer perspective of his career. In his twenties, in the French and Indian War, he had fought and killed Frenchmen alongside the British. In his forties, in the Revolution, he had done the reverse. Who could say when he might be compelled to switch again? His mildness toward his old enemies (so long as they behaved well) was joined by a certain wariness of his foreign friends. "No nation," he wrote during the war, "is to be trusted farther than it is bound by its interest."

One occasion on which he broke his own rule justified it. In the mid-eighteenth century the Iroquois Indians of western New York— six allied Indian nations—made themselves indispensable to the British Empire in North America, as warriors who could hold hostile Indians at bay, and diplomats who could influence other tribes in Britain's favor. When Britain and its colonies came to blows, the Iroquois did not know which way to turn. One nation, the Oneida, sided with the United States; the other five were neutral, or pro-British (the Anglo faction was led by Joseph Brant, a charismatic Mohawk chief who had been to London and hobnobbed with James Boswell and George III). In 1779 Washington authorized the "entire destruction" of unfriendly Iroquois villages, burning houses, crops, and orchards. Martha Washington, who saw some of the pro-American Indians before they set off on the mission, thought they looked like "cutthroats all." The punished tribes simply fled to Canada, and redoubled their raids. It was not until 1790 when Washington, then president, was able to make a treaty, promising that "all the miseries of the late war . . . be forgotten and buried together"—so long as "rash young men" did not fight alongside "bad Indians" farther west.

Beat your enemies well, then treat them well; they are not going anywhere, and they might even turn out to be your friends in the next go-round.

LEARNING FROM ENEMIES

They are wrong, they are bad, they have something you want, they want something you have—for whatever reason, they are enemies. But suppose they know something you don't?

Washington first went over the Blue Ridge Mountains to the Shenandoah Valley in 1748, age sixteen, and saw his first Indian war party; he went over the Alleghenies, almost to Lake Erie, in 1753, age twenty-one, to scout French positions, and to rendezvous with friendly Iroquois. But for all that, he had no experience fighting against, or beside, Indians, when, in 1754, he was given a lieutenant colonel's rank in the Virginia militia and the assignment of thwarting whatever the French were up to on the frontier that year.

His effort was not an entire failure. He and his men hacked a path through the wilderness, from western Maryland, halfway to the site of present-day Pittsburgh. Along the way, they encountered a small party of Frenchmen and overwhelmed them (Washington's Indian allies scalped the wounded). But when a much larger party of French and pro-French Indians came on the scene, Washington decided to defend a hastily built fort in a small clearing on low ground. The smallness of the clearing meant that enemies could get close while still under cover; the lowness of the ground meant the defenders had almost no cover. The friendly Indians, not liking the look of things, vanished. After taking one hundred casualties (a third of his force), Washington capitulated, the French graciously allowing him to retreat.

Wilderness veterans graded his performance harshly. William Johnson, Britain's agent for Indian affairs in upstate New York, and one of the smartest white men on the frontier, said the young officer had been "too ambitious of acquiring all the honor." Tanacharison, a Seneca chief who had accompanied Washington on both of his missions, in 1753 and 1754, complained that he "had no experience . . .

that he took upon him to command his Indians as slaves . . . and that he would by no means take advice from Indians. . . . [He] would never listen to them, but was always driving them on to fight by his directions." Washington wanted to be noticed, but, apart from energy and courage, he had nothing deserving of notice, certainly not savvy.

Young colonial militia officers were not the only people who had something to learn about wilderness warfare. The following year, Britain sent 2,500 troops, commanded by Major General Edward Braddock of the regular army, to drive the French out of the upper Ohio Valley for real. Washington went along as an aide-de-camp, and was present for the final debacle, when Braddock's advance guard of 1,300 men, minus any Indian scouts (Braddock had offended them), was ambushed. Some 900 British and colonials were killed (including Braddock himself) or wounded; Washington was one of the few who lived to tell the tale.

What America knows as the French and Indian War, and the world knows as the Seven Years' War, was under way. Washington would spend most of his remaining time in it commanding a regiment assigned to defend Virginia's western border. In this position, he combined the discipline and drill that he admired and envied in the British army with the tactical lessons he had learned, at such heavy cost, over the past two years.

He had 350 miles of frontier to defend. Two thousand troops, he thought, might be able to do the job, though he never had nearly that many. He built forts, better sited than the one he had thrown up in western Pennsylvania, but he put his hopes on troops that would be light, mobile, and skilled in forest skirmishing. He also wanted Indian allies to counteract the pro-French Shawnees and Delawares; since the Iroquois were fighting on other fronts to the north, he thought of Catawbas, or Cherokees. "Indians are the only match for Indians," he wrote; on another occasion, he ordered his men to speak well of them in their presence: "All of them understand English, and ought not to be affronted."

In 1758, when the British decided to make another big push into western Pennsylvania, Washington offered his expertise to the new commander, General John Forbes, who was happy to have it. "We must comply," Forbes wrote, "and learn the art of war from enemy Indians, or any[one] else who have seen the country and war carried on in it." This time, when the British and the colonials converged on France's premier wilderness fort, they found it abandoned and burning, the French having decided that they had met their match at last.

People who know a little about the American Revolution believe that we won it because Washington and his comrades repeated the frontier tactics they learned in the French and Indian War. This is mostly nonsense. Washington's strategy was different in the two wars, because the wars were different. Every siege or battle he fought in the Revolution, from Boston to Yorktown, occurred in the clear terrain of the East Coast. In a landscape akin to Europe's, fighting British and German professional soldiers, he had to prevail using European means, however Baron von Steuben tweaked them. But when Washington fought Indians where Indians lived, he learned from their methods.

In war, enemies may know the terrain, or the culture of the inhabitants; in the mock war of business (as in a "hostile" takeover), enemies may understand the corporate culture of the company that is up for grabs. In the long run, cultures and even environments may have to be changed, but in the short run, they must be understood. That means learning from enemies.

There are limits to learning. Should Washington have scalped the wounded French himself? Clearly not. Should he have prevented his allies from doing so? If he could. A leader should never learn to stop being true to himself.

CHAPTER 13

ALLIES

ALLIES ARE more than people who have signed treaties with you, or who have agreed to work with you. They are the people who are in your corner, wherever you are. Washington depended on allies all his life. There are geniuses who work alone, relying (apart from their talents) on what Stephen Dedalus called "silence, exile, and cunning," but they are not leaders. In a world full of people, some of them have to be on your side. If you are truly lonely at the top, you won't stay there long.

TAKE HELP WHEN YOU NEED IT

When you are young, or when you have failed—especially when you are a young failure—you will need allies. There will be times you will need them even when you are older and successful.

When Lieutenant Colonel Washington, age twenty-two, was beaten by French and Indians besieging his slapdash fort in the summer of 1754 (see Chapter 12, "Enemies"), the young man was criticized by old frontier hands, both red and white. But they weren't alone. Powerful figures all across the empire took critical notice of him. Thomas Penn, the proprietor of Pennsylvania, thought Washington had been "imprudent." Baron Baltimore, the proprietor of Maryland, thought he had been "unmilitary." The British ambassador to France wrote the prime minister that, although colonials like Washington "may have courage and resolution," they had no military knowledge. "Consequently, there can be no dependence on them."

There was one exception to this establishment vote of no confidence. In September 1754, John Robinson, Speaker of the Virginia House of Burgesses, wrote Washington to tell him that the legislators took "particular notice" of his "gallant and brave behavior." Robert Dinwiddie, the governor of Virginia, helped prompt the burgesses: Washington's expedition had been his idea, and he didn't want to leave his underling in the lurch, though in letters to his superiors in London he covered himself by suggesting that Washington had exceeded his orders. Washington was defended without reservation by his in-laws, the Fairfaxes. Colonel William Fairfax, Lord Fairfax's cousin and agent, sat on the King's Council, the elite, appointed upper house of the Virginia legislature. He was Washington's mentor in the family, and now he watched his protégé's back.

The timely boost from Washington's allies paid off six months later, when Major General Edward Braddock arrived in Virginia to plan a decisive counterattack on the French, and asked Washington to serve on his staff. He would not have reached out to the local colonel if the locals had not thought well of him. As Washington set out on the Braddock campaign, he did not forget to keep Speaker Robinson and the Fairfaxes apprised of his movements, and his gratitude. ("Your approbation," he wrote Robinson, "was not lost upon one who is always . . . ready to acknowledge an obligation.") He was headed for a debacle greater than the one he had presided over the year before, but this disaster would not be his fault, and it would show him in a heroic light—displaying the courage and resolution that his allies knew he had: four bullets were shot through his coat, two horses were killed under him, yet he led the survivors to safety and buried his fallen commander safe from scalpers. He would not have gotten the chance without their support.

Two decades later, in the fall and winter of 1777–78, Washington was not a militia colonel, but commander in chief. He needed allies all the same when critics in the army and Congress rallied behind the Irish-born Frenchman Thomas Conway. The Conway Cabal tried to tarnish Washington by carping and sniping; to thwart it, he needed defenders. One of the most forthright was the Marquis de Lafayette, whose passionate praise of Washington has already been quoted (see Chapter 9, "Troublemakers"). Lafayette was as valuable for who he was as what he said, the selfless young volunteer supplying the perfect contrast to the ambitious Conway. Some of Washington's allies were more than forthright. After Conway finally resigned, he was challenged to a duel by General John Cadwalader, a Pennsylvania militia officer, who shot him in the mouth. "I have stopped the damned rascal's lying tongue, at any rate," Cadwalader remarked. (Conway survived, and returned to France.) Duels were illegal, and Washington never fought one. But in the eighteenth century they were the universal last resort of gentlemen, especially officers, who believed their honor, or the honor of their commanders, was on the line. In a world of duelists, Washington would have been singular if he had had none on his side.

Washington needed his allies most when he had the fewest. His address to his angry officers at Newburgh in March 1783 impressed those who saw it as a solo performance. Captain Shaw, who described it so vividly (see Chapter 6, "Communication"), cast it in just these terms: "On other occasions," Shaw wrote, Washington had "been supported by the exertions of an army and the countenance [approval] of his friends; but in this he stood single and alone." Literally, this was true: at Newburgh Washington faced his officers all by himself. But

even at that moment, he had the approval of friends: allies in the officer corps who, however unhappy they were about not being paid, were
certain to support Washington, whatever he asked.

How many were there in the audience at Newburgh? The immediate aftermath of the speech showed there was at least one. Washington left the room as soon as he finished: the right thing dramatically
(he would have diminished his impact by lingering), though perhaps
not politically—the meeting was still in session, and resolutions were
still to come. Happily, there was a motion: Henry Knox proposed that
the officers "reciprocate . . . his affectionate expressions with the
greatest sincerity of which the human heart is capable." This motion
passed unanimously. No doubt Knox came with it in his pocket,
showing that he was as good a parliamentarian as he was an artillerist.

A cynic might call Knox a ringer. A patriot might call him a man
who was determined to do the right thing. Washington had to make
his own case and put himself on the line. But in a situation like that, it
is good to know there are at least some friendly faces in the room.

Even good leaders make mistakes, especially when they are young.
Mistaken or not, they must deal with backbiters, faint-hearts, and
worse. All these trials are made easier by allies.

Gratitude Is Not a Blank Check

Washington was grateful to his allies—sometimes more than grateful.
He had a warm spot for the Fairfaxes all his life. He loved the Marquis de Lafayette as a friend, and surrogate son. The young man left
for home after the war in December 1784. "In the moment of our separation," Washington wrote, ". . . and every hour since, I felt all that
love, respect and attachment for you, with which length of years, close
connection, and your merits have inspired me." There were no words,
he concluded, "which could express my affection for you, were I to at-

tempt it." He did not think of Henry Knox quite so warmly, but he gave him glimpses of his inner mind that he shared with few others: on the eve of his first inauguration, it was to Knox, and Knox alone, that he confided his doubts and fears.

Yet gratitude and even affection were not open-ended commitments. When duty and circumstance required it, he argued with allies, or held aloof from them, or disappointed them.

Bryan Fairfax was a son of his patron, Colonel William Fairfax. In July 1774, Washington tried to persuade him to run for the House of Burgesses: "The country never stood more in need of men of abilities." There was one small problem with Bryan Fairfax, however: Washington disagreed with him about politics—specifically, how to make Britain abandon its obnoxious imperial policies. Fairfax wanted to petition the king; Washington wanted economic warfare (see Chapter 8, "Unusual People"). Over the next seven weeks Washington wrote his friend a series of letters, expressing respect for his views while disputing them at great length. "I should think it . . . a piece of inexcusable arrogance in me," one such discussion began, "to make the least essay towards a change in your political opinions, for I am sure I have no new lights to throw upon the subject"; there followed two long paragraphs of new lights. Deep into the war, Washington kept the same attitude, writing from Valley Forge that his friendship with Fairfax was not diminished by "the difference in our political sentiments." Still, politics and war guided his conduct; in pursuit of America's rights he sailed past the Fairfaxes like an aircraft carrier.

Lafayette returned home to take a role in France's politics, becoming first a leader of its revolution, then an increasingly unhappy tool of it. In 1792, he fled his country, only to be captured by France's enemies. The Revolution considered him a traitor, while the rest of Europe considered him a dangerous revolutionary. For four years he was imprisoned in the fortress of an Austrian garrison town in what is now the Czech Republic. The walls of his cell dripped with damp, he got no exercise, he began to lose his hair. In 1795 his teenage son, George Washington Lafayette, arrived in America.

Washington was in a bind. Lafayette was the man he loved most in the world. Yet France and Austria were major powers, and Washington was the president of a weaker one. He could not compel either nation, and was anxious not to do anything that might cause diplomatic "embarrassments," without producing any "essential good." Washington waited half a year before inviting young Lafayette to live with him in Philadelphia. Finally, in May 1796 he wrote the emperor of Austria as a private person ("Official considerations," he explained, "constrain the chief of a nation"), urging "the mediation of *Humanity*" in Lafayette's case. Washington capitalized and underlined *humanity*, but official considerations forced him to make the appeal in this roundabout way.

Austria ignored both Washington and humanity, and held on to its prisoner until Napoleon forced it to free him. Lafayette never felt that Washington had abandoned him; idealist though he was, he understood reasons of state as well as his idol.

Washington tapped Knox to be his first secretary of war, and he served for five years. In 1798, he called on Knox to serve again, and it ended their friendship.

During the administration of John Adams, French bullying and rudeness exceeded even that shown by Citizen Genet. America expected war, and unofficial hostilities broke out in the West Indies, involving naval battles and American help for black rebels in Haiti. For home defense Congress voted to raise an army and called Washington out of retirement to serve as commander in chief.

The sixty-six-year-old Washington accepted, with the reservation that he did not want to take the field unless the country was actually attacked. It was essential, therefore, that he have senior officers he could rely on to get the army up to speed in the meantime. The three that he picked, to be major generals under him, were his former aide Alexander Hamilton; Charles Cotesworth Pinckney, a veteran from South Carolina; and Knox.

All three had served in the Revolution. But when that war ended, their seniority had been the reverse of what Washington now proposed: Knox had been a major general, Pinckney a brigadier general, and Hamilton only a colonel. Washington wrote Knox explaining his decision. Hamilton, he acknowledged, was a political lightning rod (there would be "some fears" of him, "I confess"), though he added he knew of no more "competent choice." Pinckney was popular in the South, which the French might be expected to attack first, given its fondness for Thomas Jefferson and the French Revolution (Washington only alluded to this, as a "leaven . . . working" in some southerners).

He said nothing at all about why he had put Knox third, because it would have been as painful as the decision itself. Knox had been a brilliant artillery commander and, in his first years as secretary of war, a hands-on overseer of Indian affairs. But as time passed, he had become gradually detached, more and more absorbed in land speculations in Maine. After the initial cabinet meetings about the Whiskey Rebellion in the summer of 1795, Knox left town; Hamilton had to take de facto charge of his department. Washington wanted Knox to serve under him for auld lang syne, but he could not count on him as an organizer. He ended his letter with the hope that "former rank will be forgot."

Knox's answer was an aria of shame and pain.

> For more than twenty years, I must have been acting under a perfect delusion. Conscious myself of entertaining for you a sincere, active, and invariable friendship, I easily believed it was reciprocal. Nay more, I flattered myself with your esteem and respect in a

military point of view. But I find that others, greatly my juniors
in rank, have been . . . preferred before me. . . . I should not have
been dragged forth to public view at all, to make the comparison
so conspicuously odious.

Pinckney, for his part, was happy to serve under Hamilton, and (if
need be) Knox. But he was not so invested in a long friendship. Washington wrote Knox again, in vain; Knox refused his appointment.

Historians argue about the whole subject of the new army and the
war scare of 1798. The lesson for leaders in Washington's dealings
with Knox is that even the oldest alliances may change when circumstances do. Sometimes they will break apart. If you don't like the ensuing distress, leadership is not your line of work.

CHAPTER 14

Sex . . .

SHOULD A LEADER have sex with his followers? With his associates? With the people he comes across in the course of business? It certainly happens all the time, the two most prominent recent examples being Bill Clinton and Jack Welch. And, while one was impeached and another lost a chunk in a divorce settlement, Clinton is still popular and powerful, and Welch is still rich as Croesus, so what's the problem?

Washington's generation knew as many sexually active leaders as ours. In the remote past, there was Anthony and Cleopatra; Plutarch, the History Channel of the ancient world, said that philosophers described four kinds of flattery, but Cleopatra "had a thousand." The recent past was clogged with royal mistresses. The "cabals" of Madame de Pompadour, wrote Alexander Hamilton in the *Federalist Papers*, "have been too often descanted upon not to be generally known."

Washington personally knew leaders who slept around, and the women who slept with them. Nathanael Greene married Caty Littlefield in 1774, when he was thirty-two and she was nineteen. Everyone who ever met her was struck by her beauty and her spirits (a "small brunette with high color, a vivacious expression, and a snapping pair of dark eyes" was the judgment of someone at whom they had snapped to good effect). Mrs. Greene liked to dance, but her husband had a limp. The commander in chief, however, didn't. At one officers' ball, when wives joined their husbands at headquarters, Caty and Washington danced for three hours without stopping. "Upon the whole we had a pretty good frisk," wrote Nathanael complacently.

Terry Golway, Nathanael Greene's most recent biographer, discusses his hero's marriage in a tone of constraint that is compounded of a lack of hard evidence, a mist of two hundred year–old gossip, and his own affection for both husband and wife. Women resented Caty Greene, and men admired her. Lafayette was smitten with her, and she was smitten with Anthony Wayne, a rough-and-ready general, and Jeremiah Wadsworth, a sleek Philadelphia merchant. The most Golway will say for certain is that, after Nathanael's death, Caty took both Wayne and Wadsworth as lovers.

No historian doubts the extramarital adventures of Washington's friend Gouverneur Morris, because he recorded them in his diary. Early in 1789 he went to Europe on business (part of which consisted of sending political observations home to Washington), and he soon became entangled with Adelaide de Flahaut, the twenty-eight-year-old wife of a sixty-three-year-old French count. Madame de Flahaut's other lover was Charles Maurice de Talleyrand-Périgord, then a Catholic bishop. Her husband was a political cipher, but her clerical lover was razor-sharp, destined for great things, and Madame de Flahaut and Morris kibitzed his career from the sidelines. After one bout of lovemaking, they drew up a list of ministers for Louis XVI, placing Talleyrand in the top spot. "This amiable woman," Morris wrote in his diary, "shows a precision and justness of thought very uncommon indeed in either sex. After discussing many points, *Enfin*, says she, *mon ami, vous et moi nous gouvernerons la France* [Then, my friend, you and I will govern France]." An "odd combination," Morris added, "but the kingdom is actually in much worse hands." Morris didn't share his diary with his friends, but they had a pretty good idea of his activities anyway: when he lost his left leg in a carriage accident, John Jay wrote that he might better have "lost *something* else."

When Washington was in his teens, he fell in love with a married woman. Worse, she was married to a Fairfax. Sally Fairfax was the sister-in-law of Bryan, and daughter-in-law of Colonel William, Washington's patron. All the materials of attraction, and disaster, were there. We don't know much about Washington's passion, since both he and Sally destroyed almost all of their letters. But when he was in his sixties, he made an oblique analysis of it, in a letter of advice to Nelly Custis, his step-granddaughter, who was then about the same age he had been when he fell for Sally.

Nelly had written, after a recent ball, that she never gave herself "a moment's uneasiness" about her young male acquaintances. "A hint here," he wrote, from his own acquaintance with such matters: "men and women feel the same inclinations to each other *now* that they always have done, and which they will continue to do until there is a new order of things. . . . In the composition of the human frame there is a good deal of inflammable matter, however dormant it may lie for a time, and . . . when the torch is put to it, *that* which is *within you* may burst into a blaze."

What then should Nelly—and George, and Gouverneur, and Caty—do? "Love is said to be an involuntary passion, and it is, therefore, contended that it cannot be resisted." Hadn't he just said that very thing, as a warning? Not quite. "This is true in part only, for like all things else, when nourished and supplied plentifully with [food], it is rapid in its progress; but let these be withdrawn and it may be stifled in its birth or much stinted in its growth." He gave an example: a young single woman can "set the circle in which she moves on fire," but as soon as she marries, the fire goes out, because her admirers can no longer hope to win her. "Hence it follows, that love may and therefore ought to be under the guidance of reason, for although we cannot avoid first impressions, we may assuredly place them under guard." Human beings are full of underbrush. Don't play with matches; if a fire starts, don't give it air.

Nelly would not have known the obvious objection to her step-grandfather's advice—that he had once burned for a woman even though she was already married. But Washington would have said the exception justified the rule; through some combination of will and duty (and his own marriage to Martha Custis) he had tamped his passion for Sally Fairfax. A few years after writing to Nelly, he wrote Sally, whom he had not seen or corresponded with for a quarter of a century (she had moved with her husband to England before the Revolution). And though he told her that the "happiest" moments of his life had been spent "in your company," he enclosed his letter inside one from his wife. I have my memories; I also have my life.

Washington did not lecture people who did not follow his advice. He knew Gouverneur Morris as well as John Jay did. Good leaders know human nature, including their own; they know what can happen, and they also know the consequences.

. . . AND DRUGS

We did not invent the drug problem. Alcohol and alcohol abuse have been around a long time, and Washington had to deal with both among his comrades and his employees.

Washington reprimanded drunkenness in his first General Orders to the army in July 1775, and sobriety or the lack of it was an element in the mental portrait he made of every senior officer under his command—portraits that stayed etched in him. Nine years after the Revolution, at a crisis point in the Ohio Indian wars (see Chapter 3, "The Future"), he jotted down estimates of all the army's generals. "No enemy, it is said, to the bottle," he remembered of General George Weedon; General Charles Scott, he recalled, was "by report . . . addicted to drinking." We have already read his harsh judgment of the "drunkard" Josiah Harmar.

But sometimes he turned to hard-drinking officers when he had to. Mad Anthony Wayne, he knew, might be "a little addicted to the bottle." But Wayne was the man he tapped to retrieve the failures of Harmar and Arthur St. Clair in Ohio. Addiction is always a liability, but in some situations some men had qualities that compensated for it.

Washington expected sobriety from his workers and overseers at Mount Vernon. He did not always get it. In May 1788 he got a letter from Thomas Green, overseer of his carpenters. Green was a good worker; he helped build an innovative two-story round barn of Washington's own design, which allowed wheat to be threshed by horses trotting a circular path over stalks spread on the second floor, the grain falling through narrow cracks to the floor below. But for all his abilities, Green was a disorganized worker and a bad manager, because he was a drunk. His 1788 letter was an apology for a bender. "I humbly beg pardon for my neglect of duty to you and I hope you will take it in consideration and over look it this time." One night after work Green "took a little grog and I found it hurt me the next day so that I was not fit to do any thing the next day." He and one of his carpenters named Mahoney, who was also hungover, went for a walk, "and then [I] was fool enough to be persuaded by Mahoney to go up to town, which he promised me that he should not stop [more than] half an hour and when we got to town I never could get sight of him any more." It rambled on—Mahoney was lost, and so was the point—until its conclusion: "Dear sir I hope you will take it in consideration and overlook it this time and you never shall have any thing to find fault with me again for I will not ever be persuaded by any person like him again."

Abject, evasive, full of empty excuses and empty promises, it is the universal language of alcoholism.

The only advice Washington could give Green was exhortation—"An aching head and trembling limbs . . . discline the hands from work"—which was no more effective than it ever is. At other moments, Washington was realistic enough to realize this. "I know full well," he wrote Green on another occasion, "that to speak to you is of no more avail than to speak to a bird that is flying over one's head." If efficiency was the only criterion, Washington should have fired Green. He kept him on, partly because of the local labor market: experienced carpenters, drunk or sober, were hard to find. But he had another reason. Green's wife, Sally, was the daughter of Thomas Bishop, a former orderly of Washington's old commander Edward Braddock, who had become Washington's servant after Braddock's death. "It is not my intention," he wrote Bishop after two decades' service, "to let you want while we both live." He felt the same responsibility for Bishop's daughter, who had her own family with the feckless Green.

Green solved the problem by taking off, leaving his family in Washington's care. Washington helped Mrs. Green set up a shop in Alexandria, the nearest town to Mount Vernon, and left her one hundred dollars in his will. Plantation owners liked to think of themselves as patriarchs, not just businessmen, but personal responsibilities still adhere to business today. Now, when it is possible to treat addiction with some success, a leader might require an afflicted employee to enter a twelve-step program.

It goes without saying that a leader will not be a drunkard or a drug addict himself. Washington was no teetotaler; he had a distillery at Mount Vernon—one of his many projects as an entrepreneurial farmer—and he served and drank wine at dinner. But he kept the clear head that his ambitions and his responsibilities demanded. In later years, Sam Houston and Ulysses Grant both had bouts of alcoholism, related to depression (the Indians among whom Houston lived for a time called him "Big Drunk"), but they managed to pull themselves out of it (good marriages helped). Otherwise, they could not have won their wars.

CHAPTER 15

COURTESY

MANY BELIEVE that good leaders are real bastards.

In his manual for princes, Niccolò Machiavelli wrote about Cesare Borgia, the ambitious son of a pope, who conquered an Italian province only to find it "completely full of rapine, factions and all other kinds of dissension." He therefore put "a cruel and efficient man," Remirro de Orca, "in full charge." But after a while Borgia "decided that such excessive authority was no longer necessary, for he feared that it might become odious." One morning he had Orca placed "on the piazza in two pieces with . . . a bloodstained knife alongside him. The atrocity of such a spectacle left those people at one and the same time satisfied and stupefied."

This Quentin Tarantino touch grabs the reader's attention. It shows what a tough guy Borgia was, and what a tough guy Machiavelli is for describing it all so bluntly. But as he develops his case, Machiavelli claims that he is not arguing for mere sadism. "Cruelties can be considered well used (if it is permissible to say good about the bad) that are performed all at once, in order to assure one's position, and are not continued. . . . Badly used are those cruelties that, although at first they are few, increase with time rather than disappear." Cruelty, then, is a condition of start-ups, the way a leader clears his throat.

But later still, in his famous discussion of fear and love, Machiavelli adds that cruelty must always hover in the air, as an option. "It is much safer to be feared than loved, if one of the two must be lacking." The reason is the nature of men: "they are ungrateful, fickle, liars and deceivers, avoiders of danger, greedy for profit." Any love they may feel toward you as a leader vanishes "every time their own interests are involved; but fear is [maintained] by a dread of punishment which will never leave you."

In his early teens, Washington copied his own manual, "The Rules of Civility & Decent Behavior in Company and Conversation," into a school notebook. Although there is nothing, at first blush, in the "Rules of Civility" about how to run a province, there is more in them than meets the eye.

The "Rules" were a list of 110 precepts, compiled by French jesuits in 1595, translated into English in the next century, then given, by some adult in the 1740s, to Washington. The "Rules" are an introduction to public life, for young men just out of boyhood—"Run not in the streets, neither go too slowly nor with mouth open" (Rule #53). They are concerned almost entirely with the externals of behavior—how to walk, talk, dress, and eat ("Cleanse not your teeth with the table cloth, napkin, fork, or knife"—#100). When they do discuss substantive matters of business, it is only to explain how they should be discussed among adults—"Be not tedious in discourse, make not many digressions" (#88)—not to offer policy advice. Any young man who took these rules to heart might become what Washington in fact became seven or eight years after he copied them down—a proper young officer on a general's staff, or at least the peacetime version of such an officer: how to fight battles or survive defeats is beyond the range of the "Rules."

Instruction of this kind is not worthless; everyone expects customary behavior, and those who don't conform—Charles Lee presenting his dogs for handshakes—are considered odd or crude. But if you read the "Rules" carefully—and since Washington wrote them out by hand, he at least read them slowly—you see that something else is going on. The "Rules" are exercises in attention. Rule #1 sets the tone: "Every action done in company ought to be done with some sign of respect to those that are present." The point of not running or dawdling, of keeping the tablecloth out of your mouth, and of getting to the point is to avoid offending or inconveniencing passersby, fellow diners, and interlocutors.

Rule #13 comes close to being explicit. It begins with simple social hygiene. "Kill no vermin, as fleas, lice, ticks, &c., in the sight of others." Not an issue in tidewater Virginia, maybe, but when young Washington made his first trip to the Shenandoah Valley a few years after writing this, he found himself sleeping under a "thread bare blanket with double its weight of vermin." The rule resumes: "If you see any filth or thick spittle put your foot dexterously upon it." Now it becomes interesting. "If it be upon the clothes of your companions put it off privately, and if it be upon your own clothes return thanks to him who puts it off." Do you say to your companions, *Look at that filth on your clothes—let me brush it off?* No, because you might embarrass them. So you draw them aside to brush it off privately. And if someone brushes filth off your own clothes, what do you do, even if you feel embarrassed? You thank them, because they have done you a service. We live surrounded by other people whose sensibilities and rights we must consider, sometimes even ahead of our own.

Once you see this pattern, it shows up over and over again in the "Rules." "Turn not your back to others, especially in speaking" (#14). "Undertake not to teach your equal in the art [he] himself professes; it savours of arrogancy" (#41). "Be not hasty to believe flying reports to the disparagement of any" (#50). "If any hesitate in his words, help him not nor prompt him without [being] desired" (#74). Unaware, arrogant, judgmental, officious—these are the qualities of people who can't be bothered to notice the people around them.

The "Rules" do not teach the brotherhood of man. They assume social rank. "Let your ceremonies in courtesy be proper to the dignity [of those] with whom you converse, for it is absurd to act the same with a clown and a prince" (#42). "*Clown*" in the eighteenth century meant "*rustic*." Washington would command many rustics during the Revolution, as well as a few noblemen. He did not treat them alike, but none of them lacked some measure, however slight, of dignity.

Even criminals were worth a thought. "When you see a crime punished," said Rule #23, "you may be inwardly pleased, but always show pity to the suffering offender." There was a lot of public punishment in Washington's lifetime—stocks, firing squads, gallows—and in his years as an officer, Washington was responsible for a fair amount of it (he drew the line at beheading: when one of his colonels during the Revolution proposed to inflict that penalty on deserters, Washington told him that the idea "had better be omitted"). Yet all these wretches merited a show of sympathy, even a phony one, for though they were bad men, they were still men. If this be hypocrisy, make the most of it.

Did Washington remember these rules later in life? There is no evidence for that, and historian Joseph Ellis suggests that one reason biographers write about the "Rules" is that there is so little else in his early life to write about. Yet there were situations that came straight out of the list. In March 1797 when Washington surrendered the presidency to John Adams, he experienced a brief traffic jam of civility. Adams had delivered his inaugural address on a dais in the chamber of the House of Representatives in Philadelphia, with the former president and the new vice president, Thomas Jefferson, sitting behind him. After Adams finished, he left the podium and the room. Jefferson, his natural reserve deepened by the fact that he and Washington were now politically estranged, held back to let the older man precede him. But Washington gestured for Jefferson to go first. He was the Father of His Country, but Jefferson was now vice president. It was Rule #33: "They that are in dignity or in office have in all places precedency." If the "Rules" was the source of this action, and others, it was no doubt the forgotten source—internalized so long ago that it did not have to be consciously recalled.

Washington needed a firm and early grounding in civility to deal with the mass and variety of men and women who passed through his life. He also needed it to supply an alternative vision to Machiavelli's. Washington never read Machiavelli, but he could not escape him. Machiavelli claimed to be the founder of the scientific study of politics, and every later political scientist, however different his conclusions, was in his debt (George Mason called him "the deepest politician who ever put pen to paper"). Washington believed in the scientific study of politics as much as any modern man. In his "Circular to the States," a valedictory message he issued in June 1783 as the Revolution was winding down, he boasted that "the foundation of our empire" was being laid at a time "when the rights of mankind were better understood and more clearly defined, than at any former period." This was so because "the treasures of knowledge, acquired by the labours of philosophers, sages and legislatures . . . are laid open for our use, and their collected wisdom may be happily applied in the establishment of our forms of government." Washington's friends and colleagues agreed. Four years later, Alexander Hamilton wrote in *The Federalist Papers* that "the science of politics . . . like most other sciences, has received great improvement."

America's first leaders thought scientific politics would help them build a great republic. But science makes its discoveries by comparing and analyzing, and analysis can be a chilling process. When practiced by Machiavelli, it was ice cold. His purpose, like Borgia's, was to end rapine, factions, and dissension, but (leaving aside his tingle in the presence of violence and vice) his view of men, as petty and feral, raises the question, Why bother? Why help them lead orderly, peaceful lives? Why not just look out for number one? The "Rules of Civility" do not explain why, but they do say, over and over again, that other men are worth the effort.

If men are shits, then a leader should be a bastard. If there is something respectable about them, then a leader should treat them with courtesy.

CHAPTER 16

Bringing Out the Best

———

MANY OF THE chapters in this section have discussed how a leader should deal with the quirks or shortcomings of the people around him—betrayal, failure, troublemaking, weirdness. But leadership is more than plugging leaks. Canceling out minuses doesn't necessarily leave you with anything. How do you bring out the best in a person? In hundreds, or thousands, of people?

A leader must believe that there is some best to be brought out. If men are wretches, they have no best. If they are machines, you have to find the right "power" switches to get them going, and they may work quite well, but that is not quite bringing out the best either. The mechanic's mode was common in the eighteenth century; it went along with the science of politics. Swatches of *The Federalist Papers* catalogue the passions of men in society with the thoroughness of a technician in a lab coat. In one paragraph, Alexander Hamilton ticks off *attachments, enmities, interests, hopes,* and *fears*. All too human, all too true. But Washington, and to a lesser degree his fellow leaders, also reached further, and looked deeper.

The near mutiny at Newburgh, in March 1783, showed Washington flipping a number of "power" switches—calling in chits, explaining consequences—but also looking for more.

He drew on the officers' bond with him, and offered himself as a model of service. The gesture with the glasses accomplished both tasks: you have known me all the years I have been growing blind, and you should be as loyal as I have been. In his remarks he also warned them of the grave consequences of the step they were considering: you may "open the flood gates of civil discord, and deluge our rising empire in blood." Hamilton, in his role as author of *The Federalist Papers*, might have said that Washington was invoking a deep attachment, and a powerful fear.

But at the end of his speech he said something else. "You will," he told the officers, "by the dignity of your conduct," allow "posterity to say . . . had this day been wanting, the world had never seen the last stage of perfection to which human nature is capable of attaining." These men had been on the point of mutiny, and now he talks of perfection. What sense does that make?

The sense it makes is that as men can fall down, make mistakes, screw up, choose wrong, they can also choose right, which is what you men will do, and will be honored and admired for doing. You may not have looked so perfect at the beginning of this meeting, angry and grumbling, but by the end of it you will. Washington throws the burden of action on others, and tells them that they can and will pick it up.

This turn is a characteristic of Washington's leadership, as unmistakable as a fingerprint, as persistent as a frog call. The man who was a master at holding people's attention and at acquiring power turns the attention back on his audience, to show them their power, and their responsibility. It is a mixture of praise and exhortation, and it happens again and again. In the "Circular to the States," issued three months after the Newburgh crisis, he told Americans, after a long description of their opportunities, that if they "should not be completely free and happy the fault will be entirely their own." Get to work; it's up to you. In his first inaugural address, in April 1789, after dilating on his own "inferior endowments," he praised "the talents, the rectitude, and the patriotism" of the new Congress. He had been dealing, not always happily, with Congresses for eight and a half years, yet he spoke as if he believed this one would be better. In his Farewell Address published in September 1796 at the end of his presidency, he told Americans that "the constancy of your support" had been "the essential prop" of his "efforts." He was retiring, but they weren't. Keep it up.

The most consistent example of the turn is a battlefield phrase that appears in numerous memories of talks he gave or shouts he made before or during combat. Washington's reported comments in the field cannot be accepted word for word: No one was taking notes; old men wrote them down, years after they had been young. Time and memory and Washington's posthumous reputation put them in capital letters. We have the sense, not the exact sounds. But one phrase appears so often that it has the ring of accuracy—*My brave fellows*. My brave fellows, I ask you to reenlist. My brave fellows, fight. Each time Washington says it, he is asserting that which is to be proved. Maybe they will go home or run away, and not be brave at all. But he gets them to be brave by telling them they are.

It is not the only way to lead. At the Battle of Kolín in 1757, Frederick the Great, Baron von Steuben's teacher, and one of the greatest generals of all time, spoke immortal words to his soldiers: *Hunde, wollt ihr ewig leben?* Do you dogs want to live forever? Shame, sarcasm, the realism of the grave—it worked then, and it works still.

Washington preferred to say, *My brave fellows*, meaning, *My fellows, be brave*.

Routine accomplishes a lot; so do the levers of interest, if they are skillfully pulled. But sometimes a leader has to see a person's best, tell him what it is, and then let him do it—because, without the best efforts of others, what can a leader accomplish?

CHAPTER 17

PERSONNEL

HERE, FOR CONVENIENCE' sake, is a chart of the people who crossed George Washington's path as a leader, listed by rank, with a summary of the particular feature of each one's relationship to him that is discussed in this section. The chart is divided into Revolutionary and post-Revolutionary periods.

REVOLUTION

Henry Laurens, president of Congress
  Superior (helpful)

Congressman Richard Henry Lee
  Superior (hostile)

Major General Charles Lee
  Weird (difficult)

Major General Horatio Gates
  Potential mutineer

Major General Henry Knox
  Ally

Major General Nathanael Greene
  Failure

Mrs. Nathanael (Caty) Greene
  Flirt

Major General Thomas Conway
  Troublemaker

Major General Benedict Arnold
  Traitor

Mrs. Benedict (Peggy) Arnold
  Traitor, flirt

Major General Baron von Steuben
  Weird (useful)

Major General Marquis de Lafayette
  Ally

Col. Alexander Hamilton
  Smart, friend of potential mutineers

Col. Lewis Nicola
  Worst advice in history

continues...

REVOLUTION, *continued*

Major John Armstrong
Potential mutineer

Assistant Adjutant Joseph White
Subordinate (cheeky)

Private William Lloyd
Subordinate (cheeky)

Officers
Potential mutineers

Soldiers
What will they do?

New Englanders
Weird ("dirty & nasty")

Fairfaxes
Allies, lover

Indians
Allies, enemies, models

POST-REVOLUTION

Secretary of State Thomas Jefferson
Troublemaker

Secretary of State Edmund Randolph
Not a traitor

Treasury Secretary Alexander Hamilton
Smart

Rep. James Madison
Smart

Gouverneur Morris, Minister to France
Troublemaker, flirt

George Mason
Smart

Henry Knox
Ally (disappointed)

Edmond Charles Genet, Minister to the United States
Troublemaker

Lafayette
Ally (not saved)

Eleanor Parke (Nelly) Custis, step granddaughter
Flirt?

Thomas Green
Drunkard

Americans
What will they do?

Note: A complete organizational chart of all of Washington's personnel would be several hundred pages longer

Part Three

SELF

Washington's office at Mount Vernon is a small room, with a built-in bookshelf, a desk, and a globe. On top of a cabinet is a souvenir of his one trip abroad, a piece of coral from Barbados. There is also an unusual contraption, a chair with pedals that work small fans. Why have such a thing? So that on even the hottest Virginia summer days, Washington could be absolutely alone, without servant or slave, when he read, wrote, or thought. But even then, he was with George Washington.

You are a dimension of every problem or personal interaction you face. Some problems, at least, get solved, and people go off to do or not do their jobs. You remain. You are the tool that is never put back in the box.

Washington was not an introspective person, at least not in writing. His diary is a bald record of engagements and weather reports, with few of his own thoughts. Yet Washington was well aware of himself, and of what he brought to the table, both good and bad.

CHAPTER 18

Identify Your Strengths

LIKE CARS LEAVING a factory, we come equipped with certain features, physical, intellectual, and temperamental. Some of these are helpful to a leader.

A leader's strengths can operate unconsciously. But they will be stronger yet if he knows what they are—if he knows what he has, and what he can draw on.

Appearance

Abigail Adams was not easily impressed, but she was impressed the first time she met George Washington. Mrs. Adams had gone from the family home in Braintree to be presented to Washington when he took command of the American troops outside Boston in July 1775. She described their meeting in a letter to her congressman husband who was chained to his desk in Philadelphia.

> I was struck with General Washington. You had prepared me to
> entertain a favorable opinion of him, but I thought the one half
> was not told me. . . . Those lines of Dryden instantly occurred to
> me:

Mark his majestic fabric! He's a temple
Sacred by birth, and built by hands divine.
His soul's the deity that lodges there,
Nor is the pile unworthy of the God.

The features of this temple were straight, pulled-back hair, once chestnut colored, now graying and powdered; deep-set blue-gray eyes; a strong nose and jaw; height over six feet; long, powerful arms and legs; and, more than any one thing, the balance and command of the whole. Washington was in command of his body, and it commanded the space around him. Thomas Jefferson was also a six-foot-plus redhead, and, in his own way, an impressive man. But Senator William Maclay, in a description that historians have been citing for decades, because it is both vivid and unawed, wrote that "a laxity of manner seemed shed about" Jefferson. No one ever saw a laxity of manner in Washington.

There are two quotations in Abigail Adams's letter. Those over-the-top lines of John Dryden, written out as verse, come from a 1690 play, *Don Sebastian, King of Portugal;* in quoting them, Adams gave them a sex-change operation, for they are spoken of the play's heroine: "Mark her majestic fabric," and so forth. (Why did Abigail turn a woman into Washington? No doubt, from her powerful identification with the mighty events she was living through.)

But the other quotation, unsignaled by punctuation, is even more over-the-top, for it is the Bible's description of the Queen of Sheba meeting Solomon (Adams kept her sexes straight in this one). "And she said to the king, It was a true report that I heard in mine own land of thy acts and of thy wisdom. Howbeit I believed not the words, until I came, and mine eyes had seen it; and, behold, the half was not told me" (I Kings 10:6–7). It's pretty good, on a first meeting, to make Abigail Adams think of King Solomon.

Solomon impressed Sheba with his mind, his judgment, and his surround: "And when the queen of Sheba had seen all Solomon's wisdom, and the house that he had built, And the meat of his table, and the sitting of his servants, and the attendance of his ministers, and their apparel, and his cupbearers . . . there was no more spirit in her" (I Kings 10:4–5). George impressed Abigail by his looks and manner alone. It should be no surprise that such qualities, by themselves, could have such powerful effects. Malcolm Gladwell's book on the importance of first impressions is called *Blink*, not *Sniff*, or *Hi!* Every sense tells us vital information, but sight rules. The eyes have it. That is why all of us, from children who have first learned the tyranny of fashion to Missionaries of Charity in their blue-striped veils, are concerned with personal appearance. That includes leaders.

We all know what Washington looked like, but it is hard to know, in the twenty-first century, what looking at him was like. He was painted many times, yet the best painter to do his portrait, Gilbert Stuart, caught him when he was already in his midsixties, the beginning of the end. Stuart's full-length image, which hangs in the Smithsonian, gives us a powerful, and powerfully guarded, face, but the body is stiff and static, missing in inaction. Stuart's so-called Athenaeum portrait, which hangs on every dollar bill, is a head shot, with no body at all. How did Washington move? This was a man who rode a horse every day of his life, and who danced with Caty Greene for three hours. A relatively crude production like Emanuel Leutze's *Washington Crossing the Delaware* captures some of this energy by displacing it onto other elements in the painting—the floating ice, the straining flag, the rowing men. We are left with written descriptions, as entranced, and inadequate, as Abigail Adams's. Norman Mailer wrote a whole book about Marilyn Monroe, but what explains more—his words, or a few frames of *The Seven-Year Itch*? Books about Franklin

D. Roosevelt still roll off the presses, but you can learn as much from photos of his million-dollar smile and his jaunty cigarette holder.

When did Washington become conscious of his own appearance? Certainly by the time he began ordering his own clothes. When he was eighteen or nineteen he wrote a "memorandum to have my coat made by the following directions," describing in some detail the lapels ("six button holes") and the length ("very long waisted . . . down to or below the bent of the knee, the [distance] from the armpit to the fold to be exactly as long or longer than from thence to the bottom"). All Virginia gentlemen wrote such directions; they had to be particular because their tailors lived across the ocean in England, and their orders often came back wrong. Washington kept up a keen interest in dress all his life, designing every uniform he wore from the French and Indian War to the possible war with France that called him out of retirement in 1798. One benefit of uniforms for him was that epaulettes compensated for his narrow shoulders, one of the few limitations of his physique.

American military style began to change forty years after Washington died. The two great generals of the Mexican War were Winfield Scott and Zachary Taylor. Scott, a tall, stout peacock, was nicknamed Fuss and Feathers; Taylor was a slob (no tailor he). Ulysses Grant, who served under both men, imitated Taylor's relaxed style during the Civil War, and the cult of simplicity marches on in the American military. Washington, who preceded it, knew he looked good, and he wanted to make sure he looked as good as possible.

America in Washington's lifetime was a republic of words. Americans read everything, from Thomas Paine to the Bible (no American would have needed an explanation of Abigail Adams's allusion to the Queen of Sheba). Washington lived in the midst of that literary ferment. But he was also an intensely visual person, trained as a surveyor, the designer of his own house, a lover of performances and plays.

Having the raw materials of an impressive appearance, he improved them and then broadcast them. The dissemination took a lot of effort in a world that did not even have the technology for cheap reproductions of prints until shortly after he died, but he had unusual opportunities to get his image out, and he made use of them. No magazines or newspapers? He visited all thirteen states. No TV or YouTube? He was seen, in person, by tens of thousands of people. He was the biggest, and longest-running, show in America.

Now, when kids mug for each other via cell phone and every Web site links to a podcast, leaders have more chances, and more need, to make use of their appearance. No one looks like George Washington (though an Italian stylist did try to bring his long-behind haircut back in the nineties: "It can be a very white-trash look. But for me, there's a rebel in that hairstyle, something hard-edged"). Every leader has to know what he does look like, what that can mean for him, and how to present himself to his audience.

Strength

If strength only mattered in the NFL, why do so many corporate headquarters have gyms?

For most of Washington's life, it was obvious to him, and to everybody else, that he was strong, and that this was noteworthy; tales of his physical prowess go back to his boyhood. We owe the story that he threw a rock across a river to his first biographer, Parson Weems. "The trouble with Weems," one historian told me, "is that he isn't lying all the time." Weems actually scratched around and interviewed people who had known Washington when he was a boy. He attributed the rock-throwing story to Colonel Lewis Willis, a cousin of Washington's who "often [saw] him throw a stone across Rappahannock, at the lower ferry of Fredericksburg. It would be no easy matter to find a man, nowadays, who could do it." I made an experiment, for a PBS documentary, with a half-dozen young men on the baseball team of Stafford High School, near Fredericksburg, taking them to the former ferry site with a bucket of rocks, and seeing what they could do. Two of the guys managed, twice each, to hurl their stones to the other side: not a superhuman feat, but hard enough. It would have been even harder in the mid-eighteenth century when the Rappahannock, not yet dredged, was broader.

Washington's strength was an aspect of his compelling appearance; the temple built by hands divine drew much of its attraction from being a powerhouse. The array of tools produced by human culture—handheld rocks, Blackberries, paintbrushes, rosaries—have modified the premium we place on sheer physical force. But strength lingers in our hard wiring as an object of respect. An old-fashioned phrase for going to war is "making an appeal to arms." Our first arms are the two at our sides. One delegate to the Continental Congress, Dr. Solomon Drowne of Rhode Island, fantasized that the issues dividing England and the colonies might be settled by a single combat between Washington and George III.

But sometimes—usually in the military, though not only there— the millennia of culture peel off, and Dr. Drowne's primal fantasy becomes reality. When James Monroe was president, his treasury secretary, William Crawford, called him a "damned infernal old scoundrel" and threatened to beat him with a cane. Monroe, by then an old, small man, but a brave one—he had been shot at the Battle of Trenton—grabbed a pair of fireplace tongs to defend himself. The two calmed down before they came to blows. Nobody was calm in Cambridge, in the winter of 1775, when the Virginians and the Marblehead men began their rumble in the snow (see Chapter 8, "Unusual People"). Washington went to the center of the fight and pulled two combatants apart and held them by their necks, like dogs, until they settled down, and the other brawlers ran away or settled down themselves. Luckily for the discipline of the army, this was not a daily occurrence. But if the lid blew off, Washington could deal with it, with his bare hands if necessary, and everyone knew it.

A very practical manifestation of his strength was his skill on horseback. Almost everyone, even urbanites, rode horses in those days; Boston-bred Sam Adams was taught how to ride by his cousin John on their way to the Continental Congress. Washington was peerless. He honed his skills with frequent fox hunts, which his step-grandson, George Washington Parke Custis, remembered rapturously: "He rode, as he did every thing, with ease, elegance, and with power. . . . [A] horse might as soon disencumber itself of the saddle, as of such a rider." Young Custis saw Washington's riding with the hero worship of a boy, but no adult ever contradicted his estimate. A remarkable instance of horsemanship in action was recorded by a lieutenant in a Connecticut regiment, who saw it on the predawn march to Trenton in December 1776, after the crossing of the Delaware. The road the Americans took, slick with snow and sleet, crossed a pair of steep ravines. "While passing a slanting, slippery bank," the lieutenant wrote, Washington's "horse's hind feet both slipped from under him, and he seized his horse's mane and the horse recovered." It is hard enough to catch your own balance in midfall; how much harder to catch a half-ton creature?

Such feats can save lives—Washington's, for instance, who might have tumbled down the bank—or battles. While Ulysses Grant was besieging Fort Donelson in February 1862, he was away from his main force when the enemy made a breakout. "The roads," he noted drily in his memoirs, ". . . were unfit for making fast time, but I got to my command as soon as possible." The roads were rutted mud, suddenly frozen solid, as dangerous a surface as the slippery bank outside Trenton; only Grant's uncanny affinity for horses allowed him to gallop back in time to bottle the enemy up. In July 1898 Theodore Roosevelt's regiment lay below the San Juan heights outside Santiago, Cuba, being peppered by bullets that the Spaniards poured down on them from state-of-the-art Mauser rifles. Time to charge, though who would want to in such a situation? "Are you afraid to stand up when I am on horseback?" Roosevelt shouted to a hesitating man. That man was shot and killed where he lay, but Roosevelt's other men stood up, despite the fusillade, and followed him up to the heights.

Though war is now mechanized, and computerized, the physical remains a factor. The capabilities of a Ranger put televised strongman competitors, hauling trucks around, into perspective. Horses even were used in attacking the Taliban in Afghanistan in 2001, along with Predator drones. But the arts of peace call for their own stamina. Sitting in a negotiation or at a desk on a deadline, or making a presentation after a transcontinental flight, is not heroic, but it is hard in its own way, and if you flag, you lose—not least the confidence of those working with you.

In January 1992, George H. W. Bush vomited at a state dinner in Japan. This moment of feebleness (he was suffering a twenty-four-hour bug) symbolized both physical and political weakness—this despite his having been a war hero and a college athlete. Gerald Ford was possibly the most athletic man ever to reach the White House—he was recruited by the Green Bay Packers after college, though he chose instead to go to law school—yet a few well-publicized stumbles as president and the mockery of Chevy Chase, the TV comic, fixed an image of him as a klutz. By contrast, Franklin D. Roosevelt, crippled but relentlessly upbeat, conveyed personal force, which translated to political power. In October 1944, during his fourth presidential campaign, he made a daylong swing through four of New York City's five boroughs in an open car in the pouring rain, relieved only by two changes of clothes and some fortifying bourbon. He was in fact dying at the time, of an enlarged heart and other ailments, but he seemed lively, and he won his election.

Until that Rapture of geeks, the Singularity, we are stuck with our bodies. A leader should pull his weight at least, and if he has got something more, flaunt it.

AMIABILITY

Not every leader is likable, but Washington was. His heroic qualities came to overshadow his amiability as his career progressed, and they have obliterated it since his death. The face on Mount Rushmore wears no trace of a smile, and why should it? He had wars to fight, and a country to found. But his contemporaries attested to his amiability—what biographer James Thomas Flexner called his "sweetness"— and he made use of it in his grand roles.

When Abigail Adams described her first impressions of Washington as commander in chief to her husband, she spent most of her letter on his physique. But she also wrote some sentences about his manner. "Dignity with ease and complacency . . . look agreeably blended in him." *Complacency* now means smugness: the complacency of the Academy Awards ceremony. In the eighteenth century it also meant, and clearly means here, a pleasant manner, or a disposition to please: a manner that puts people at ease.

It's not that Abigail Adams was a soft touch. Everybody likes Benjamin Franklin, from Walter Isaacson to Walt Disney. But Abigail Adams was immune to his charms. In 1784, nine years after meeting Washington, she described an evening with Franklin and a French lady friend. "After dinner she threw herself upon a settee, where she showed more than her feet. She had a little lap-dog, who was, next to the Doctor, her favorite. This she kissed, and when he wet the floor she wiped it up with her chemise. This is one of the Doctor's most intimate friends, with whom he dines once every week, and she with him." Franklin's ménage did not put her at ease. But Washington did.

Abigail Adams noted a quality of Washington's that was related to his complacency: "Modesty marks every line and feature of his face." Eliphalet Dyer, one of the congressmen who voted him into the commander in chief's job, praised the same quality: he was "no harum-scarum, ranting, swearing fellow." Harum-scarum fellows can do just fine in the military; Baron von Steuben ranted and swore to good effect, Charles Lee ranted and swore, and George Patton's pep talks to the Third Army before D-day are classics of profanity. "The quicker we clean up this goddamn mess, the quicker we can take a jaunt against the purple pissing Japs . . . before the Marines get all the goddamn credit." Washington had a different approach.

He had made use of his amiability in his first long-term military command, as colonel of the Virginia Regiment, formed in 1755 to guard the frontier during the French and Indian War. "Our colonel," wrote one of his men, "is an example of fortitude in either danger or hardships, and by his easy, polite behavior, has gained not only the regard but affection of both officers and soldiers." Fortitude won him the regard of officers and men, but easy, polite behavior won their affection. When Washington resigned his commission in 1758, twenty-seven officers signed a testimonial, hailing him not only as an "excellent commander" but also as a "sincere friend" and an "affable . . . companion." "How rare it is," they went on, "to find those amiable qualifications blended together in one man." For good measure, they called him "the man we know and love." Serving in the Virginia Regiment was not lovers' duty. It struggled with inadequate supplies and murderous raids, and Washington hanged his share of deserters. Yet at the end of it all, his officers wrote him a tribute that seems better suited to the retirement of a popular high school teacher than a commander in a war zone. They asked him to stay on another year, but he was not intending to, and in fact went straight to married life, so they had nothing to gain by their warmth. They offered it anyway: sign that they had been warmed by their commander.

Washington was still amiable when he stepped into the presidency. Once again he was described by Abigail Adams. "He is polite with dignity, affable without familiarity, distant without haughtiness, grave without austerity." Other qualities—distance, gravity—have joined the mix of his public personality, appropriate to his political station and his age; Washington was twenty-three when he took on the Virginia Regiment, forty-three when Abigail Adams first met him, fifty-seven when he was first inaugurated. But affability is still there. "[He] has so happy a faculty of appearing to accommodate and yet carrying his point, that, if he was not really one of the best-intentioned men in the world, he might be a very dangerous one." There is the Adams sharpness; she knows full well that not every smiling face is friendly. But Washington's good intentions had been ringing true for years.

One reason we have forgotten Washington's amiability is that it did not come in the most memorable form that amiability can wear, a sense of humor. He enjoyed other people's jokes, but told few himself. So Franklin and Abraham Lincoln, still cracking wise into the twenty-first century, have come down to us as the all-time great guys of American history. We need to remind ourselves—perhaps Abigail Adams could help us—that humor isn't always what it seems. Lincoln (not Franklin) had a vein of deep sympathy, alloyed with depression, but both men used their humor to keep other people at a distance, and in the dark. Washington's distance and gravity were more forthright.

Men who kill and risk death must feel bound to the men who command them. Politics and business lack the pressure of danger, but each has its own pressures, and its own occasions for bonding. Overbearing harum-scarum fellows rise to the top in both worlds, as they do in the military. Former press lord Conrad Black (no shrinking violet himself) tells a story about a French Canadian politician of his youth. The boss was sitting on a podium, as a flunky praised him, calling the roll of his many virtues. "Broadminded!" he interjected. The flunky dutifully added this trait to the list. But amiable leaders are equally capable of taking men into battle, and keeping big men, petty men, and men who are a combination of both in harness. A leader should not force himself to rant and swear if it does not come naturally, and he should cultivate any geniality that he has. It can see him through much dullness, wrangling, and bloodshed.

BRAVERY

People look for bravery wherever they can, even in metaphors: so we speak of political campaigns and hostile takeovers. Pacifists are proud of their courage in maintaining that fighting is wicked and senseless.

Accounts of Washington's bravery in battle fill his wars. After his first battle in 1754, he wrote a brother, "I heard bullets whistle and believe me there was something charming in the sound." At Yorktown in 1781, his last battle, he was inspecting the field when one of his aides, Lieutenant Colonel David Cobb, worried that he was too exposed. "Had you not better step a little back?" "Colonel Cobb," Washington replied, "if you are afraid, you have liberty to step back."

That answer was a little hard on Cobb, who was only trying to make sure the commander in chief was not blown away. But Washington's rebuke, like his letter about the bullets' whistle, makes him seem indifferent to the danger around them. Two days after the Inchon landing in September 1950, Douglas MacArthur went ashore to inspect the beachhead. At one point a Marine lieutenant tried to block his way. "We just knocked out six Red tanks over the top of this hill." "That was the proper thing to do," MacArthur said, and went to the crest to see for himself.

Such bravery is not necessarily the product of insensibility. (God help the man for whom it is—and the men under him even more.) In 1786, Washington's secretary, David Humphreys, was working on a biography of his boss, which he offered to Washington for comments and corrections. The longest comment Washington wrote, and the most vivid writing of his life, concerns Edward Braddock's defeat in 1755, and the subsequent retreat, which Washington had to lead, all the other senior officers having been killed or wounded.

> The shocking scenes which presented themselves in this night's march are not to be described. The dead, the dying, the groans, lamentations, and cries along the road of the wounded for help . . . were enough to pierce a heart of adamant—the gloom and horror of which was not a little increased by the impervious darkness . . . of thick woods, which in places rendered it impossible for the two guides which attended to know when they were in or out of the track, but by groping on the ground with their hands.

Bullets were not so charming when they found so many marks. Washington learned fast that every battlefield is a charnel house. In the moment of action, however, he was too engaged to worry, or to fear.

A leader's bravery in combat inspires his men. It can also prepare a leader for other less obvious exercises of courage. Though Washington was ambitious, for his country and himself, he always hesitated to take on his great assignments, not only because he wanted to show that he was a modest man and no harum-scarum fellow but also because he sensed how difficult they would be—so difficult that they might be beyond his powers. When the Continental Congress tapped him to be commander in chief, he warned them that his "abilities and military experience may not be equal" to the trust they were laying on him. There were times it looked that way, and in fact he had never held a command so complex. As he cruised to his unchallenged election as first president, he was full of foreboding. He told his old comrade Henry Knox that he felt like "a culprit . . . going to the place of his execution." He told his diary, in a rare expression of feeling, that he had "the best dispositions," but "less hope." And what good would hope have done him? The world was full of generals before he came along, but not of presidents; he was walking into a job that was not only new to him but new in history. History had some precedents, though—all the nations that had smashed up through mistakes at the top. Most culprits bring only themselves to grief; Washington might damage his country.

He might also damage something of little consequence to the world, but important to him—his reputation. After the victory of the Revolution, he was the greatest man in America, one of the greatest on the planet. Now he was sliding his pile of chips onto the table one more time. Knox understood exactly what was at stake. "Secure as he was in his fame," he wrote Lafayette, "he has again committed it to the mercy of events." At the end of his first term of office he yearned for retirement, in part, no doubt, out of a desire to protect his fame, still (amazingly) secure. Yet he put the fame on the table one more time. It is never hard to do less; only the brave take risks.

One of Washington's last executive decisions was so long in coming that we see little courage in it, though it may have looked different to him. Despite careful management, Mount Vernon was clearly losing money by the 1780s. Only rents from his large landholdings kept him flush (the landholdings themselves were quite valuable, but he sold parcels only out of necessity). The war, and his absence, had been a drag on Mount Vernon's balance sheet. So were the many slaves he had to support, more and more as time passed. In 1799 he made an inventory of the slaves at Mount Vernon, 277 people in all. Their labor was free, but more than half of them were too old or too young to work. Workers and nonworkers alike had to be clothed and fed.

This was a common dilemma of slaveholders who were reluctant to maximize their labor force by selling off the unproductive. "I am . . . against selling negroes, as you would do cattle in the market," Washington wrote in 1794, and other slaveholders shared this view, not wanting to break up families, nor to think of themselves as slave traders rather than patriarchs. In 1799 Washington took a step beyond his peers by writing a will that freed all his slaves after his wife's death.

This was no simple matter. Many slaves, after a lifetime of bondage, were unable or unwilling to fend for themselves; Washington stipulated that they could continue to be supported at Mount Vernon. (The estate made payments until 1839, totaling $10,000.) Washington's will covered only the 124 slaves he owned; the other 153 belonged to the estate of Martha Washington's first husband, Daniel Custis, and so to his heirs (in 1799, her grandchildren). Neither George—nor Martha, had she wished—could free them.

At least some of Washington's legatees—he divided his estate among Martha's descendants, and the many descendants of his brothers and sisters—must have been unhappy about the disposal of so much real property. The emphatic language of Washington's will suggests as much: "I do . . . most pointedly and most solemnly enjoin it upon my executors . . . to see that *this* clause respecting slaves, and every part thereof be religiously fulfilled at the epoch at which it is directed to take place, without evasion, neglect or delay." A will is already a pointed and solemn document; why be doubly so unless there is a need for it? Martha Washington, at least, had good reason to be concerned by what George was planning; since his slaves were to be freed after her death, might not some of them take steps to hasten it, if she survived him (as she did)? "She did not feel as though her life was safe in their hands," Abigail Adams wrote after visiting the old lady after her husband passed. Martha freed George's slaves a year after he died, a year and a half before she followed him.

Washington's will did not show the bravery of the battlefield, or of the high-stakes political player. It shows the courage it takes, akin to determination, to grasp a gnarled fact of life. Slavery is gone, but other problems remain. Do you dislike illegal immigration? Who cleans your offices? Do you think the earth is out of balance? Is buying carbon offsets enough of a contribution to the solution? Every leader has (or should have) a moral code—a spur that gets him up in the morning, and a matrix that tells him what he may, what he must, and what he must not do. He has to decide if his moral beliefs are sensible, and if his line of work suits them, and he should know that those decisions may cost him time and money, perhaps popularity and power.

The varieties of bravery are not necessarily connected. Benedict Arnold was as brave a warrior as George Washington, and had a shattered leg to prove it, but he did not have the courage of his convictions, because he had no convictions. Bravery is a quality a leader must show whenever it is needed. If he does not have it naturally, then he must acquire it. Life supplies many opportunities for training.

CHAPTER 19

BUILD YOUR STRENGTHS

———

SOME LEADERSHIP qualities may be in us ready-made; they only need to be identified and exploited. Others exist in a rudimentary state, and have to be developed, matured, built up, if we are to succeed, or succeed beyond a certain point. They take work.

When Benjamin Franklin was in his early twenties, he drew up a list of thirteen virtues, and a plan for acquiring them. He intended to devote a week to each in turn, going through four cycles in a year, and he made himself charts in which to record his daily lapses. "I was surprised to find myself so much fuller of faults than I had imagined," he wrote. In his thirties, he gave up this punctilious method for another: inserting bright little maxims in the pages of the almanacs he published. What he could not learn by drill, maybe he could teach his readers and himself by cleverness. "Lying rides upon debt's back." "The sleeping fox catches no poultry." "All would live long, but none would be old." Each smile administers a homeopathic dose of responsibility, industry, or self-knowledge. Today, magazines vary their text with photos, spot art, or (in *The New Yorker*) other people's goofs. Franklin filled his blank spaces with good advice.

Franklin built his strengths the way a scientist or a wit would do it, by careful observation or by cracking jokes. Washington did it his own way.

Financial Independence

One of Franklin's maxims was, "An empty bag cannot stand upright." That appeared in his almanac for 1740, when Washington was a boy. There is no evidence that Washington read any of Franklin's almanacs, but he didn't need to, to know that it is almost impossible for a poor man to be independent, and quite impossible for a dependent man to be a leader.

George's father, Augustine Washington, died in April 1743, when George, the third of his six sons, was eleven. The Washingtons were successful gentry—Augustine's father and grandfather had served in the colonial legislature—but Augustine died before he had truly made it in the world, and his estate was split many ways, with the lion's share going to his two elder sons, George's half brothers. George got a 260-acre farm on the Rappahannock River, four less important properties, and ten slaves, all to be managed by his mother until he was an adult. Mortality was high in eighteenth-century Virginia, and in time, death would make George the master of other Washington family assets, including Mount Vernon. But his boyhood inheritance left him a minor sprig of his clan.

He got something much more important from the marriage in July 1743 of his oldest half brother, Lawrence. Lawrence's wife, the former Ann Fairfax, was a cousin of Thomas, Lord Fairfax, the inheritor of a royal grant of 5 million acres of the colony of Virginia. The Fairfax holdings ran from the tidewater over the mountains into what is now West Virginia.

In the webs of family patronage that bound the British Empire in the eighteenth century—and have not entirely blown away, in Britain or anywhere else—a cousin's husband's half brother was entitled to little, except consideration. In 1748, at age sixteen, George Washington was tapped to help survey the Fairfax property; with a good word from the Fairfaxes, he also became the surveyor for Culpeper County. His work as a surveyor, which lasted for four years, gave him an eye for land, a chance to see a lot of it, and wages, which he used to start buying it. He made his first purchase in 1750: 1,459 acres in the Shenandoah Valley. A dependent younger son could spend his whole life doing jobs for his family. When Washington bought land with his earnings, he showed he intended to stand on his own.

The French and Indian War opened a box of new opportunities—the upper Ohio Valley, beyond the Alleghenies. The royal governor of Virginia offered land to induce men to enlist, and at war's end the king promised land to veterans. Washington was determined to get his share, and in the mid-1760s he embarked on a series of transactions that would concern him for the next ten years.

He knew exactly what he wanted. "Ordinary, or even middling land would never answer my purpose," he wrote. "No: a tract to please me must be rich," that is, fertile. He did not intend to reap its richness himself, but planned to lease it to tenants as settlers moved west. He was a speculator, who hoped in time to become a developer.

Sometimes he speculated very publicly. In October 1770 he canoed 250 miles down the Ohio to its juncture with the Great Kanawha River (now in West Virginia) to do a preliminary inspection of the governor's bounty land. The next year he sent out a surveyor, a former ensign in his unit, to map out the land in parcels. Washington acted as the agent of a group of veterans, assuming some of the expenses himself (he was reimbursed for hiring the surveyor, but not for his own time). Not surprisingly, he got prime tracts.

At other times, he operated in the shadows. The king's grant to veterans might not apply to him, since he had resigned his commission before the war's end. He ultimately persuaded the royal governor to give him a colonel's share, but in the meantime, he bought up the shares of other veterans, acting through his youngest brother, Charles, whom he coached like a real estate mogul in a Tom Wolfe novel. "I should be glad if you would (in a joking way, rather than in earnest at first) see what value they seem to set upon their lands . . . " "If you should make any purchases, let it be done in your own name . . . " "I should be obliged to you if you would inquire in a roundabout way . . . " "You need not let your reasons for inquiring . . . be known . . . " "I would have the title given to you, and not to me, till matters are riper than they appear at present . . . " "Show no part of this letter . . ." George Washington was already so prominent a speculator that he feared asking in his own name would jack up prices. (Sellers must have been naive if they did not suspect his younger brother of working with him.) One way or another, he bought or was awarded 32,000 acres of veterans' land. The French and Indian War made Washington famous. It also helped make him rich.

Washington pursued the land business with an avidity that somewhat contradicted the code of the Virginia gentleman, who was supposed to be above all that. Other articles of the code he followed to the letter. Washington was hospitable and grand: Any presentable person who showed up at Mount Vernon, including perfect strangers, got dinner and a room for the night, if necessary; their host never stinted on horses, hounds, carriages, or clothes. But he always knew his acreage, and his rents.

Another giant step up the social ladder for Washington was his marriage to Martha Custis. Martha Dandridge was the daughter of an obscure if respectable family. At age eighteen, she married Daniel Parke Custis, whose family was crazy—capricious, miserly, violent—but wealthy. At age twenty-six, her husband died, leaving the wealth to her and her children. When she married again in January 1759, her second husband became the custodian of a fortune. This was the beginning of Washington's life as a planter, and farmer; it was also the beginning of Mount Vernon's progress from a poky house on a commanding bluff to the jewel tourists visit today.

Washington was not the only American leader, then or now, who benefited from marrying well. In 2004 John Kerry's enemies mocked his marriage to Teresa Heinz, the widow of the ketchup heir. But he followed a long tradition. Thomas Jefferson's marriage to Martha Wayles, and the death of her father shortly thereafter, tripled his holdings; Jefferson owned 5,000 acres, Martha owned 11,000; Jefferson owned 50 slaves, Martha owned 135. Alexander Hamilton's marriage to Elizabeth Schuyler was a jackpot. He jumped from being an illegitimate immigrant in the army to the beloved in-law of the most powerful Anglo-Dutch family in New York. John Adams did not rise nearly so far in the world when he married Abigail Smith, but he did rise, for while he was the son of a farmer, she was the daughter of a minister, still a prominent position in post-Puritan Massachusetts. One of the few founding fathers who did not marry up was the one who wrote about the flimsiness of empty bags: Benjamin Franklin made a common-law marriage with a printer's daughter, expecting to get on in life entirely on his own.

Shrewdness put Washington on the track to independence; shrewdness and marriage put him on the track to financial preeminence.

What did wealth have to do with leadership? When he was an old man, discussing Washington's "talents" as a leader, John Adams included in the mix his "large, imposing fortune." Adams believed, incorrectly, that Washington's father had left him "a great landed estate." But he well understood the importance of the Custis inheritance and the "immense tracts of land of his own acquisition." What was the effect of these holdings on Washington's ability to lead? Wealth was impressive; it got people's attention, and their awe. "There is nothing," Adams explained, "except bloody battles and splendid victories, to

which mankind bow down with more reverence than to great fortune."
Adams gave an example. The First Continental Congress in 1774 was
the first time that most of the future leaders of America met each
other. As in any group of patriots or players, they checked each other
out. Whenever hard data were lacking, they gossiped. Thomas Lynch,
a delegate from South Carolina, reported to Adams a grand offer that
"Colonel Washington" of Virginia had made. "If the English should
attack the people of Boston, he would raise a thousand men at his own
expense and march at their head to New England to their aid."

Washington never said such a thing, and could not have done it
(land was not ready cash, as Washington and many other landowners
have found over and over). But he was certainly willing to fight himself, and his station in life gave weight to his willingness. War, at best,
would take time from his business; in the worst case—defeat—his possessions might be confiscated, or destroyed. The most precious things a
man can risk are common to all men: life, freedom, family. But wealth
is another marker, and Washington was willing to lay it down.

Wealth was also a testimonial for a leader, and a character reference. This was a truism of the political theory of the day, which held
that leaders and citizens alike had to be at the very least financially independent, since if they were poor, the wealthy would bribe or bully
them. The people, Adams argued, believe the wealthy are not out for
themselves; the word he used was *disinterested*. If a political leader has
already made his pile, he has less temptation to make it on the job.
Adams, wiser than theory, knew that this was in fact not true. There
are as many rich crooks as poor ones. People were frequently "deceived
and abused in their judgments of disinterested men. . . . But such is
their love of the marvelous, and such their admiration of uncommon
generosity, that they will believe extraordinary pretensions to it." He
quoted a cynical Renaissance pope, who had said, "If the good people
wish to be deceived, let them be deceived." Then Adams added this

kicker: "Washington, however, did not deceive them." Wealth creates a presumption of honesty in office, and that presumption is often false. Yet Washington lived up to it.

Washington's financial independence allowed him to take the last act of leadership in his life. As early as the 1780s, it was clear that the twin pillars of his wealth were really only one. Agriculture at Mount Vernon, despite all his innovations and attention, had become a money pit. Mount Vernon was kept afloat by the rents he was able to collect on his western land, or by selling off swatches from it. He died wealthy because of the great liquidation, in his will, of the real estate empire he had built up after the French and Indian War. His sharp dealing as a younger man guaranteed his bequests to his many nieces and nephews—and the liberation of his slaves.

Money and leadership keep their symbiotic relationship today, both in private and in public life. Once a businessman has made money, people believe that he is likely to make more. Displays of success, from the grandiloquent to the grotesque, have a business function, though the public is often, as Adams said in a different context, abused and deceived. Yet sometimes even tinsel fortunes retrieve their luster. Donald Trump, son of a wealthy but quiet developer, turned himself into a celebrity, overbuilt, then went bankrupt. But his celebrity allowed him to recoup and offer his brand name as an add-on for other developers. In some times and places there is a fashion of self-restraint; old money often likes to look different from new money. Yet it is money all the same.

The image of money in politics has changed since Washington's day. As democracy has broadened the franchise, the rhetoric of democracy encourages us to believe that our leaders have humble roots, which they remember. But does reality match our rhetoric? Historian Edward Pessen shows in his book *The Log Cabin Myth* that only six presidents were born below the middle class, in anything like log cabins: Millard

Fillmore, Abraham Lincoln, Andrew Johnson, James Garfield, Richard Nixon, and Ronald Reagan. Pessen was a stern grader; Lyndon Johnson did not make his log-cabin cut because he was born on the right side of the tracks, even though his family sank into poverty during his boyhood. Pessen wrote before the election of Bill Clinton. Where would he fall? He ran as the Man from Hope, though his stepfather owned a Buick dealership in Hot Springs. So, despite our democratic professions, Americans turn to men of substance, sometimes (John F. Kennedy, the Roosevelts) very rich men. Even the log-cabin veterans on Pessen's list raised themselves up in the world financially before they began their political careers: Fillmore, Lincoln, and Nixon were lawyers, Johnson was a tailor who opened his own shop, Garfield taught Latin and Greek, Reagan was a movie star.

A leader should strive for financial independence (wealth is an extra) to win people's respect, and to be worthy of it. People admire a man who has made it, and a leader must not be in a position to be made or unmade by other men.

EDUCATION

In 1785 Washington was asked to do what any leader today in his position—more than a year into retirement—would already have begun: write a memoir. David Humphreys, a former aide-de-camp, suggested that "a good history of the revolution" would be both a "rational amusement" and a "noble . . . employment" for "the evening of your days." Humphreys was in no position to offer what a retired leader would now be guaranteed—a fat advance.

Washington declined. He told Humphreys he lacked the time; farming and the demands of fame—answering letters, sitting for painters—took it all. There was another problem: he lacked the "talents." "I am conscious of a defective education, and want of capacity" for writing "commentaries." (Humphreys took on the assignment himself, though he never completed it.)

Washington's father and his two elder half brothers all attended a school in the North of England; had Augustine Washington not died when he did, George might have been sent there too. Instead, he seems to have attended a local school in Virginia, and also to have had a tutor; his biographer James Thomas Flexner rated these fragments of training the equivalent of elementary school, plus the additional math he learned to be a surveyor. Whatever his schooling was, it was over by his midteens. Washington felt that his education did not suit him to write a history of the Revolution; that was a task for Humphreys (Yale class of 1771). Yet Washington's education had suited him to winning the Revolution, and would suit him, a few years later, to be president. What had he learned, and where?

Lawrence Washington's marriage to Ann Fairfax was an educational as well as a financial opportunity for George. The Fairfaxes had a grand estate, Belvoir, next to the Washington family farm that Lawrence had inherited and named Mount Vernon. Living with his brother, and visiting his in-laws, Washington acquired gentlemanly polish as well as connections, and that polish included additional learning. He read Seneca and Caesar in translation (he never learned any foreign language). Seneca was a Roman philosopher whose exhortations to live a virtuous life had made him popular for centuries with Christian audiences; Caesar was the greatest general, and clearest stylist, of the Roman world. These were well-known authors in eighteenth-century England and America, but they had special meaning for a future leader.

From Seneca Washington would have learned contempt for difficulty: not the brainless euphoria of a Nike ad ("*Impossible* is a word") or the slightly less giddy optimism of Colin Powell ("It can be done!"), but contempt for the power of adversity to darken or degrade us.

Seneca knew that life was full of difficulties, and impossibilities. But he argued that even when a man could not control them, he could control his reactions to them; he could choose not to whine, or fret, or do evil. Lying "at ease upon a bed" may be worse than torture, "if we suffer the latter with honor, and enjoy the other with infamy. It is not the *matter*, but the *virtue*, that makes the action *good* or *ill*; and he that is led in triumph may be yet greater than his conqueror." Seneca's intention was to talk up virtue; his writing is one long pagan sermon, as relentless as a Calvinist in a pulpit. But implicitly, and maybe to greater effect, he inculcates an attitude: Life is hard; conquests happen all the time, often to you; get over it.

Caesar's most famous work was his *Commentaries* on the conquest of Gaul in the 50s BC (when Washington declined Humphreys's suggestion to write his memoirs, he used the word *commentaries,* without needing to explain the reference). From the *Commentaries* the young Washington would have gotten a foretaste of the difficulties that military leaders were likely to encounter. During the French and Indian War, one of the Fairfaxes reminded him that "you have therein read of greater fatigues, murmurings, mutinies and defections than will probably come to your share, though if [they do come] I doubt not but you would bear them with equal magnanimity." Washington would read history, and military history, all his life—from Gibbon on the Roman Empire to Voltaire on Charles XII of Sweden, an almost contemporary figure—widening his frame of reference and multiplying examples of problems solved, and not solved. Seneca told him to keep a cool head; Caesar and other historians showed him what to do with it.

After the French and Indian War, he began reading up on another subject: politics, which, in his forties, was history in the making. The early 1760s saw local quarrels over clerical salaries and paper money that pitted Virginia against its London overlords. In 1765 there came a quarrel that agitated all thirteen colonies, over the Stamp Act, a

British tax on publications and legal documents. Washington bought the pamphlets generated by these controversies. By his marriage, he acquired the Custis family's library, which included a collection of English antiestablishment writers of the early eighteenth century. These men—John Trenchard and William Gordon on the Left; Henry St. John, Viscount Bolingbroke, on the Right; all three on the angry margins—were familiar, and largely ignored, figures in England. But their denunciations of corrupt London insiders resonated in America, as America began to chafe at London. Washington studied the problems of the day, and acquired a framework for understanding them that was inhospitable to the status quo. When his neighbor George Mason and his younger acquaintance Thomas Jefferson began making their own critiques of the imperial system, he bought and read their works as well.

The American Revolution did not fall upon him as some eruption of ill fortune out of Seneca. No one in America, except perhaps Samuel Adams, saw the Revolution coming very far in advance. But thanks to his reading, Washington had a good grasp of the problems that caused it, and when it came he not only did what was needful for a patriotic American to do but also understood why he was doing it.

He kept reading after the war. Now intellectuals and polemicists sent him their work, since he was their most famous fellow citizen. The *New York Times Book Review* has strict rules for avoiding conflict of interest; a reviewer should not have close relations, friendly or hostile, with an author whose book he is judging, and if he does, he must say so in the review. Washington could never have been assigned to review *The Federalist Papers*. He had known Alexander Hamilton, James Madison, and John Jay for years, and consulted them before, during, and after the Constitutional Convention; he arranged to have *The Federalist Papers* reprinted in Richmond, and told Hamilton approvingly that it "candidly discussed the principles of freedom and the topics of government which will be always interesting to mankind so long as they shall be connected in civil society." Today, a publisher would put that on the jacket (A BOOK FOR MANKIND—*George Washington*). Washington could not write for the *Book Review*, but he had prepared himself for the presidency.

He kept in touch with more abstract thought. Madison made him an executive summary of Montesquieu's *Spirit of the Laws* (1748), a classic of political philosophy, and Humphreys made another of Adam Smith's *Wealth of Nations* (1776), a classic of political economy. He owned a copy of John Locke's magnum opus on epistemology, *An Essay Concerning Humane Understanding* (1690). Locke argued that all knowledge derives from the impressions of our senses, and Washington read enough Locke to say that the reason Americans disagreed about the Constitution was because different minds perceived "the same object in different points of view." Locke was actually a little old-fashioned by the time Washington got around to him; more recent philosophers had posited a sixth moral sense, in addition to the bodily five, and Thomas Jefferson echoed them in his first draft of the Declaration of Independence, when he accused England of giving "the last stab to agonizing affection" in the colonies. Jefferson thought his appeal to affection was the climax of his argument, but the Continental Congress was unimpressed, and cut it out. The point of learning, for a leader, is not to be a polymath, or on the cutting edge of everything, but to know what you must know for the task at hand.

Washington read whatever he could about the task of farming. It was fashionable for late-eighteenth-century English gentlemen and aristocrats to write about their farms, and Washington kept abreast of this literature. The most useful and prolific author was Arthur Young, an English clergyman's son who had tried his hand at journalism and fiction, then found his vocation in managing farms and describing what he had learned. Young was also a clearing house for seeds and tools. In 1784 he began publishing a journal, *Annals of Agriculture*, which Washington subscribed to. (Another subscriber, and contributor, was George III, who wrote under the name "Ralph Robinson.") Young sent encouraging letters to Washington; when he learned that the American had given up tobacco, he wrote approvingly that "you might be as great a farmer as a general." Washington replied modestly. "I never possessed much skill in the art, and nine years' total inattention to it, has added nothing to [my] knowledge." Washington knew that American farmers had a lot to be modest about. Land seemed so plentiful that they did not bother to care for it. "Much ground has been *scratched* over," he told Young, "and none cultivated or improved as it ought to have been." He was determined to learn all he could to do otherwise.

Washington supplemented a meager education with a lifetime of self-education. Other leaders who were as badly schooled as he did the same. Most of the poor presidents on Edward Pessen's list were adult readers and writers. Ronald Reagan, scorned by his enemies as a genial dunce when he lived, turns out, with the publication of his letters, radio scripts, and diaries, to have been a careful and thoughtful writer.

But Washington had thought of a way to avoid his, and their, problem. He wanted Congress to establish a national university in the capital, whose "primary object" would be "the education of our youth in the science of government. In a republic," he added, "what species of knowledge can be equally important?" Washington called for a national university in his State of the Union addresses, and thought of hiring the faculty of the University of Geneva, Switzerland, on the run from the French Revolution, to jump-start it. The University of America, if its name commemorated its mission, or the University of Washington, if it remembered its founder, would guarantee a supply of future Washingtons.

Congress never established a national university, and it was probably right. There is no reason to think it would have fulfilled the mission Washington assigned to it. Would such a school have admitted the young Abraham Lincoln? Even if it had, would education in the science of government have made him a better leader? Woodrow Wilson was the best-educated president ever, according to Washington's criteria—he had a doctorate in political science, and was a political science professor—yet though he is often ranked among the better presidents, no one has ever claimed that he was the best.

There is no formula for educating a leader, because he must be responsible for much of his own education himself. He should receive the basic equipment that society gives its top tier, so as not to seem freakish. But the rest of his education will be governed by the problems he encounters, and the answers he must supply, and it will be a lifelong process.

CHAPTER 20

AVOID WEAKNESSES

———

WE COME INTO our careers with strengths, and the potential for strengths. But we also come with weaknesses—holes that will never be plugged, shortfalls that no amount of effort will ever push over the finish line. A leader has to know what he can't do, and not do it, whenever possible.

PUBLIC SPEAKING

Studies show that fear of public speaking is widespread, right up there with fear of death. Studies do not show how many public speakers are deadly, though the number must be large.

Washington's first inauguration, from his swearing-in to the evening celebrations in the streets of New York, was a dramatic triumph, a cathartic ceremony of commitment binding hero and crowd. Washington's performance as a speaker was the least part of it. Representative Fisher Ames, describing the inaugural address to a Boston friend, skipped Washington's words entirely, concentrating on physical details, several of them endearingly vulnerable: he shook; his voice wavered. Senator William Maclay left an even sharper portrait of Washington on the podium: "This great man was agitated and embarrassed more than ever he was by the leveled cannon or pointed musket. He trembled, and several times could scarce[ly] . . . read" his text, "though it must be supposed he had often read it before." We can count on Maclay to see everything and understand nothing: Washington might have rehearsed his speech fifty times, and still not have been completely comfortable giving the first inaugural address in history. Yet Maclay was acute enough to realize that his own sour judgment flowed from disappointed admiration: "I felt hurt that he was not first in everything."

Washington was far from first in speaking, in an age when oratory was at its height. Parliament never heard more eloquence; Edmund Burke's maiden speech in 1765 called for the repeal of the Stamp Act, and his greatest, ten years later, pleaded for England to avoid the Revolutionary War. Americans who were lucky enough to visit London went to Parliament, as we would go to the opera, or a rock concert; stay-at-homes could buy the published records of the debates, like owning a DVD of favorite performances.

Sermons had been an American genre for 150 years. Older revolutionaries remembered the preachers of the Great Awakening. In 1740, the English evangelist George Whitefield addressed a crowd of 30,000 on Boston Common. People came from far and wide to hear him; the population of Boston was then only 16,000. Samuel Adams, a senior at Harvard, heard him preach; Benjamin Franklin was Whitefield's friend and publisher. American politicians rivaled ministers in eloquence. John Adams gave the finest speech of his life to the Continental Congress on July 1, 1776, the last day of debate on Richard Henry Lee's motion for independence. He spoke for several hours; deep into his speech, he had to back up and recap for the New Jersey delegation, which arrived late. Everyone who heard him knew they had heard something great. Jefferson called him "our Colossus on the floor"; another delegate called him "the Atlas of American independence."

Adams was out of the country during the summer of 1787 when the Constitutional Convention met, but his place was well supplied by other orators. One of the best was Gouverneur Morris. "He charms, captivates, and leads away the senses of all who hear him," wrote a fellow delegate. His speech of August 8 was no charmer, but a philippic against slavery as "the curse of heaven," which still stings in James Madison's notes.

The greatest of all the founding orators was Patrick Henry, a homeschooled lawyer from the Virginia backcountry who began his political career, like Edmund Burke, with a speech against the Stamp Act, and was in and out of local and national politics for the next three decades. Jefferson, who disliked him—they were political rivals and temperamental opposites—nevertheless paid him a high compliment, saying that he spoke "as Homer wrote." By this he meant that Henry was a force of nature. Jefferson had no low opinion of his own abilities, but he knew that he was not a force of nature. (He and Henry were both skillful violinists: Jefferson read music; Henry played by ear.) Henry's greatest effort was his speech of March 23, 1775, to the Virginia Convention, a meeting of the House of Burgesses without the permission of the colonial governor in a Richmond church. The question before the delegates was whether Virginia should prepare for war (British troops garrisoned Boston, though the Battles of Lexington and Concord had not yet happened). In 2006 the Library of America included Henry's remarks in *American Speeches,* two volumes of political oratory from colonial times to Bill Clinton. Henry's is still one of the best speeches in the collection, and one of the only ones in the first hundred years that could be given to a modern audience. Everyone knows the ending: "I know not what course others may take, but as for me, give me liberty, or give me death!" But the speech's urgent power springs from another source: the insistent rattle of questions leading to the climax. There are twenty-two questions in a speech of fewer than 1,500 words; the last short paragraph has four in a row: "Why stand we here idle? What is it that gentlemen wish? What would they have? Is life so dear, or peace so sweet, as to be purchased at the price of chains, and slavery?" Henry turns a solo performance into dialogue, forcing his listeners (and his readers, two hundred years later) to ask themselves: What will I do?

Did Henry actually ask these questions? The text everyone knows, and that the Library of America used, was printed in 1817, in a biography of Henry by William Wirt, a younger contemporary (Henry had died in 1799). Was Wirt a posthumous collaborator? In fairness to Henry, the speech reads nothing like Wirt's own efforts, one of which also makes it into *American Speeches*. Those who heard Henry in 1775 were stunned. Edward Carrington, soon to be an artillery officer, listened through a window of the church, and told his wife that he wanted to be buried on the spot. Henry certainly had a talent for the brilliant improvisation and the inspired outburst. In the last public appearance of his life, campaigning for a seat in the Virginia legislature, he overheard a Baptist minister, irked at the attention being lavished on him, say, "Mr. Henry is not a god." Henry replied, "No, indeed, my friend. I am but a poor worm of the dust—as fleeting and unsubstantial as a shadow of the cloud that flies over yon fields and is remembered no more." Pretty good for off-the-cuff.

Washington didn't have it in him. He was so far from being a born speaker that his first speech in the House of Burgesses was a blank. When he took his seat in 1759, the house thanked him for his "faithful services" and "brave and steady behavior" in the French and Indian War. He rose to respond—and could not utter a word. Speaker John Robinson considerately took him off the hook. "Sit down, Mr. Washington, your modesty equals your valor, and that surpasses the power of any language I possess." This was no doubt a case of first-day jitters, similar to what he would feel at his inaugural thirty years later.

But he never acquired the ease of a good speaker. "In public, when called on for a sudden opinion," wrote Jefferson, long after he was dead, "he was unready, short and embarrassed."

Washington's lack of ability as a speaker was related to his character. Self-possession was a lifelong value of his. He once told a diplomat's wife that his face "never yet betrayed my feelings." If faces could be traitors, how much more so words? A speaker can impose himself on his listeners, but he also exposes himself to them. What they learn, from mistakes he makes or the way he says things, may give them as much power over him as he gains over them. Shortness of speech, once Washington fell into the habit, breeds more of the same. The need for control encourages reticence; lack of practice then encourages yet more reticence.

Washington went with his reticence, and spoke as little as possible. He served sixteen years in two legislatures—the House of Burgesses and the Continental Congress. The only memorable address he made during that time was his acceptance, in June 1775, of the position of commander in chief—three short paragraphs. At the Constitutional Convention he spoke only three times in four and a half months, equally briefly and less memorably. As presiding officer, he felt it was not seemly for him to speak, yet he no doubt enjoyed the protection that the role afforded him. For the first presidential inauguration, David Humphreys, a former aide, wrote a seventy-three-page speech. Washington was in a bind: Humphreys was living at Mount Vernon at the time, working on the future president's biography; his oration could not be rejected out of hand. Washington turned to James Madison for help. "I have not the smallest objection," he wrote, "to you conversing freely with Col. H— on all matters respecting this business." Madison then ghosted the four-page speech that Washington actually gave. Washington's Farewell Address is delivered every year in the Senate, but he never delivered it; the nation read it in the newspapers in

September 1796. "I never heard" him, Jefferson recalled, "speak ten minutes at a time, nor to any but the main point."

Yet there were many times when speaking was unavoidable. For example, the Constitution directs the president to "give to the Congress Information of the State of the Union" (Article II, Section 3). How did Washington manage his command performances? As time went on, his reputation helped him. Senator Maclay might feel disappointed by the gap between Washington's accomplishments and his words, but most people heard the words in light of the accomplishments. It was sufficient that he showed up. He also made use of his instinct for the dramatic. It may seem odd that a man who was tongue-tied should have been so theatrical. Yet although plays are full of talk and poetry, not all drama is verbal: dancers are silent, and so for years were movie actors. In a public forum, Washington could sometimes call on one skill to reinforce the other.

On some occasions—asking soldiers to reenlist when going home would leave no army, telling officers to be patient when anger might destroy the country—he relied on honesty. He had to mean what he said. His audiences felt he did.

In an age of television and all its mutant forms—teleconferencing, podcasts—the opportunities for leaders to speak are endless. A leader has to shape them to his inclinations and his abilities. When Jefferson, who disliked public speaking as much as Washington, became president, he interpreted the constitutional requirement to inform Congress to mean that he could submit his messages on the state of the union in writing. It was not until Woodrow Wilson, who liked to speak and was good at it, that the practice of giving them in person was revived. Some leaders speak well, or well enough; others might do better to emulate Jefferson: Jimmy Carter has a sickly smile and George W. Bush a little smirk that flash across their faces uncontrollably, like tics.

But leaders must also acknowledge custom and expectation. Changing the delivery system might take effort that they prefer to spend elsewhere.

Polemical Writing

The eighteenth century was a golden age of American editorializing. For a small, remote country, America had more newspapers per capita than England, more absolutely than France. Journalists could get away with more here. In colonial times, juries ignored sedition laws, which made it a crime to criticize public officials. A New York editor named John Peter Zenger was prosecuted for calling the governor and his friends "monkeys" and "spaniels," but was acquitted, in a display of sheer jury nullification. After independence, Congress passed and President John Adams signed a national sedition act; its unpopularity was one of the reasons Adams and his congressional backers were wiped out in the next election.

There was a small but feisty corps of professional journalists, many of them foreign born. James Rivington, an Englishman, edited the *Royal Gazette*, a New York newspaper that kept publishing during the British occupation; he also slipped information to Washington's spies on the side. William Cobbett, another Englishman, was a sergeant major in the British army who had to quit because of his radical views; when he moved to America in the 1790s, he became a staunch supporter of the Washington administration, writing under the name Peter Porcupine. "Professions of *impartiality* I will make none," Cobbett said. "They are always useless, and are besides perfect nonsense, when used by a newsmonger." Washington thought he was a little too staunch, disapproving of his "strong and coarse expressions." Greatest of all the professionals, foreign born or homegrown, was Thomas Paine. An English excise collector at loose ends, Paine came to America at the end of 1774, and found his calling and immortality: *Common Sense*, his argument for independence, was read by, or to, every other free adult in the thirteen colonies. Paine became an intimate of the founders; in 1789, at the beginning of the French Revolution, when Lafayette sent the key of the demolished Bastille to President Washington, Paine was the messenger who delivered it.

The founders did not leave polemical writing to journalists, but immersed themselves in publication and controversy. Samuel Adams and Alexander Hamilton both published newspapers (Hamilton's, the *New-York Evening Post*, is still going strong). Benjamin Franklin was a patron of other publishers, who got his start as a teenager writing for his older brother's newspaper in Boston, then went on to found a printing empire in Philadelphia, with former employees sown through the colonies, publishing their own newspapers. Even when he was a seventy-year-old scientist, sage, and diplomat, he kept his hand in; while he was America's ambassador to France during the Revolution, he had a printing press at his suburban Parisian estate, which ran off anti-British propaganda, as well as humorous pieces for his lady friends.

Franklin had the light touch of a master. John Adams did not, but that did not prevent him from writing often and at length. When he was vice president, he began a series of essays for a Philadelphia newspaper, ostensibly a commentary on sixteenth-century French history, actually a commentary on the best forms of government. When Adams alarmed his old friend Thomas Jefferson by writing too many kind words about monarchy, Jefferson launched a sly counterattack: he blurbed Thomas Paine's newest book, praising it as an antidote to "heresies which have sprung up among us." Everyone knew whose heresies Jefferson had in mind; Adams certainly did. Today, Jefferson might have written a bitchy letter to the *New York Review of Books*.

The most prolific founder-journalist was Hamilton. He had gotten his start in the Virgin Islands, describing hurricane damage for a local newspaper when he was fifteen. While he was a college student in New York City, he defended the colonies in two long pamphlets totaling 50,000 words, published by James Rivington, happy as always to work both sides of the street. His great service for the Constitution was to organize *The Federalist Papers*, a series that ran in the newspapers of New York, where opinion on the Constitution was sharply divided. He picked two collaborators, John Jay and James Madison, and wrote more than fifty of the eighty-five essays, for a contribution of 100,000 words. During Washington's second term, he produced another long series of essays, defending the treaty that Jay had negotiated with England against its critics. Washington praised their "clear, distinct and satisfactory manner," while Jefferson, who was one of the critics, ruefully conceded that Hamilton was a "host within himself." His contribution to this batch of thirty-eight essays was 70,000 words. (This book, by way of comparison, is 68,000 words long.) Besides these major efforts, he wrote numerous short series over the years, of a half-dozen pieces or less.

The goal of polemical writing is to persuade. Sometimes it persuades by instructing, but the purpose is always to move the audience in some direction. Politics is the obvious field for polemics. The people, Jefferson wrote, "may be led astray for a moment, but will soon correct themselves. . . . [G]ive them full information through the channel of the public papers, and . . . contrive that those papers should penetrate the whole mass of the people." Business is also rife with polemics. Advertising is a specialized form of it, but polemics are also used to build businesses and businessmen up *(The Art of the Deal)* or tear them down *(Unsafe at Any Speed, Roger and Me)*.

The best polemics lay down markers. When the shouting stops, the arguments remain, to guide future controversies. The purpose of *The Federalist Papers* was to influence the debate over ratifying the Constitution in New York. They were only partly effective: New York City, where they appeared, elected a strong, pro-Constitution delegation to the state's ratifying convention, but delegates from upstate were lopsidedly anti. Even so, Hamilton used so many arguments from *The Federalist* on the floor of the convention that someone on the other side asked if he was bringing out a second edition. Washington had *The Federalist* reprinted in Richmond, to influence the debate of the Virginia ratifying convention. (Both states voted narrowly in favor.) Now, two centuries after the authors and their opponents are dead, *The Federalist* marches on in college curriculums, Supreme Court decisions, and later generations of polemics. John Locke and Niccolò Machiavelli have been dead even longer, but their polemics about seventeenth-century England and Renaissance Italy are still studied.

Today, polemical writing is generally left to hired hands and ghosts. Our political class is so illiterate, or so pressed for time, that it is news when Al Gore writes a book, Barack Obama writes a readable book, or Fred Thompson blogs. But in the late eighteenth century, all the important leaders were in there scrapping, except for two.

One of the holdouts was Jefferson, despite his writerly gifts and the role he assigned the public papers. He wrote one long political essay before the Revolution, *A Summary View of the Rights of British America;* its passion and swiftness encouraged the Continental Congress to appoint him to the committee for drafting a declaration of independence, and encouraged his fellow committee members, Adams and Franklin, to let him do the work. He wrote other official papers, as a congressman, secretary of state, and president, and kept up a large correspondence all his life. But after the *Summary View*, he kept himself out of public back-and-forth as much as possible. *Notes on Virginia* (1784) was written as a scientific description of his home state, though the author's opinions, on everything from religious liberty to black intelligence, intruded. His anti-Adams blurb for Paine was a slippery little operation; he claimed that the blurb had been printed without his knowledge (though if he had wanted to protect his privacy, he would hardly have been corresponding with a publisher). He never did such a thing again. When he wanted something written, he got James Madison to do it, or he asked Philip Freneau, a State Department translator whom he had hired, not to read letters from foreigners (Jefferson himself was multilingual) but to publish a pro-Jefferson newspaper in the nation's capital. Jefferson would not write for the papers, even his own. Shyness held him back; so did a combination of patience and optimism: he always suspected he would be on the winning side, and he was often right.

The other significant bystander in the polemical wars among the founders was Washington. Jefferson's opinion of Washington's prose—ready, diffuse, easy, and correct—has been quoted above (see Chapter 6, "Communication"). If Washington was no great writer, he was certainly good enough to have been accepted by the newspaper editors of his time.

He declined to write for them, in part, for the same reason that he declined to write his biography. He was surrounded by men of many words, many of them well educated. *The Federalist Papers* were produced by two alums of King's College, today's Columbia University (Hamilton and Jay), and one of Princeton (Madison). His aides had been to college (Humphreys was a Yale man). Hacks had been to college (Philip Freneau went to Princeton). Why pick fights when you are lightly armed?

Washington's silence was encouraged by early experience, for he had appeared in print in his early twenties, to mixed effect. In 1753, the colonial governor of Virginia sent him over the mountains to scout French activity in the upper Ohio Valley. He was gone two and a half months in the late fall and early winter, submitting a 7,500-word journal of "the most remarkable occurrences that happened to me." They were not dull. He spoke to French officers and Indian chiefs, whose words he reported at length; an Indian took a shot at him, and he almost froze after falling into the Allegheny River. His account was laconic, as far as the messenger was concerned—he rarely offered his own thoughts on what he had seen—and when it was printed in colonial and British newspapers, it ran with a preface explaining that he never imagined it would be published. Modesty can be a rhetorical strategy, but his journal does have the quality of a private report, not for public consumption.

In the spring of 1754 he was off again, in command of 160 men assigned to occupy the forks of the Ohio (the site of modern Pittsburgh). He ambushed a small French party, then was surrounded and beaten by a much larger one, which allowed him, after surrendering, to march home in July. This time he made the papers twice. The letter to a younger brother, written after the first skirmish, in which he described whistling bullets as "charming," was reprinted in a London magazine, where it was read by King George II. "He would not say so," observed His Majesty, a combat veteran, "if he had been used to hear many." Washington never knew that, but he did know that a private boast had become public knowledge. After his defeat, the French published the journal he had been keeping of his journey, which, they said, showed him to be shifty and dishonorable: was the first skirmish honest combat or unprovoked murder (the two countries were formally at peace)? Virginians, whose opinion Washington cared most about, supported their young officer, but this time publicity had done him little good.

From then on he made it a practice never to publish anything that was not official: orders, proclamations, official correspondence, speeches. He could leak information skillfully: his back-and-forth with the British in the summer of 1776 about how he should be addressed (see Chapter 4, "Small Stuff") impressed Congress, and the public. His little note to Thomas Conway in the fall of 1777 (see

Chapter 9, "Troublemakers") was intended for a smaller audience, Conway's coconspirators; it depressed and alarmed them. But he never stepped out of uniform, military or presidential.

He must also have made a judgment of the talent level of the writers around him. He was very familiar with their work. He bought and read their relevant productions; most of them wrote to him or for him, at one time or another. So many of them were good; four—Jefferson, Franklin, Paine, Gouverneur Morris—had real genius. They did not write as Homer wrote, but they wrote as well as Patrick Henry spoke. Washington knew he was not first in everything. Unlike William Maclay, he was not hurt by that fact, but he drew a prudential conclusion.

Theodore Roosevelt wrote a famous tribute to "the man . . . in the arena, whose face is marred by dust and sweat and blood," which Richard Nixon quoted as he was leaving the arena (though he came back). Washington, Roosevelt, and Nixon all spent their lives in the arena of politics. But it has many playing fields. Roosevelt and Nixon were both capable polemicists, before and after their time in the White House. Washington left polemical writing to others.

CHAPTER 21

Control Your Flaws

———

A WEAKNESS is the absence of a good quality; a flaw is the presence of a bad one. Everyone has flaws, and no one is ever rid of them all.

Jefferson thought that Washington's character was "in its mass, perfect, in nothing bad, in few points indifferent." This was a generous judgment, and a mistaken one, for Washington, like all of us, had flaws. To succeed as a leader, he had to know them, and to control their effects.

OBSTINACY

Washington's mother is supposed to have greeted news of one of her son's victories in the Revolution by saying, "George generally carries through anything he undertakes"—a good trait in a leader who undertakes causes as risky as the Revolution. But there are projects, or strategies, that should not be carried through, because they are mistaken or hopeless. Obstinacy is persisting beyond all reason.

Washington showed obstinacy in each of his wars. One of the focal points of the French and Indian War was control of the upper Ohio Valley. The area was a geographic and economic prize; it was a short portage to the Great Lakes and an easy sail to the Mississippi, and the Indians who lived there controlled the fur trade.

The first two times Washington went to the Ohio Valley, in 1753 and 1754, he traveled northwest, over the Alleghenies from the upper Potomac. This was the most direct path for a Virginian, and it suited the political goals of his colony, since Virginia, from its inception, claimed the region. Washington's path also suited the financial agenda of his friends and patrons, who had formed a partnership, the Ohio Company, which intended to develop the area. When Washington went a third time, in 1755, as an aide to General Edward Braddock, he took the same route out—and back, after Braddock was killed and his army shattered.

In 1758, he joined in one more effort. There had been a change of government in London; new, competent officers were sent to America, with orders to clean the French out of the continent once and for all. General John Forbes, who was assigned to capture the upper Ohio, was intelligent, organized, and concerned to avoid Braddock's mistakes. When the young Virginia militia officer gave him advice on forest tactics, Forbes listened gratefully (see Chapter 12, "Enemies"). When Washington suggested that Forbes follow his and Braddock's old route, he was thanked for his "openness and candor." Then he was told that the new army would march due west from central Pennsylvania. Forbes's engineers had concluded that this route was shorter, and would avoid river crossings that were both tedious and dangerous.

Washington was enraged. The new road was an affront to Virginia and a blow to the Ohio Company, since it would give Pennsylvanians their own path to the interior. It also represented a rejection of the efforts he had been making, to scout and conquer the Ohio Valley, for five years. He lobbied Forbes's second in command to change the plan, and wrote one of Forbes's aides that "all is lost!" He wrote the governor of Virginia that the Pennsylvania road was "indescribably bad," and he told Speaker John Robinson of the House of Burgesses that the king himself should know "how grossly his honor and public money have been prostituted." Forbes's second in command begged him, in vain, to "yield to the evidence," while Forbes thought him "singularly impertinent." Washington had been seeing this part of the world through one prism, from age twenty-one to twenty-six, and now he was being asked to abandon it.

Twenty years later, Washington was fighting the British alongside the French. His allies and his enemies had changed, but not his temperament. The new instance of his obstinacy concerned the endgame of the Revolution.

All the episodes of the Revolution that have left a trace in popular memory or imagery—Paul Revere's ride, signing the Declaration, crossing the Delaware, Valley Forge—belong to its first two years. They begin the struggle, and take it to the end of the beginning—the point at which Americans showed that neither cold, hunger, many losses, nor heavy odds would defeat them. The beginning of the end, our recollection of high school history tells us, was the Battle of Saratoga in the fall of 1777—the American victory that brought France into the war on our side, and changed the strategic equation. But the fighting went on for four more years—as long as the entire Civil War, longer than our share of World War II. Not losing the Revolution was heroic; winning the Revolution was boring, bloody, and strategically perplexing.

The heroic phase of Washington's war was dominated by a simple arc. After the curtain-raiser, lifting the siege of Boston, all the various events—he called them "the strangest vicissitudes"—fitted into a binary pattern: He was driven out of New York; then he was driven out of Philadelphia; then he followed the British back to New York. Now, people commute between New York and Philadelphia every day. Washington and the British made the same 150-mile round-trip in two years, and at the cost of thousands of casualties. He was mindful of the pattern. "It is not a little pleasing," he wrote in August 1778, "nor less wonderful to contemplate, that after two years maneuvering . . . both armies are brought back to the very point they set out from." Washington wasn't quite back where he set out from, though, for he had begun in New York, and the British were still there. In 1778, however, he was hopeful. "The hand of Providence has been so conspicuous in all this, that he must be worse than an infidel that lacks faith."

Washington put his faith in winning the war by recapturing New York. But to do it, he needed help. When he lost New York in 1776, he had no navy to put up against Britain's. Now there was one, but it belonged to America's new ally, France. Any attack on a city of islands would have to be a joint Franco-American operation.

The first attempt was scheduled for July 1778, but when the French admiral, the Comte d'Estaing, found that his largest ships could not cross the bar of the lower bay, he decided instead to drive the British from Newport. A gale dispersed both navies, and the French had to sail on to Boston to refit.

The French took their fleet to the West Indies, where it lost and won various sugar islands, each as valuable as the entire United States. In the fall of 1779 d'Estaing sailed north again, to besiege Savannah. He had a French fleet and army, and the help of an American army from Charleston; when the siege dragged, he tried to take the city by storm. The attack was repulsed, with heavy casualties, and the French returned to the West Indies.

In 1780 and 1781, the war shifted to the South (see Chapter 11, "Failure and Betrayal"). The British took three states, and Nathanael Greene took them back. Lord Cornwallis, the British commander in the southern theater, moved his operations to Virginia, where he almost captured Governor Jefferson. Washington remained in the North, with his eyes on New York. It was the British command center, and the source of their reinforcements; the more pressure Washington could keep on them there, the less they would be free to do in the South. But he still dreamed of a knockout blow. In the summer of 1780 the possibility revived: a new French army and a small fleet, won by Lafayette's lobbying, appeared in American waters.

French officers had a mixed attitude toward Washington. Lafayette idolized him. Many admired his easy dignity, and romanticized him as a simple patriot, a rustic Roman. But their commanders understood, as professional soldiers, that he had few troops, no ships, and no money, while they had all three. They were determined to use their strength as they thought best.

Washington and the French commanding general, the Comte de Rochambeau, held two meetings as 1780 turned to 1781. Both times Washington pressed the New York option. Rochambeau met him with a mix of delay and generalities, agreeing that New York could be a target "under present circumstances." In July 1781 he and Washington even reconnoitered northern Manhattan from the Bronx, once getting themselves marooned at high tide on a tongue of land near Throgs Neck. Rochambeau did not tell Washington that he had dispatched an order to the Comte de Grasse, the new admiral of the West Indies fleet, to sail north that autumn—to Virginia.

Obstinacy is the brother of determination. There is no easy way to tell them apart; in the heat of the moment, they can look and feel the same. But when the moment lengthens and lengthens, it becomes time to try some other way; the obstinate leader won't. Recognizing when it is time to let go takes experience, wisdom, and instinct. Some leaders are slow to see it; others see it too soon. A twentieth-century governor of Louisiana, Earl Long, was told by an aide, "I'm with you when you're right, Governor. But not when you're wrong." "You stupid sonofabitch," Long said, "I don't need you when I'm right." But a leader must learn to know when he is no longer right.

Washington did not become truly less obstinate with age, but his attitude toward the quality changed. He was sometimes able to recognize it, which meant that, when the stakes were high enough, he could turn it off. Where the route to the Ohio Valley was concerned, he never changed. He accompanied Forbes all the way over the Alleghenies, resenting every step. When they came to the forks of the Ohio late in the fall of 1758, they found that the French had burned their fort and fled. They had captured a heap of ashes, a linchpin of the continent. Washington was deprived even of the satisfaction of fighting bravely. The next month he resigned his commission in the militia in disgust.

He carried his infatuation with the Potomac route over the mountains into peacetime: his interest in inland navigation and canals was the same project, translated to civilian life (see Chapter 3, "The Future"). His sense that the country had to be linked, east to west, was right, but he never gave up the paths he had walked himself in his twenties. When James Madison heard him, after the Revolution, going on and on about canals, he thought it was a symptom of postwar boredom. "[A] mind like his . . . cannot bear a vacancy." He did not know his man.

Washington abandoned his dream of retaking New York after four years. The French told him in August 1781 that de Grasse and the West Indies fleet would be sailing directly for Virginia, but he had already come around by the end of July. "It is more than probable," he wrote Lafayette on the thirtieth, "that we shall . . . entirely change our plan of operations." In Washington's favor, Rochambeau's alternative plan was insanely complex, summoning fleets and armies hundreds of miles apart to a Virginia rendezvous. In Rochambeau's favor, insane complexity sometimes takes the enemy by surprise, as in D-day or MacArthur's landing at Inchon. Ironically, Washington's tenacious focus on New York assisted the surprise, convincing the British command that New York really was the target, until it was too late to warn Cornwallis, their man in Virginia, of his fate.

Washington came close to admitting that he had been mistaken. On the same day he wrote Lafayette, he wrote in his diary that one of the French admirals had declined a recommendation of his to cruise past New York, preferring to wait until de Grasse arrived and link up with him. "This induced me to desist . . . [lest any] damage to his fleet should be ascribed to my obstinacy." This was only a conditional admission: *if* the French admiral followed Washington's suggestion, and *if* something went wrong, then unnamed others *might* blame his obstinacy. He had not invited the thought that he was mistaken into his mind, but he had opened the door to it.

Once the new plan was in motion, Washington threw himself into it with his usual energy and will to succeed. His army and Rochambeau's marched and sailed 450 miles, from northern New Jersey to southern Virginia, in forty days; the siege took nineteen; the endgame was won.

The mature Washington had fulfilled his mother's judgment, and carried through what he had undertaken, if not his way, then some other.

TEMPER

There were no voice-activated recording systems in the Washington administration, but there was one note taker, so we have occasional records of scenes as vivid as anything on the Watergate tapes.

The problem of how to deal with Citizen Genet (see Chapter 9, "Troublemakers") consumed many hours of cabinet meetings in the summer of 1793. At night, Thomas Jefferson would scribble down what he had said and heard. On August 2 he recorded a presidential outburst. The question before the cabinet that day was whether Genet's bad behavior should be made public (they had already unanimously agreed to demand his recall). Alexander Hamilton and Henry Knox, enemies of France, were for maximum publicity; Jefferson and

Edmund Randolph wanted the matter handled in diplomatic channels. Washington listened as the discussion unfolded. Then, Knox, in
order to show the bad effects Genet was having on popular opinion,
mentioned a satire that had recently run in Philip Freneau's *National
Gazette*, "A Funeral Dirge for George Washington," in which Washington was led to the guillotine. Genet's American admirers were im-
porting the symbolism of revolutionary France, if not actual
guillotines, into American politics.

Washington did not need to be told about the piece; he had already
seen it. He became, Jefferson wrote,

> much inflamed, got into one of those passions when he cannot
> command himself, ran on much on the personal abuse which had
> been bestowed on him, defied any man on earth to produce one
> single act of his since he had been in the government which was
> not done on the purest motives. [He said] that he had never re-
> pented but once . . . having slipped the moment of resigning his
> office, and that was every moment since; that *by God* he had
> rather be in his grave than in his present position; that he had
> rather be on his farm than to be made *emperor of the world* . . .
> that that *rascal Freneau* sent him three of his papers every day, as
> if he thought he would become the distributor of his papers; that
> he could see nothing in this but an impudent design to insult
> him. He ended in this high tone.

"There was a pause," Jefferson added, and they had "some difficulty in
resuming our question."

There are three noteworthy things about this passage. One is its
uncanny liveliness. This is how most of us lose our tempers. The blood
goes up; we like the feeling; we're off. We defend ourselves (he "defied
any man on earth") and thrash our tormentors ("that *rascal Freneau*").

Jefferson's nighttime memoranda are not completely trustworthy, for they never show him in a bad light—he doesn't mention, for instance, that Freneau was on his payroll. But this scene has the ring of truth. The second point is that this outburst was not unique: Jefferson calls it "one of those passions" of Washington's. We infer there have been others, probably also witnessed by Jefferson himself. The third point is that Washington's tantrum ended, and that it had no effect. Washington did not segue from his high dudgeon into action. On the question of whether to embarrass Genet, he decided not to decide; Jefferson quoted him: "Perhaps events would show" whether publicity "would be necessary or not." In the event Washington decided to handle Genet officially and discreetly.

This was the pattern of his public life. Hamilton, who was at the explosive cabinet meeting, had also witnessed such outbursts: a February 1781 explosion had blown him off Washington's staff. The commander in chief asked to see his aide, Hamilton showed up a few minutes late, and they quarreled (see "Smart People" in Chapter 8). Hamilton's encounter with Washington's temper was like Jefferson's in two ways: it was not his first ("the great man . . . shall for once at least repent his ill-humor," Hamilton wrote a friend while he was still nursing his wounds, implying that the case had not been unique), and it did not last long (Washington offered to make things up a half hour after their spat). When Hamilton proved to be uninterested in reconciliation, Washington bided his time, offering the younger man a field command he desired, turning to him for political advice, and, finally, placing him in his cabinet. Washington tried not to let his temper deflect policy or personnel, and if it did, he worked to repair the damage.

He had gotten good advice about his temper all his life. The "Rules of Civility" warned him against bad temper: "Be not angry at table whatever happens & if you have reason to be so, show it not but [put] on a cheerful countenance" (#105). Seneca discussed anger at great length, calling it, among other things, "a wild impetuous blast, an empty tumor, the very infirmity of women and children, a brawling, clamorous evil: and the more noise, the less courage; as we find it commonly, that the boldest tongues have the faintest hearts." But so what? Everybody knows that bad temper is bad, but not everybody controls it.

John Adams got the chance to preside over his own cabinet when he succeeded Washington as president in March 1797. He decided to retain Washington's last officeholders, a distinctly second-rate group (the glory days of Jefferson, Hamilton, and Knox were long past). That might not have mattered, except that the most important men in the cabinet were all closer to Hamilton than they were to Adams (James McHenry, secretary of war, had written a poem for Hamilton's wedding), and this came to matter a great deal as Adams and Hamilton drifted apart. By May 1800 Adams felt that it was time to clean out the Hamilton loyalists, but the way he did it was grotesque. He summoned McHenry from his dinner table to come see him, ostensibly to settle a minor appointment. "The conversation now paused," and then Adams "introduced a new subject."

The note taker at this meeting was McHenry himself, who sent an account to Adams afterward, by way of putting it all on the record. McHenry's account, like Jefferson's, has the ring of truth, despite his obvious bias. Adams launched into a tirade in the form of an inquisition, interrupted by McHenry's futile protests. He called Hamilton an intriguer ("the greatest . . . in the world") and a bastard, called McHenry his tool ("You are subservient to him"), said McHenry was incompetent ("Everybody says so"), and said that the entire cabinet was ignorant ("You are all mere children"). Adams's outburst went on much longer than Washington's—eight printed pages to Jefferson's paragraph. It was also a shouting match with the man at whom he was angry, rather than an explosion at a distance, as if Washington had accosted the rascal Freneau in the street.

McHenry reported his tongue-lashing to his old friend Hamilton, who correctly diagnosed one of the factors at play: "The ungovernable temper of Mr. Adams" makes him "liable to paroxysms of anger, which deprive him of self command, and produce very outrageous behavior to those who approach him." True enough. Hamilton rendered his judgment, however, in a 15,000-word attack on Adams that he wrote later in the year. The president's bad treatment of James McHenry was one item of Hamilton's indictment, but there were many others: Adams, he wrote, was "a man of an imagination sublimated and eccentric . . . vanity without bounds . . . disgusting egotism . . . distempered jealousy . . . ungovernable indiscretion." Hamilton intended his essay for a small audience of like-minded friends, but when it leaked (as it was bound to do) to the whole political world, the veteran polemicist was pleased: now everyone could read his brilliant put-downs. Everyone read them for what they were, a printed tantrum.

Adams and Hamilton each had reasons for what they said and did. Adams deserved a cabinet of wholehearted supporters, and Hamilton was not the only man, then or since, to conclude that Adams, for all his greatness, was a less-than-great president. But both men brought passion to their judgments, and both men surrendered to it. Like Washington in the discussion of Genet, they finally achieved release, but unlike him, they kept going. They fell in love with the sound of their own words; mostly, they fell in love with the emotions that the words conveyed. "I am in a very belligerent humor," Hamilton admitted, as he was planning his anti-Adams jeremiad. Washington's fits of temper ended, not because they were weaker than Adams's or Hamilton's but because he decided to end them, and because he had decided, as a general principle, that, in such situations, he must make the effort to decide. There was a norm for a leader's behavior, a range within which he should act, and when Washington felt he had been tugged away from it, he would tug himself back.

Washington's youthful preceptor, Seneca, argued that anger was a completely bad thing, undermining the power of reason. Some leaders, heeding such advice, try to eliminate anger from their public characters entirely, but they have their own problems. Jefferson was so adept at segregating his hostile actions and sometimes even his hostile thoughts from his own consciousness that many of his colleagues, and even some of his friends, accused him of duplicity. He is "like the great rivers, whose bottoms we cannot see and make no noise," wrote John Adams, after knowing him for forty years. "In deceiving others," wrote Adams's eldest son, John Quincy, who knew him as long, "he seems to have begun by deceiving himself." Jefferson's enemies were more blunt: Hamilton called him "a contemptible hypocrite." Jefferson never got mad, he got even, but this quality made other people mad, or confused.

In condemning anger root and branch, Seneca contradicted Aristotle, the greatest thinker of the ancient world, who said, sensibly enough, that there was such a thing as good anger: being angry "with the right people, at the right things, in the right way" (berating Charles Lee at Monmouth, for instance). But that assumes that one can control one's anger. Men with quick tempers—Washington, Adams, Hamilton—find that hard to do, and impossible if they don't make the effort. It is not so bad for people to know that a leader has a temper. But if his temper has him, then they will hold him in contempt. Enemies and rivals will be able to call him disgusting and ungovernable, and the fact that they may be equally guilty will not lessen the sting of the charge or the damage of the offense.

The late-twentieth-century presidency was scarred by temper. All Lyndon Johnson's emotions, including rage, were operatic. "Lyndon feeling sorry for himself," one aide recalled, "was like a billion Chinese crying." He believed he manipulated his emotions for effect, but they often burst their bounds. Richard Nixon seemed better controlled, but appearances were false, maintained only by the after-hours whining and sniping recorded on the nemesis of tape. The tempers of these men reflected more serious failings: Johnson was a bully, Nixon a plotter.

Washington went through life burdened with cares, and surrounded by difficulties and failures. There was daily cause to be angry, and no doubt he often was. Some of his flare-ups were revealed by his associates only to close friends or diaries, to protect the hero's reputation. Why did they protect him? Because he had earned their admiration over the long haul by keeping his eye on the task at hand, resisting (among other things) the distraction of losing his temper. Why did they feel like protecting him? Because he had spared them much of his anger, and leavened it, when he had not, with impartiality and consideration ("His justice," wrote Jefferson, was "the most inflexible I have ever known"). He had more important things to do than lose his temper. So does everyone, but he kept it in mind.

CHAPTER 22

SUCCESSION

———

YOU ARE the tool that is never put back in the box—until you stop working. There comes a time when every leader steps down or is struck down. How can a leader preserve his legacy after that? Succession crises are the bane of businesses, when innovators lose control of their companies, or unfortunately keep it, handing them off to unsuitable acolytes. An innovator may become unsuitable himself, locked into his first discoveries, like Henry Ford churning out Model Ts long after Americans stopped wanting them. Transfers of power in a democracy are controlled by the laws, not the will of the outgoing leader, yet these are always supplemented by the laws of politics, in which the soon-to-be ex-leader's choice may in fact count for a great deal—for good or ill.

Washington had his favorite and unfavorite generals during the Revolution, and he made sure he praised the former to Congress. His most important recommendation came in October 1780, when Congress let him choose the man who should take over from the disgraced Horatio Gates in the southern theater. Washington tapped his able loyalist Nathanael Greene. "I think I am giving you a general," he wrote a southern congressman laconically, meaning, *I am sure I am giving you a good one.* So he was. But Washington usually had no power to choose American commanders; he had to live with whomever Congress selected, as well as the possibility (which occasionally hovered over the horizon of reality) that Congress might supersede him.

Washington was succeeded in the presidency by his vice president, John Adams, but he took no direct role in picking him for either the number-two or number-one slot. It was clear, in late 1788, that the first vice president should be a New Englander, for regional balance; Washington told James Madison that he could work with either Adams or Massachusetts governor John Hancock. Adams prevailed in that election, and the next one, thanks to his own prominence as a patriot and the maneuvers of lesser political figures on his behalf. In the presidential election of 1796, Washington preferred Adams to his rival Thomas Jefferson, because Washington's relations with his fellow Virginian, personal and ideological, had soured, and because of national pride: the French ambassador publicly threatened economic warfare unless Jefferson was elected, a gross interference in American politics. Adams won narrowly, though without Washington's active support. At the new president's inauguration, the outgoing president seemed to feel relief more than anything else; Adams thought Washington gave him a look that said, "See which of us will be happiest!"

Washington's aloofness had several sources. The whole system was newborn. Party lines did not emerge until the end of his first term, and party organizations took a few years more to coalesce. Thanks to his fame, Washington won two elections essentially by acclamation, and felt that he should maintain his nonpartisan stance. Although Adams had nominated him for the commander in chief's job in 1775, the two men did not know each other that well, Adams having spent a decade abroad during and after the war; the vice presidency was not an office calculated to bring them closer together (Adams was the first in a long line of vice presidents to complain that he had nothing to do). As a result Washington was followed by a man who broadly agreed with his policies, without being particularly similar to him in experience or temperament.

The best service Washington performed for his successor was to stay out of his way, with one glaring exception: in 1798, when Congress, fearing a war with France, tapped Washington to lead the army once more, he insisted that his second in command be Adams's bête noire, Alexander Hamilton. Adams never forgave Washington for this, though he realized that Congress, packed with Hamilton's allies, would have forced Hamilton on him even if Washington had not. Once Washington was sure of his former aide's assistance, he supported Adams's efforts to tone the war fever down, and rejected all entreaties that he, not Adams, run for president a third time in 1800. (Washington died in December 1799, but even the memory of third-term talk would have made the endgame of Adams's administration more bitter than it was.)

The era of parties and partisanship arrived, but it has not made arranging presidential successions any easier. Even if the handoff is successful, the new runner may stumble. Andrew Jackson and Ronald Reagan, two-term presidents who gave their names to movements (Jacksonian Democracy, the Reagan Revolution), were succeeded by vice presidents—Martin Van Buren and George H. W. Bush—who were closer to their chiefs than Adams and Washington had been. Both successors, however, proved to be unpopular one-termers.

Some presidents undermine their successors. Theodore Roosevelt groomed his secretary of war, William Howard Taft, to follow him in the White House in 1908. Roosevelt, however, wearying of retirement, claimed that Taft had betrayed his legacy, and challenged him in the 1912 election cycle, splitting their party and guaranteeing that both men went down to defeat. Dwight Eisenhower had a shade of contempt for his vice president, Richard Nixon; in August 1960, as Nixon was running to succeed him, Eisenhower was asked by a reporter what ideas Nixon had contributed to the administration. "If you give me a week," Ike said, "I might think of one." Lyndon Johnson subjected his vice president, Hubert Humphrey, to exquisite tortures of domination and fickleness that he had perfected during the years they served together in the Senate. Humphrey managed to win the nomination in 1968 after Johnson announced he would not run again, but lost the election to Nixon, making his second (Eisenhower-free) run.

The only successful string of successors in American political history was the Virginia dynasty (1800–1824): two terms of Jefferson, followed by two terms of his secretary of state, Madison, followed (after a rebellious moment of wanting to jump ahead in line) by two terms of Madison's secretary of state, James Monroe. The three men remained friendly enough after their twenty-four years in the White House that they all served on the Board of Visitors of the University of Virginia—more important positions, in Jefferson's view, than the presidency. Franklin Roosevelt solved the succession problem by making himself into a dynasty, winning four elections in a row. The strength of this strategy was that, since FDR never retired, he was never a lame duck. The weakness of it was that he won his last election in 1944 as a dying man (see Chapter 18, "Identify Your Strengths"). When he did die, three months after his inauguration, he was succeeded by a vice president, Harry Truman, who had been so badly briefed he was unaware of the atomic bomb. The Twenty-second Amendment made this strategy unconstitutional.

All the pitfalls of presidential succession—the incompetence of the incomers, the malice, envy, and ego of the outgoers—afflict transfers of power in the business world, for the same reason that they affect them in politics: leaders do not want to know that they are dispensable, or mortal. Some CEOs, like some presidents, make an honest effort to find competent replacements, but often enough they fail, wittingly or unwittingly, or they tear down the replacements they have found, or they hang on, without term limits, smiling from the covers of business magazines or group portraits at Sun Valley, with their wrinkles and their trophy wives.

Washington knew that he was mortal, and replaceable. One prominent twentieth-century biography of him is called *The Indispensable Man*, yet he dispensed with himself twice, at the end of the Revolution, and after his second term as president. The ceremony for his retirement from military life in December 1783 was prescribed by Congress. A committee headed by Thomas Jefferson directed Washington to appear in the statehouse in Annapolis, Maryland, where Congress was meeting, on the twenty-third. When Washington rose to make his remarks, Congress would remain seated. When the president of Congress rose to respond, Washington would remain standing. At the end of their exchange, Washington would bow; members of Congress would not bow, but would take off their hats.

This protocol, designed to demonstrate the subservience of the military to the civilian power, was not intended by Jefferson, in any demeaning spirit, to put Washington in his place. That may well have been the intention, however, of the president of Congress, Thomas Mifflin, Washington's old enemy from the Conway Cabal (see Chapter 9, "Troublemakers"). If Mifflin had malice in mind, however, he had not calculated on one thing: Washington's complete acceptance of the principles that the ceremony was meant to express. "It was a solemn and affecting spectacle," wrote a young congressman. "When [Washington] commended the interests of his dearest country to almighty God, and those who had the superintendence of them to His holy keeping, his voice faltered and sunk, and the whole house felt his agitations. After the pause which was necessary for him to recover himself, he proceeded to say in the most penetrating manner, 'Having now finished the work assigned me I retire from the great theater of action.'" He performed the part that had been written for him with conviction—because it was the part he would have written for himself.

Toward the end of Washington's second presidential term, Jefferson, who was by then Washington's political enemy, knew enough not to try to run him down. Philip Freneau and other journalistic warriors in Jefferson's party had been trying that, for almost four years, without effect. Washington had emerged from every controversy, foreign or domestic, with his reputation and his popularity intact. In June 1796 Jefferson wrote Monroe resignedly that "one man outweighs [Congress] in influence over the people. . . . Republicanism must lie on its oars, [and] resign the vessel to its pilot." Three months later Washington told the country, in his Farewell Address, that he was resigning the pilot's chair. At the inauguration of President Adams and Vice President Jefferson the following spring, Washington, by his own little ceremony of giving way to Jefferson (see Chapter 15, "Courtesy"), showed once again where he stood, once his job was done.

Washington retired to private life, twice. But private life, after his second retirement, confronted him with another decision. He had kept his estate going in the 1760s by moving from planting to farming: from being a tobacco crop master to a multipurpose agricultural entrepreneur. But now farming no longer paid. Slave labor was not productive enough, and he had too many nonlaboring mouths to feed. Thanks to his investments in land, he was still a very rich man, but the heart of his self-made empire had become hollow.

In his will he freed his slaves (see Chapter 18, "Identify Your Strengths"). But he also addressed the troubled condition of Wash-Corp by breaking it up. Martha was given the use of his estate while she lived, and he gave blocks of stock to various schools. After his wife's death, more than 9,000 acres, including Mount Vernon, would go to three nephews and two step-grandchildren. The rest, 60,000 acres plus miscellaneous stocks, bonds, and livestock, he valued at $530,000. He directed that it be sold and divided into twenty-three equal shares, to be distributed to his many nieces and nephews. The careful itemizing in his will still shows the eye of a surveyor (he said he was "but little acquainted" with one tract in southern Maryland, though he knew that it was "very level") and the instincts of a bar-gainer (he urged his executors "not to be precipitate" in selling off land, since prices "have been progressively rising"). He still plugged canals: "I particularly recommend it to [my] legatees" to hold shares in Potomac canal stock, rather than cash them in, "being thoroughly convinced myself, that no uses to which the money can be applied will be so productive as the tolls arising from this navigation."

So the engine of his energy and ambition still spun, but it was mo-mentum merely, and Washington knew it. None of his heirs would become rich as a result of his legacy. The occupants of his glorious es-tate house found themselves saddled with a white elephant, increas-ingly chipped and sagging as the decades passed, until the 1850s when a patriotic woman from South Carolina, appalled by its condition, raised the money to buy it for the Mount Vernon Ladies' Association, which owns it still.

Washington gave no one a windfall. He left each of his relatives somewhat better off than he had been left when his father died a half century before. Two of them would have notable careers—his nephew Bushrod Washington was already an associate justice of the Supreme

Court, and his step-grandson George Custis would be a successful memoirist, evoking his youth at Mount Vernon. But their lives, as he planned, would be up to them.

Washington's careers ended with his retirement, or his life. He did what he had to do, then handed the work off to others, or wound it up. He left his successors with the burden, and the freedom, of making their way.

Conclusion: We Must Take Men

MAYBE GOUVERNEUR Morris was wrong, and it is possible to write a book about leadership. But how is it possible to summarize one?

Lessons come from examples, which are as diverse as a day's messages, the people you know, and the surprises that walk through your door. Some lessons tug in different directions: communicate, but keep quiet; find a strategy, while sweating the small stuff; learn from enemies, and deny your allies. One thought of George Washington's, though, gets to the gist.

He expressed it at a low point in his career (one of many low points—if you want a pleasant life, don't be a leader). In April 1778 he wrote a letter from his headquarters at Valley Forge to John Banister, a congressman from Virginia. The winter, thankfully, had ended, but the commander in chief was worried, as he so often was, that his army might be about to end too. Ninety officers from Virginia had submitted their resignations to him personally, and "the same conduct," he told Banister, "has prevailed among the officers from the other states." They were resigning not because of privation or battle fatigue—that they could handle—but because they weren't being paid. Washington wrote Banister to urge Congress to find some remedy, and in doing so he made a general statement: "We must take the passions of men as nature has given them."

What he meant by this in April 1778 was that men want to provide for their futures, and for their families. As things then stood, officers were losing money, not making it or even treading water; they had to "break in upon [their] private fortune[s] for present support, without a prospect of future relief." The Declaration of Independence had pledged the lives, fortunes, and sacred honor of its signers, and of America, to the cause of liberty and independence, but such promises could be pushed only so far.

Taking the passions of men as nature has given them is a counsel of realism, and Washington had been learning it for a long time. In 1778 he was forty-six years old. He had been in leadership roles since he first reconnoitered the French in the Ohio Valley at age twenty-one. He had experience with merchants, workers, battles, sex, sickness, patronage, and politics. He would keep learning for twenty-one more years. Among the many things he had observed was that people who did not learn from experience, including their experience of the passions of men, ended up dependent, or shunted aside, or dead.

In his letter to Banister, Washington went on in this realistic vein.

> I do not mean to exclude altogether the idea of patriotism [as a motive]. I know it exists, and I know it has done much in the present contest. But I will venture to assert that a great and lasting war can never be supported on this principle alone. It must be aided by a prospect of interest or some reward. For a time, [the idea of patriotism] may of itself push men to action, to bear much, to encounter difficulties. But it will not endure unassisted by interest.

We must, therefore, take the passions of men as nature has given them.

But there was a second meaning in Washington's general statement, hidden, no doubt, even from himself as he wrote it in April 1778, though it was demonstrated by the thrust of his life. *To take* can mean *to accept* or *to consider:* to take account of. But it can also mean *to choose*, or *to grasp:* to take hold of. Men have many passions, which can counteract each other; they also have reason, if they take their thoughts seriously. They can be warned, or persuaded, or inspired. They can be led. That goes for anyone you meet; that goes for yourself. Take a good look at people as they are and where they are; then take them someplace else. Washington was doing it even as he wrote Congressman Banister.

A leader must know who he is, and who he is dealing with; and then he must lead.

Notes

Washington's papers at the Library of Congress—65,000 items—can be read online at: http://memory.loc.gov/ammem/gwhtml/gwhome.html. In these notes, any reference using the initials GW is from this source.

Abbreviations

AH Hamilton, Alexander. *Writings*. New York: Library of America, 2001.

FC McClellan, James, and M. E. Bradford, eds. *Debates in the Federal Convention of 1787 as Reported by James Madison*. Richmond: James River Press, 1989.

FP Hamilton, Alexander, James Madison, and John Jay. *The Federalist Papers*. New York: New American Library, 1961.

TJ Koch, Adrienne, and William Peden. *The Life and Selected Writings of Thomas Jefferson*. New York: Modern Library, 1944.

W Washington, George. *Writings*. New York: Library of America, 1997.

Introduction: Founding CEO

1 "first in war" Marshall, 5:366.

2 "excellent commander" Flexner, 2:222.

2 "The spectators" Rhodehamel, 796.

2 "first in peace" Marshall, 5:366.

3 "These delays" Brookhiser *(Washington)*, 57.

3 John Adams remarked Bowling and Veit, 28.

3 "Few can realize" W, 752.

3 "forests" Chateaubriand, 1:122–23. *Cherchez les bois où brilla l'épée de Washington: qu'y trouvez-vous? Des tombeaux? Non: un monde!*

5 "inclined to gloomy" TJ, 175.

5 "his character" TJ, 174.

5 "None know how" Davenport, 2:54.

5 "with the tenderness" Irving, 295.

5 "On other occasions" Rhodehamel, 788–79.

5 "Mr. Madison" FC, 601.

6 "Such a pen" W, 1052.

PART I: PROBLEMS

9 "constantly on" W, 1050.

CHAPTER 1: START-UPS

12 "cursing, swearing" W, 175.

13 "void[ing] excrement" Golway, 62.

13 "The regimental quartermasters" GW's General Orders, January 5, 1776.

14 "all filth" Golway, 87.

14 "Out of tender regard" GW's General Orders, March 13, 1778.

15 "When a regiment" Steuben, 81.

15 "On the arrival" Steuben, 133.

15 "the quartermaster must" Steuben, 84.

15 "The preservation" Steuben, 125.

15 "The Commander-in-Chief" GW's General Orders, April 11, 1779.

16 "Everthing . . . depends" Rose, 15.

16 "fully sensible" Rose, 17.

16 "He was too good-looking" Rose, 2.

17 "Get some intelligent" Rose, 78.

18 "medicine" Rose, 108.

18 "write on the blank leaves" Rose, 175.

18 five hundred pounds Rose, 264.

18 "He will be able" Rose, 171.

18 "Let not an hour" Rose, 190.

19 "[His] powers" McDonald, 209.

19 "We are acting" FC, 450–51.

19 "a bad edition" TJ, 435.

20 "was introduced" Bowling and Veit, 128–32.

21 "be damned" Flexner, 3:217.

Chapter 2: Strategy

23 "the defence" Marshall, 2:487.
24 "It is notorious" AH, 21–22.
25 "But as her finances" Paine, 113.
25 "Our business" Billias, 85.
25 "about as gentle" Billias, 25.
25 "If the Americans" Billias, 41.
26 "I have never" W, 241.
27 "In the worst" Flexner, 3:73.
27 "perhaps the strongest" TJ, 173.
27 "The General does want" Golway, 142.
29 Tobacco was a demanding Breen, 46–53.
30 Successful planters Breen, 61–62.
30 "The quality of" Breen, xix, 22–23.
30 "Our plants" Dalzell and Dalzell, 252.
30 "I am at a loss" Breen, 82.
31 "neat and fashionable" Dalzell and Dalzell, 54.
32 "Many families" W, 131.
32 "This is the seventh" Flexner, 2:399.
33 "respectable and prosperous" W, 517–59.
34 "Thirteen sovereignties" W, 622.
35 "Like a house" W, 635.
35 "O.K., let's go." Ambrose, 139.
35 "Refraining if he saw" TJ, 173.

Chapter 3: The Future

37 "servants, possessions, dignity" L'Estrange, 134.
38 "We went through" W, 11.
38 "New states" W, 592.
39 "ignorant" W, 14.
39 "How much more" W, 592.
39 "The General sent" Brookhiser *(Washington)*, 49.
40 "which put them" W, 12–13.
41 "That it is" W, 538.
42 "bad Indians" W, 775.

42 "I expected *little*" W, 768.

42 "More active" Flexner, 3:303.

43 one refugee from Fenn, 46–47.

44 "with some reluctance" Fenn, 14.

44 "fishing or on any" W, 176.

44 "It is a very" Fenn, 75–76.

45 "I find it impossible" Fenn, 93–94.

45 "the disorder began" Fenn, 98.

45 In one month Fenn, 306.

45 "the first large-scale" Fenn, 102.

46 "About 747 Negroes" Fenn, 132.

Chapter 4: Small Stuff

47 "to the great points" TJ, 60–61.

48 "invincible obstinacy" Fischer, 70.

48 "relieved from the" Fischer, 74.

48 "peace and lasting union" Abbot, 5:296.

48 "George Washington Esq." Abbot, 5:297.

49 "much regretted" Abbot, 5:398–402.

50 "The Hessians" Fischer, 97.

50 "acted with a dignity" Continental Congress to GW, July 17, 1776.

52 "What sort of a town" GW to Edmund Randolph, October 14, 1793.

53 "extends to *place*" Alexander Hamilton to GW, October 24, 1793.

53 "a novel proceeding" GW to Edmund Randolph, October 14, 1793.

53 "extraordinary Occasion" Edmund Randolph to GW, October 24, 1793.

54 "the only alternative" Flexner, 4:98.

Chapter 5: Management Style

55 "He formed" McDonald, 226.

56 All the others Golway, 65–66.

57 "If we could" Fischer, 264.

57 "Some doubts" Reed, 397.

58 "Should an attempt" Elkins and McKitrick, 475.

59 "If the Laws" W, 874.

59 "The very existence" Elkins and McKitrick, 478–80.

61 "act as occasion" Flexner, 2:298.

61 "would have done honor" AH, 52.

62 "partial attack" Flexner, 2:299.

62 "To speak" Flexner, 2:300.

62 "Was it not" Brookhiser *(Founders)*, 172.

62 "I was disconcerted" Flexner, 2:305.

62 "His coolness" AH, 54.

63 "Only by full" Hook, 238.

67 "dispenses happiness" Flexner, 2:43.

67 "jubilant personality" Flexner, 2:70.

67 "damned sharp" Brookhiser *(Hamilton)*, 77.

66 "history" TJ, 521.

67 "Our forefathers" Pliny, 5:217–19.

67 "Sat down therefore" Dalzell and Dalzell 129; GW's diary, February 5, 1760.

67 "As you are now" Ellis *(His Excellency)*, 47.

68 "I . . . has whipped them" Dalzell and Dalzell, 141.

68 "a rogue" W, 118.

69 "The bridge" Haven, 38.

Chapter 6: Communication

71 "wrote readily" TJ, 174.

72 "the exercise" W, 767.

72 "Those about me" Brookhiser *(Hamilton)*, 29.

73 "very minute" Brookhiser *(Washington)*, 101.

74 "It was a very" Ames and Allen, 1:568.

74 "idleness" Brookhiser *(Washington)*, 154.

74 he was only the first Emery, 26.

75 "The temper of the army" W, 479.

75 "the senior officer" Flexner, 2:505.

75 "unexpected[ly]" Rhodehamel, 787–78.

76 "For a dreadful moment" Rhodehamel, 789.

76 "I can't tell a lie" Weems, 24.

77 "great Art," Rhodehamel, 781.

77 "secret Artifice" Rhodehamel, 784.

77 "the most solemn" Bowling and Veit, 137.

78 "His colloquial talents" TJ, 174.

78 "he scattered information" Bowling and Veit, 275.

78 "His Highness" Ferling, 302.

79 "He got on the subject" Bowling and Veit, 17.

79 "possessed the gift" Schutz and Adair, 107.

Chapter 7: Timing

83 "He that has lost" Brookhiser *(Washington)*, 123.

Chapter 8: Unusual People

88 "was strengthened" TJ, 43.

88 "a man who spends" Broadwater, 55.

89 "Much abler heads" W, 157.

89 "a youth" Irving, 370.

90 "There is no skimming" Brookhiser *(Washington)*, 58.

90 "probable" AH, 169.

90 "sedentary and studious" Leibiger, 6–7.

91 "measures of relief" Leibiger, 51.

91 "our first man" Ames and Allen, 1:569.

92 "it would end" FC, 616.

92 "Pride on the one hand" GW to James Craik, September 8, 1789.

93 "absolute absurdity" Leibiger, 208.

93 "I am not conscious" AH, 94.

93 "That he is ambitious" W, 1013.

95 "taken familiarities" Brookhiser *(Founders)*, 40.

95 "You say" Bobrick, 334.

96 "first object" Steuben, 135.

96 "A certain great man" Bobrick 225.

97 "have obtained" W, 184.

97 "I can bear" Flexner, 2:38.

98 "leaped from his saddle" Fischer, 25.

98 "Virginian geese" Schutz and Adair, 106.

Chapter 9: Troublemakers

99 "General Conway's merit" Bobrick, 298.

100 "a weak general" Flexner, 2:248.

100 "there are prompters" Flexner, 2:275.

101 "Sir, A letter" Flexner, 2:249.

102 "I am here" Brookhiser *(Morris)*, 42.

102 "Yes, Sir" Schama, 28.

102 they had unmasked Brookhiser *(Hamilton)*, 35.

103 "He has I think" Davenport, 2:595–97.

104 "It is beyond" Brookhiser *(Washington)*, 92.

104 "I live here" Elkins and McKitrick, 343.

104 "too much warmth" Elkins and McKitrick, 341.

104 "diplomatic subtleties" Elkins and McKitrick, 348.

104 "appeal from the President" Flexner, 3:58.

104 "What must the world" Elkins and McKitrick, 351.

405 "As long as" Elkins and McKitrick, 373.

406 "My dear general" Brookhiser *(Morris)*, 24.

407 "You were charged" W, 799–800.

407 *"I now promise"* Davenport, 2:403.

108 "He pursued steadily" Flexner, 3:356.

109 "mutual forbearances" W, 817, 819.

109 "some instrumentality" AH, 789.

109 "not a syllable" TJ, 521.

109 *"We think in English"* AH, 523.

109 "The liberty" TJ, 522.

109 "I would rather" Sidey, n.p.

110 "For our citizens" Elkins and McKitrick, 348.

110 "affectionate" Elkins and McKitrick, 344.

110 "look and gesture" Elkins and McKitrick, 350.

110 "After I had read" Flexner, 4:58–59.

110 "T.J. has had a fever" Flexner, 4:59.

111 "scenes of greater" Flexner, 4:75.

111 "any communication" Flexner, 4:76–77.

Chapter 10: Superiors and Subordinates

113 "Nothing now" GW to John Robinson, September 1, 1758.

114 "Don't think my Lord" Ellis *(His Excellency)*, 30.

114 "every gentleman" W, 167.

114 "I have a grateful" W, 290.

115 "not having received" Bobrick, 436.

115 "It is not within" W, 407–8.

116 "mixed government" Lewis Nicola to GW, May 22, 1782.

117 "The same abilities" W, 1106.

117 "surprise" W, 468–49.

118 "Pray sir" "The Good Soldier White" (online), n.p.

118 "saw General Washington" Dann, 125.

Chapter 11: Failure and Betrayal

121 "Thy steady temper" Quintana, 7 (1.1.7).

122 "I would burn" Golway, 92.

122 "What valuable purpose" GW to Nathanael Greene, November 8, 1776.

122 "I cannot conceive" Nathanael Greene to GW, November 9, 1776.

123 "with the tenderness" Irving, 295.

123 "I feel mad" Golway, 103.

123 "Oh, general!" Irving, 296.

124 "determined . . . to risk" GW to Congress, November 16, 1776.

124 "Fortune seems" Golway, 106.

125 "virulent" FC, 468.

125 "the very verge" Rhodehamel, 774.

126 "the precipice" Rhodehamel, 779.

126 "to guide the torrent" AH, 122.

126 "will see you starve" Brookhiser *(Morris)*, 70.

126 "I have never" Rhodehamel, 782.

126 "It is easier" Rhodehamel, 779.

127 "the fury" Brandt, 133.

127 "I wish America" Brandt, 181.

128 "In proportion" Bobrick, 413.

128 "Whom can we trust" Bobrick, 417.

128 "[Washington] went up" AH, 90.

130 "a *special reason*" Elkins and McKitrick, 425.

130 "well disposed" Flexner, 4:224.

130 "immoral and impolitic" Elkins and McKitrick, 427–48.

130 "make such explanations" Flexner 4:234.

131 "one second" Flexner 4:236.

132 "glowering hack" Elkins and McKitrick, 625.

Chapter 12: Enemies

133 "Be assured" Brookhiser *(Washington)*, 71.

133 impertinent, drunk W, 147.

134 "pursue[d] each other" Golway, 240.

134 "widely differs" Brookhiser *(Morris)*, 45.

134 "hearty assent" Goebel, 314.

135 "No nation" W, 329.

135 "entire destruction" W, 365.

135 "cutthroats all" Flexner, 2:346.

135 "all the miseries" W, 772–75.

136 "too ambitious" Longmore, 24.

136 "had no experience" Flexner, 1:100–101.

137 "Indians are the only" Ellis *(His Excellency)*, 25.

138 "We must comply" Ellis *(His Excellency)*, 32.

Chapter 13: Allies

139 "silence, exile" Joyce, 247.

140 "imprudent," Longmore, 24.

140 "may have courage" Flexner, 1:108.

140 "particular notice" John Robinson to GW, September 15, 1754.

140 "Your approbation" GW to John Robinson, April 20, 1755.

141 "I have stopped" Bobrick, 306.

141 "On other occasions" Rhodehamel, 788.

142 "reciprocate" Marshall, 4:91.

142 "In the moment" GW to Lafayette, December 8, 1784.

143 "The country never" W, 152.

143 "I should think it" W, 157.

143 "the difference in" W, 293.

144 "embarrassments" W, 917.

144 "Official considerations" GW to the emperor of Germany, May 15, 1796.

145 "some fears" GW to Henry Knox, July 16, 1798.

145 "For more than twenty" Henry Knox to GW, July 29, 1798.

Chapter 14: Sex . . . and Drugs

147 "had a thousand" Dryden, 2:498.

147 "cabals" FP, 55.

147 "small brunette" Golway, 42.

148 "Upon the whole" Golway, 196.

148 Caty took Golway 158.

148 "This amiable woman" Davenport, 1:235.

149 "lost *something* else" Brookhiser *(Morris)*, 59.

149 "a moment's uneasiness" W, 900.

150 "happiest" W, 1003.

150 "No enemy" Opinion of General Officers, March 9, 1792.

151 "I humbly beg" Thomas Green to GW, May 15, 1788.

152 "An aching head" Dalzell and Dalzell, 146.

152 "I know full well" Dalzell and Dalzell, 147.

152 "It is not" GW to Thomas Bishop, April 10, 1779.

153 "Big Drunk" Haley, 74.

Chapter 15: Courtesy

155 "completely full" Musa, 55–57.

155 "Cruelties can be" Musa, 73.

156 "It is much safer" Musa, 139.

156 "The Rules of Civility" Many editions. Mine is Brookhiser *(Rules)*.

157 "thread bare blanket" W, 11.

158 "had better be" Bobrick, 440.

158 Joseph Ellis suggests Ellis *(His Excellency)*, 9.

159 "the deepest politician" Longmore, 155.

159 "the foundation" W, 517.

159 "the science" FP, 72.

Chapter 16: Bringing Out the Best

161 *attachments, enmities* FP, 54.

162 "open the flood gates" W, 500.

162 "should not be" W, 517.

163 "inferior endowments" W, 731–32.

163 "the constancy" W, 963.

163 *Hunde, wollt ihr* Fraser has *kerls* (literally, *guys* or *fellows*; here, *rogues* or *bums*). But it is also remembered as *Hunde*.

Chapter 18: Identify Your Strengths

169 "I was struck" Longmore, 182.

170 "a laxity" Bowling and Veit, 275.

172 "memorandum to have" W, 17.

173 "It can be" Maume, n.p.

173 "often [saw] him" Weems, 39.

174 "damned infernal old" Brookhiser *(Adamses)*, 81.

175 "He rode" Custis, 386–87.

175 "While passing" Fischer, 227.

175 "The roads" Grant, 163.

176 "Are you afraid" Roosevelt *(Rough Riders)*, 104.

177 "sweetness" Flexner, 1:159.

177 "Dignity with ease" Longmore, 182.

177 "After dinner" O'Brien, 15.

178 "Modesty marks" Longmore, 182.

178 "no harum-scarum" Flexner, 1:343.

178 "The quicker we clean" Widmer, 2:451.

178 "Our colonel" Flexner, 1:159.

178 "excellent commander" Flexner, 1:222.

179 "[He] has so happy" Flexner, 3:200.

180 "Broadminded!" Black, 246.

180 "I heard bullets" W, 48.

180 "Had you not" Flexner, 2:456.

180 "We just knocked out" Manchester, 692.

181 "The shocking scenes" W, 616.

181 "abilities and military experience" W, 167.

182 "a culprit" W, 726.

182 "the best dispositions" W, 730.

182 "Secure as he was" Flexner, 3:111.

183 "I am . . . against" W, 900.

183 "I do . . . most" W, 1023–24.

183 "She did not feel" Hirschfeld, 214.

CHAPTER 19: BUILD YOUR STRENGTHS

185 "I was surprised" Franklin, 1389.

185 "Lying rides" Franklin, 1219.

185 "The sleeping fox" Franklin, 1230.

185 "All would live" Franklin, 1254.

186 "An empty bag" Franklin, 1216.

187 "Ordinary, or even" W, 124.

188 "I should be glad" W, 135–37.

189 "talents" Schutz and Adair, 106–7.

190 "deceived and abused" Schutz and Adair, 106.

192 "a good history" David Humphreys to GW, January 15, 1785.

192 "talents" W, 580.

194 "at ease upon a bed" L'Estrange, 99.

194 "you have therein" William Fairfax to GW, May 13, 1756.

195 "candidly discussed" W, 692.

196 "the same object" W, 707.

196 "the last stab" TJ, 27.

197 "you might be" Arthur Young to GW, January 17, 1784.

197 "I never possessed" W, 602.

197 "Much ground" W, 798.

197 "primary object" W, 983.

CHAPTER 20: AVOID WEAKNESSES

199 "This great man" Bowling and Veit, 13.

200 "our Colossus" Brookhiser *(Adamses)*, 29.

201 "He charms" Brookhiser *(Morris)*, 78.

201 "the curse of heaven" FC, 392.

201 "as Homer wrote" TJ, 6.

201 "I know not" Widmer, 1:20–21.

202 "Mr. Henry" Meade, 448.

202 "faithful services" Flexner, 1:227.

202 "Sit down" Lewis, 273.

203 "In public" TJ, 174.

203 "never yet betrayed" Flexner, 4:493.

203 "I have not" Leibiger, 103.

204 "I never heard" TJ, 61.

205 "monkeys" Brookhiser *(Morris)*, 4.

205 "Professions of *impartiality*" Burns, 340.

205 "strong and coarse" Cobbett, 37.

206 "heresies which have" Brookhiser *(Adamses)*, 46.

207 "clear, distinct" Brookhiser *(Hamilton)*, 124.

207 "may be led" TJ, 411.

209 "the most remarkable" W, 34.

210 "charming" W, 48.

210 "He would not say so" W, 1057.

211 "the man" Roosevelt *(Letters)*, 782.

Chapter 21: Control Your Flaws

213 "in its mass" TJ, 174.

213 "George generally" Smith, 4.

214 "openness and candor" Ellis *(His Excellency)*, 33.

214 "all is lost!" Flexner, 1:208–15.

215 "the strangest" W, 320.

217 "under present" Flexner, 2:430.

217 "I'm with you" Gold, epigraph (n.p.).

218 "[A] mind like his" Brookhiser *(Washington)*, 49.

220 "much inflamed" Jefferson, 2:382.

221 "the great man" AH, 97.

222 "a wild impetuous" L'Estrange, 271.

222 "The conversation" Syrett, 24:555–65.

223 "The ungovernable" AH, 960.

223 "a man of" AH, 937–41.

223 "I am in a" AH, 930.

224 "like the great" Ellis *(Passionate Sage)*, 115.

224 "In deceiving others" Nevins, 409.

224 "a contemptible" AH, 977.

224 "with the right" McKeon, 391.

224 "Lyndon feeling" John Roche, personal communication.

225 "His justice" TJ, 173.

Chapter 22: Succession

227 "I think I am" Golway, 230.

228 "See which of us" Flexner, 4:333.

230 "If you give me" Ambrose, 525.

231 "It was a solemn" Rhodehamel, 796.

232 "one man outweighs" Elkins and McKitrick, 517.

233 "but little acquainted" W, 1039.

233 "not to be" W, 1035.

233 None of his heirs Dalzell and Dalzell, 220.

Conclusion: We Must Take Men

235 "the same conduct" W, 298–99.

236 "I do not mean" W, 299–300.

Bibliography

Abbot, W. W., Dorothy Twohig, and Philadner D. Chase, eds. *The Papers of George Washington: Revolutionary Series*. 12 vols. Charlottesville: University Press of Virginia, 1985—.

Ambrose, Stephen E. *Eisenhower: Soldier and President*. New York: Simon and Schuster, 1990.

Ames, Seth, and W. B. Allen, eds. *Works of Fisher Ames*. 2 vols. Indianapolis: Liberty Classics, 1983.

Billias, George Athan, ed. *George Washington's Generals*. New York: William Morrow, 1964.

Black, Conrad. *Render unto Caesar*. Toronto: Key Porter Books, 1998.

Bobrick, Benson. *Angel in the Whirlwind*. New York: Simon and Schuster, 1997.

Bowling, Kenneth R., and Helen E. Veit, eds. *The Diary of William Maclay*. Baltimore: Johns Hopkins University Press, 1988.

Brandt, Clare. *The Man in the Mirror: A Life of Benedict Arnold*. New York: Random House, 1994.

Breen, T. H. *Tobacco Culture*. Princeton: Princeton University Press, 1985.

Broadwater, Jeff. *George Mason, Forgotten Founder*. Chapel Hill: University of North Carolina Press, 2006.

Brookhiser, Richard. *Alexander Hamilton, American*. New York: Free Press, 1999.

_____. *America's First Dynasty: The Adamses, 1735–1918*. New York: Free Press, 2002.

_____. *Founding Father: Rediscovering George Washington*. New York: Free Press, 1996.

_____. *Gentleman Revolutionary: Gouverneur Morris, the Rake Who Wrote the Constitution*. New York: Free Press, 2003.

_____. *Rules of Civility*. Charlottesville: University Press of Virginia, 2003.

_____. *What Would the Founders Do?* New York: Basic Books, 2006.

Burns, Eric. *Infamous Scribblers*. New York: Public Affairs, 2006.

Chateaubriand, François-René de. *Mémoires d'outre-tombe*. 2 vols. Philadelphie: Carey and Hart, 1848.

Cobbett, William. *Peter Porcupine in America*. Edited by David Wilson. Ithaca: Cornell University Press, 1994.

Custis, George Washington Parke. *Recollections and Private Memoirs of Washington*. Bridgewater, Va.: American Foundation Publications, 1999.

Dalzell, Robert F., Jr., and Lee Baldwin Dalzell. *George Washington's Mount Vernon*. New York: Oxford University Press, 1998.

Dann, John C. *The Revolution Remembered*. Chicago: University of Chicago Press, 1980.

Davenport, Beatrix Cary. *A Diary of the French Revolution by Gouverneur Morris*. 2 vols. Boston: Houghton Mifflin, 1939.

Dryden, John, trans., and A. H. Clough, ed. *Plutarch's Lives of the Noble Grecians and Romans*. 2 vols. New York: Modern Library, 1992.

Elkins, Stanley, and Eric McKitrick. *The Age of Federalism*. New York: Oxford University Press, 1993.

Ellis, Joseph J. *His Excellency*. New York: Vintage Books, 2004.

_____. *Passionate Sage*. New York: W. W. Norton, 1993.

Emery, Noemie. "What George Knew." *Weekly Standard*, February 19, 1996.

Fenn, Elizabeth A. *Pox Americana*. New York: Hill and Wang, 2001.

Ferling, John. *John Adams: A Life*. New York: Henry Holt, 1996.

Fischer, David Hackett. *Washington's Crossing*. New York: Oxford University Press, 2004.

Flexner, James Thomas. *George Washington*. 4 vols. Boston: Little, Brown, 1965–1972.

Franklin, Benjamin. *Writings*. New York: Library of America, 1987.

Goebel, Julius, Jr., ed. *The Law Practice of Alexander Hamilton*. New York: Columbia University Press, 1964.

Gold, Vic. *I Don't Need You When I'm Right*. New York: William Morrow, 1975.

Golway, Terry. *Washington's General*. New York: Henry Holt, 2005.

"The Good Soldier White." *American Heritage*, June 1956, 74–79.

Grant, Ulysses S. *Personal Memoirs*. New York: Penguin Books, 1999.

Haley, James L. *Sam Houston*. Norman: University of Oklahoma Press, 2002.

Haven, C. C. *Thirty Days in New Jersey Ninety Years Ago*. Trenton: printed at the "State Gazette" office, 1867.

Hirschfeld, Fritz. *George Washington and Slavery*. Columbia: University of Missouri Press, 1997.

Hook, Sidney. *Marx and the Marxists*. New York: D. Van Nostrand, 1955.

Irving, Washington. *George Washington: A Biography*. New York: Da Capo Press, 1994.

Jefferson, Thomas. *The Writings of Thomas Jefferson*. Edited by Andrew A. Lipscomb and Albert Ellery Bergh. 20 vols. Washington, D.C.: Thomas Jefferson Memorial Association, 1903–1904 (known as the Memorial Edition).

Joyce, James. *A Portrait of the Artist as a Young Man*. New York: Viking Press, 1964.

Leibiger, Stuart. *Founding Friendship*. Charlottesville: University Press of Virginia, 1999.

L'Estrange, Sir Roger, Knt. *Seneca's Morals by Way of Abstract*. London: printed for S. Ballard . . . , 1756.

Lewis, Thomas A. *For King and Country*. New York: John Wiley and Sons, 1993.

Longmore, Paul K. *The Invention of George Washington*. Berkeley and Los Angeles: University of California Press, 1988.

Manchester, William. *American Caesar*. New York: Dell Publishing, 1978.

Marshall, John. *The Life of George Washington*. 5 vols. New York: Wm. H. Wise, 1925.

Maume, Chris. "Hair Today, Gone Tomorrow." *The Independent*, August 1, 1999.

McDonald, Forrest. *The American Presidency*. Lawrence: University Press of Kansas, 1994.

McKeon, Richard, ed. *Introduction to Aristotle*. New York: Modern Library, 1947.

Meade, Robert Douthat. *Patrick Henry: Practical Revolutionary*. Philadelphia and New York: J. B. Lippincott, 1969.

Musa, Mark, trans. and ed. *Machiavelli's "The Prince."* New York: St. Martin's Press, 1964.

Nevins, Allan. *The Diary of John Quincy Adams*. New York: Longmans, Green, 1928.

O'Brien, Conor Cruise. *The Long Affair*. Chicago: University of Chicago Press, 1996.

Paine, Thomas. *Collected Writings*. New York: Library of America, 1995.

Pessen, Edward. *The Log Cabin Myth*. New Haven: Yale University Press, 1986.

Pliny. *Natural History*. With an English translation by H. Rackham. 10 vols. Cambridge: Harvard University Press, 1950.

Quintana, Ricardo. *Eighteenth Century Plays*. New York: Modern Library, 1952.

Reed, Joseph. "General Reed's Narrative . . . " *Pennsylvania Magazine of History and Biography* 8 (1884).

Rhodehamel, John, ed. *The American Revolution*. New York: Library of America, 2001.

Roosevelt, Theodore. *Letters and Speeches*. New York: Library of America, 2004.

_____. *The Rough Riders: An Autobiography*. New York: Library of America, 2004.

Rose, Alexander. *Washington's Spies*. New York: Bantam, 2006.

Schama, Simon. *Citizens*. New York: Alfred A. Knopf, 1989.

Schutz, John A., and Douglass Adair. *The Spur of Fame*. Indianapolis: Liberty Fund, 2001.

Sidey, Hugh. "L.B.J., Hoover, and Domestic Spying." *Time*, February 10, 1975.

Smith, Richard Norton. *Patriarch*. Boston: Houghton Mifflin, 1993.

Steuben, Frederick William Baron von. *Baron von Steuben's Revolutionary War Drill Manual*. New York: Dover Publications, 1985.

Syrett, Harold C., et al., eds. *The Papers of Alexander Hamilton*. 26 vols. New York: Columbia University Press, 1961–1987.

Weems, Mason. *A History of the Life and Death, Virtues and Exploits of General George Washington*. Cleveland: World Publishing, 1965.

Widmer, Ted, ed. *American Speeches*. 2 vols. New York: Library of America, 2006.

Index

Acting, of leaders, 77
Adams, Abigail, 94
    Adams, John, marrying, 189
    Franklin evening described by,
       177–178
    King Solomon thought of, 170
    Washington, George, amiability
       described by, 179
    Washington, George, impressing,
       169–171, 177–179
Adams, John, 20, 51, 200
    Adams, Abigail, marrying, 189
    administration of, 144
    cabinet presided over by, 222–223
    Hamilton and, 223
    as public speaker, 79
    as Vice President, 3
    Washington, George, succeeded by,
       228
    writings of, 206
Adams, Samuel, 195, 200, 206
Addiction, 151–152
Addison, Joseph, 121
Administration, of John Adams, 144
Aeneid (Virgil), 27
Alcohol abuse, 150–153
Algernon, Sidney, 88
Allen, Woody, 70
Alliances, 146
Allies
    gratitude for, 142–146
    Washington, George, depending on,
       139–142

Aloofness, 228–229
Ambassador to France, 106–107
America
    American Revolution of, 103–104
    challenges to, 33
    constitution of, 3
    eighteenth century newspapers in,
       205–206
    first immunization campaign in,
       45–46
    French helping, 114–115
    Indian war fought by, 42
    inoculation experience in, 43, 45
    laws of, 59
    politics in, 104–105, 230–231
    regional differences of, 98
    tariff collection in, 34
    taxes/tariffs funding, 64–65
American army
    congress creating, 12
    experienced officers needed by, 94–95
    Knox best general of, 98
    New Englanders supplying, 115
    not paying, 75
    preserving health of, 14–15
    smallpox dealt with by, 43–46
American Revolution
    characteristics of, 134
    early episodes of, 215
    first battle of, 49–51
    France supporting, 103–104
    Washington, George, strategies of,
       24–29

American Revolution, *continued*
   Washington, George, understanding
      causes of, 195
   worst defeat in, 121–125
Americans
   Genet agitating, 129–130
   as land-hungry, 38–39
   reading everything, 172–173
Ames, Fisher, 73–76, 199
Anger, 224
Appearance, of George Washington,
   171–172
Armstrong, John, 125, 166
Arnold, Benedict, 44, 131, 165, 184
   court-martial of, 127–128
   as Philadelphia military governor, 127
   treason of, 18–19, 128–129
Arnold, Mrs. Benedict, 128, 165
Artillery retrieval mission, 63–64
Assunpink Creek, 69–70
Astor, John Jacob, 31
Attention, 157

Baltimore, Baron, 140
Banister, John, 235
Battle
   of American Revolution, 49–51
   of Bunker Hill, 26
   of Fallen Timbers, 42
   of Kolín, 163
   of Long Island, 49–51, 56–57
   Monmouth Court House, 62, 96–97
   of Princeton, 58
   sanitation, 12–15
   of Saratoga, 215
   of Trenton, 68–69
Betrayal, 125–132
Biological warfare, 45–46
Bishop, Thomas, 152
Black, Conrad, 179
Bolingbroke, Viscount, 195
   See also Henry St. John
Borgia, Cesare, 155
Boston, 56
Bowel movements, 14

Braddock, Edward, 137, 140–141, 152,
   181
Bradford, William, 59
Bravery
   leader quality of, 184
   of Washington, George, 180–184
Breen, T.H., 30
"Bring out the best" of people, 161, 163
British
   Fort Washington surrendered to,
      122–123
   Greene, Nathanael, and, 216
   Indians indispensable to, 135
   leaving Philadelphia, 134
   Manhattan conquered by, 17–19
   New York attack preparations of,
      26–27
   Pennsylvania entered by, 138
   Philadelphia captured by, 61
   policy change desired from, 24–25
   Randolph, John, connections with,
      131
British army
   Assunpink Creek forced by, 69–70
   countering movements of, 118
   Gates defeat of, 100
   Gates veteran of, 25
   Hudson river entered by, 122
   letter of truce from, 48–49
   Monmouth Court House battle
      with, 62, 96–97
   New England volunteers v., 11–15
   New York Harbor arrival of, 48–49
Bunker Hill, battle of, 26
Burke, Edmund, 200
Bush, George H. W., 176, 229
Bush, George W., 204
Businessmen, 31–32
Butler, Pierce, 21

Cabinet members
   Adams, John, presiding over,
      222–223
   Jefferson as, 55
   Washington, George, trusting, 65–66

Cadwalader, John, 141
Caesar, Julius, 32, 193, 194
Canada, invasion of, 102
Careers, 31–32
Carrington, Edward, 202
Carter, Jimmy, 204
Cary, Robert, 31
Catastrophes, 54
Cato, 121
Changing conditions, 36
"Channel of information," 16
Character reference, 190–191
Chase, Chevy, 176
Chastellux, Marquis de, 32
Chateaubriand, 3
Civilian superiors, 117
Civility, 159
Clarkson, Mathew, 51
Cleopatra, 147
Clinton, Bill, 147, 192
Cobb, David, 180
Cobbett, William, 205
Combat bravery, 181–182
Commander in chief, 2, 11–15, 82
Commentaries (Caesar), 194
Common Sense, 206
Congress, 115–116
    army created by, 12
    Conway commissioned by, 99–100
    excise tax levied by, 58
    impotence/paralysis of, 33–34
    new session of, 52–54
    retired Washington, George, called
        by, 144–145
    Washington, George, relationships
        with, 114–116, 162–163
    Washington, George, reporting to,
        124
Consensus, 61
Constitutional Convention, 92
    Hamilton's joking offer at, 106
    Madison notes of, 5
    presidency rules written at, 19
    Washington, George, attendance
        decision of, 34–35

Constitution, U.S., 3
Continental army, 2
Conway Cabal, 100–102, 114, 126
Conway, Thomas, 99–100, 141, 165,
    210
Cornwallis, Lord, 28, 46, 216
Corruption, 127
Council of war, 57–58, 61–62
Countering movements, 118
Courtesy, 160
Court-martial, 97
    of Arnold, 127–128
    of Lee, Charles, 97
Crawford, William, 174
Credit crunch, 30–31
Creek Indians, 41
Criminals, 158
Cromwell, Oliver, 32
Custis, Daniel Parke, 188
Custis, George Washington Parke, 175,
    234
Custis, Martha. *See* Washington,
    Martha
Custis, Nelly, 149, 166

Dandridge, Martha, 188
Deane, Silas, 127
Declaration of Independence, 196, 236
Dedalus, Stephen, 139
Defeats, 121–125, 181
Delegation, of leaders, 66
Determination, 217
Dinwiddie, Robert, 140
Distillers, 58
Distillery, 152–153
Diversification, 31
Don Quixote, 74
Don Sebastian, King of Portugal, 170
Drowne, Solomon, 174
Drunkenness, 150–151
Dryden, John, 170
Dyer, Eliphalet, 178

Economics, of land rush, 38–39
Economic warfare, 24–25, 28

Education
    leaders, 198
    of Washington, George, 192–198
Eighteenth-century armies, 127
Eisenhower, Dwight, 35
Ellis, Joseph, 158
Emery, Noemie, 74
Employer, exacting, 67
Enemies
    learning from, 136–138
    living with, 133–135
    Washington, George, dealing with,
        134–135
An Essay Concerning Humane
        Understanding (Locke), 196
Estaing, Comte de, 216
Excise tax, 58
Experienced officers, 94–95
Extramarital adventures, 148–149

Fairfax, Ann, 166, 186, 193
Fairfax, Bryan, 143, 149
Fairfax property, 186–187
Fairfax Resolves, 88–89
Fairfax, Sally, 149–150
Fairfax, William, 140, 143
Fallen Timbers, battle of, 42
Family business, 4–5
Farewell address, 73, 82, 203–204
Farming, 196–197, 232
Father of the Constitution, 91
Federalist Papers
    Hamilton and, 147
    Madison collaborator of, 207
    passions of men catalogued in, 161
    purpose of, 207–209
    science of politics written in, 159
    Washington, George, commenting
        on, 195–196
Fenn, Elizabeth, 45
Fillmore, Millard, 191–192
Financial independence, 191–192
First Continental Congress, 81
    British policy change desire of,
        24–25

future leaders first meeting at, 190
Fischer, David Hackett, 68
Flahaut, Adelaide de, 148
Flexibility, 36
Flexner, James Thomas, 177, 193
Forbes, John, 138, 214
Ford, Gerald, 176
Ford, Henry, 227
Foreign policy, 92–93
Fort Lee, 122
Fort Washington, 122, 123
Founder-journalist, 206–207
Founding CEO, 1
France, 103–104, 166
Franklin, Benjamin, 6, 51, 95, 125, 189,
        200
    Adams, Abigail, describing,
        177–178
    publishing of, 206
    virtues sought by, 185–186
Frederick the Great, 163
Freedom, 70
Freeman, Douglas Southall, 10
French
    America helped by, 114–115
    officers, 217
    revolution, 103–104, 109
    Washington, George, retreating
        from, 136
French and Indian War
    land opportunities after, 187–188
    Ohio Valley control sought in,
        213–215
    Washington, George, during,
        113–114, 137–138
Freneau, Philip, 209, 220, 232
Furst, Alan, 108

Garfield, James, 192
Gates, Horatio, 96, 124, 165, 227
    British army defeated by, 100
    as British army veteran, 25
    strikes against, 126–127
Genet, Citizen. See Genet, Edmond
        Charles

Genet, Edmond Charles, 166, 219–220
    American agitation from, 129–130
    privateer commissions mission of,
        103–105
    privateer outfitted by, 109–111
Gentleman outlaw, 50–51
George III (King), 13, 210
Germantown, 54
Gladwell, Malcolm, 171
Golway, Terry, 148
Gordon, William, 195
Gore, Al, 208
Government
    Congress and, 33–34
    Washington, George, influencing,
        133–134
Governor, 127
Grant, Ulysses, 153, 172, 175
Grasse, Comte de, 217
Gratitude, 142–146
Great Awakening, 200
Green Bay Packers, 176
Greene, Caty, 147–148, 165, 171
Greene, Nathanael, 34, 98, 127, 134, 165
    advice of, 26
    British and, 216
    judgments warped, 123–124
    Knox letter from, 123
    Littlefield married to, 147–148
    rapid rise of, 121–122
    sanitation problem faced by, 12–15
    Washington, George,
        recommending, 227–228
    Washington, George, supported by, 56
Green, Thomas, 151, 166
Guare, John, 85

Hale, Nathan, 16, 19
Hamilton, Alexander, 58, 61, 165, 166,
        207–209, 221
    Adams, John, and, 223
    background of, 89–90
    economics/law abilities of, 90
    economic warfare defense of, 24–25
    farewell address help from, 73

Federalist Papers and, 147, 195–196
as first treasury secretary, 64–65, 90
headaches from, 93–94
Jefferson at odds with, 108–109
joking offer of, 106
major general appointment of, 145
military pressure thoughts of, 126
passions of men catalogued by, 161
polemical writing of, 206
policies of, 65–66
presidential powers and, 53
as prolific founder-journalist,
    206–207
Schuyler marriage to, 189
science of politics written by, 159
treasury department work of, 82
with yellow fever, 51
Harmar, Josiah, 42, 151
Harrison, Robert Hanson, 72
Health, of army, 14–15
Heinz, Teresa, 189
Henry, Patrick, 201–202
Heroic phase, 215–216
Hessians, 57–58, 68
Honesty, 133
Hoover, J. Edgar, 109
Horseback skills, 175–176
House of Burgesses, 202–203
Houston, Sam, 153
Howe, Richard, 48–50, 81–82
Howe, William, 48–50, 81–82
Howland, John, 69
Hub and wheel, 55–63
Hudson river, 122
Human nature, 150
Humphrey, Hubert, 230
Humphreys, David, 181, 192, 203
"Hyde Park tactics," 25

Immunization campaign, 45–46
Imprisonment, of Lafayette, 143–144
Inaugural address
    Madison writing, 72–73
    Washington, George's, 73–74,
        199–200

Indians
     American war with, 42
     Creek, 41
     Iroquois, 135
     nations, 135
     Oneida, 135
     Seneca, 42
     in Shenandoah Valley, 40–41
     southern, 19–20
The Indispensable Man, 231
Information agents, 17–18
Inland navigation, 39–40, 218
Inoculation, 43, 45
Intelligence agents. *See* Information
     agents
Invalid Corps, 116–117
Iroquois Indians, 135
Irving, Washington, 123

Jackson, Andrew, 229
James river, 39–40
Jay, John, 73, 77–78, 108, 195, 207
Jefferson, Thomas, 19, 54, 88, 91, 104,
     166
     Declaration of Independence and,
          196
     dies bankrupt, 4
     Hamilton at odds with, 108–109
     laxity of manner about, 170
     Madison writing for, 209
     as party leader, 109
     political essay of, 208–209
     as presidential cabinet member, 55,
          65–66
     presidential outburst recorded by,
          219–221
     troublesome, 108–109
     urgent letters from, 110–111
     as Vice President, 158–159
     Washington, George, comments of,
          5, 27, 71–72, 78
     Washington, George, political
          enemy of, 232
     Wayles marriage to, 189

Johnson, Andrew, 192
Johnson, Lyndon, 109, 224, 230
Johnson, William, 136
Judgments, 123–124

Keeping-mouth-shut strategy, 77–79
Kerry, John, 189
Kipling, Rudyard, 118
Knox, Henry, 20, 41, 59, 81, 126, 165,
     166
     as army's best general, 98
     artillery retrieval mission of, 63–64
     Greene, Nathanael, letter to, 123
     officer proposal of, 142–143
     Washington, George, appointment
          refused by, 145–146
     Washington, George, comments to,
          181–182
Kolín, battle of, 163

Lafayette, Marquis de, 62, 141, 165,
     166, 217
     imprisonment of, 143–144
     Washington, George, affection for,
          142–143
     Washington, George, defended by,
          101–102
Land opportunities, 187–188
Land rush, 38–39
Latrines, problem of, 12–15, 81
Laurens, Henry, 114, 165
Laxity of manner, 170
Leaders
     acting performance of, 77
     alliances and, 146
     bad contingencies preparations of,
          37
     best effort of others sought by, 163
     betrayal dealt with by, 132
     bravery quality of, 184
     "bring out the best" by, 161
     combat bravery of, 181–182
     courtesy and, 160
     dealing with catastrophes, 54

delegation by, 66
detail addressed by, 47, 51
educating, 198
financial independence and, 192
First Continental Congress first
    meeting of, 190
flexibility needed by, 36
future interest of, 42
hub and wheel system benefiting,
    60–61
human nature known by, 150
judging people by, 98
opportunity given to, 124–125
presenting problems to, 55–56, 83
presenting themselves, 173
pulling their weight, 177
retreat led by, 69–70
sexuality and, 147–150
smart people and, 94
strategies of, 23–29
strengths of, 169
unexpected planned for by, 46
Washington, George, as, 5–6
weaknesses known by, 199
Leadership, 7, 27
    Washington, George, characteristic
        of, 162–163
    Washington, George, failure of,
        129–130
    Washington, George, roles in, 236
    wealth and, 189–190
Lear, Polly, 51
Lee, Charles, 25–28, 62, 95, 156, 165,
    178
    court-martial of, 97
    problems presented by, 96–97
Lee, Henry, 45
Lee, Richard Henry, 114, 165, 200
Leslie, Alexander, 46
Letter of truce, 48–49
Leutze, Emanuel, 57, 171
Lincoln, Abraham, 179, 192, 198
Littlefield, Caty. See Greene, Caty
Livingston, Robert, 78

Livingston, Sarah, 78
Lloyd, William, 118, 166
Locke, John, 88, 196, 208
The Log Cabin Myth (Pessen), 191
Long, Earl, 217
Long Island, battle of, 49–51, 56–57
Love, involuntary passion, 149–150
Lynch, Thomas, 190

MacArthur, Douglas, 180
Machiavelli, Niccolò, 7, 155–156, 159,
    208
Maclay, William, 20, 21, 77, 82, 170,
    199
Madison, James, 53, 82, 109, 166, 195,
    218, 230
    Constitutional Convention notes
        of, 5
    convention called for by, 34
    farewell address written by, 203–204
    as Father of the Constitution, 91
    as Federalist Papers collaborator, 207
    first inaugural address written by,
        72–73
    as Jefferson writer, 209
    qualities of, 90–91
Mailer, Norman, 171
Major general appointment, 145
Management style, 62–63
Manhattan, 17–19, 48
Marrying well, 188–189
Martinet, 119
Maryland, 29
Mason, George, 87–89, 92–93, 166, 195
Mather, Cotton, 43
McGillivray, Alexander, 41, 82
McHenry, James, 222
Memoirs, 192–193
Mexican War, 172
Middle class, 191–192
Mifflin, Thomas, 59, 100, 231–232
Military, 1–2, 126
Modesty, 178
Money, 191–192

Monmouth Court House, 62, 96–97
Monroe, James, 109, 133, 174, 230
Montesquieu, 196
Montgomery, Richard, 44
Moral beliefs, 184
Morris, Gouverneur, 5, 6, 103, 166
    as ambassador to France, 106–107
    as excellent orator, 201
    extramarital adventures of, 148–149
    Reign of Terror and, 107–108
Morris, Robert, 4, 20, 58, 64
Mount Vernon, 82–83
    distillery at, 152–153
    Ladies Association, 233
    slave inventory at, 182–183
    sobriety expected at, 151–152
    troubles of, 30
    Washington, George, inheriting,
        29–31
    Washington, George's, office at,
        168
Mutiny
    near, 82, 141–142
    Washington, George, diverting, 126,
        161–162
"My brave fellows" phrase, 163

Napoleon, 144
National bank, 64–65
National university, 197–198
Newburgh
    near-mutiny at, 82, 141–142
    officer complaints at, 125–126
New Englanders
    army food supplies from, 115
    British army v., 11–15
    Washington, George, dealing with,
        97–98
New Jersey, 121–122
Newspapers, 205–206
New York
    British attack preparations on,
        26–27
    British concentrating forces in, 61

Washington, George, recapturing,
    216, 218–219
New York Harbor, 48–49
Nicola, Lewis, 116–117, 165
Nixon, Richard, 192, 211, 224
Normandy invasion, 35
Notes on Virginia, 208

Obama, Barack, 208
Obstinacy, 213–219
    determination v., 217
    Washington, George, showing,
        213–215
Officers
    American army needing, 94–95
    complaints of, 125–126
    drinking by, 150–151
    French, 217
    Knox proposal to, 142–143
    testimonials of, 178–179
Ohio Valley, 213–215
Oneida Indians, 135
Operation 'Culper,' 18
Opportunity, leaders with, 124–125
Orators
    Henry, Patrick, as, 201–202
    Morris, Gouveneur, as, 201
Orca, Remirro de, 155

Paine, Thomas, 25, 205
"Passions of men" statement, 235–237
Patterson, James, 48–49
Patton, George, 178
Pennsylvania, 138
Penn, Thomas, 139
People
    judging/managing, 85
    leaders judging, 98
    Washington, George, crossing path
        of, 165–166
Perimeter defense, 26–27
Pessen, Edward, 191, 197
Philadelphia
    Arnold military governor of, 127

British capturing, 61
British leaving, 134
as new capital, 51
Washington, George, riding to, 54
yellow fever striking, 51–52
Physical prowess, 173–177
Pickering, Timothy, 130, 132
Pinckney, Charles Cotesworth, 145
Pliny the Elder, 67
Polemical writing, 205–211
Policy change, 24–25
Political essay, 208–209
Political scientific study, 159
Politics
    in America, 104–105, 230–231
    money in, 191–192
    Washington, George, reading,
        194–195
Pompadour, Madame de, 147
Potomac river, 39–40
Powell, Colin, 193
Pre-Revolutionary experience, 66
President
    Constitutional Convention rules for,
        19
    below middle class, 191–192
    Monroe as, 174
    successor undermining, 229–230
    Washington, George, as, 3
    Washington, George, surrender of,
        158–159
Presidential outburst, 219–221
Presidential powers, 53
Presidential successors, 230–231
The Prince (Machiavelli), 7, 155
Princeton, battle of, 58
Prisoners, 49
Privateer
    commissions, 103–105
    outfitting of, 109–111
Problems, 81–83
Prussian military habits, 95
Public life, 156
Public punishment, 158

Public speaker, 199–205
    Adams, John, as, 79
    Washington, George, as, 200–205
Publisher, 206
Putnam, Israel, 94

Quarantine, 44
Queen of Sheba, 170
Quincy, John, 224

Randolph, Edmund, 52, 59, 130–131,
        166
Randolph, John, 131
Reagan, Ronald, 74, 192, 197, 229
Regional differences, 98
Regulation for the Order and Discipline of
        the Troops of the United States,
        14
Reign of Terror, 107–108
Reputation, 182, 225
Retirement, 232–233
Retreat, 69–70, 124
Rhode Island militia, 121–122
Rivington, James, 205, 207
Robinson, John, 140, 215
Rochambeau, Comte de, 217
Roosevelt, Franklin D., 171–172, 176,
        230
Roosevelt, Theodore, 176, 211, 229
Rose, Alexander, 17
Rules, 19–22
"The Rules of Civility & Decent
        Behavior in Company and
        Conversation," 156–160,
        221–222
    public life introduction from, 156
    social hygiene from, 157
    social rank assumed in, 158
Rush, Benjamin, 52
Rutledge, Edward, 51

Sanitation battle, 12–15
Saratoga, battle of, 215
Schuyler, Elizabeth, 189

Science of politics, 147
Scott, Charles, 151
Scott, Winfield, 172
Self-education, 197
The Senate, 20–22
Seneca (Roman philosopher), 6, 37, 193
Seneca Indians, 42
Sermons, 200–202
The Seven Year Itch, 171
Seven Years' War. *See* French and Indian
    War
Sexuality, 147–150
Shaw, Samuel, 75–76
Shays, Daniel, 34
Shenandoah Valley
    Indian party net in, 40–41
    Washington, George, first land
        purchase in, 187
    Washington, George, first visiting,
        157
    Washington surveying, 38
Sidney, Algernon, 88
Silence, gift of, 79
Six Degrees of Separation, 85
Slaves
    freedom and, 70
    labor of, 68
    Mount Vernon inventory of,
        182–183
    used for biological warfare, 45–46
    Washington, Martha, freeing, 183,
        233
Smallpox, 43–46, 81
Smart people, 87–94
Smith, Abigail. *See* Adams, Abigail
Smith, Adam, 196
Sobriety, 151–152
Social hygiene, 157
Social rank, 158
Solomon, King, 170
Southern Indians, 19–20
Spectacles gesture, 76–77
Spirit of the Laws (Montesquieu), 196
Spy, 16–17
Spymaster, 19

Stalin, Joseph, 63
Stamp act, 194
Start-ups
    establishing routines during, 15–16
    rules guiding, 19–22
St. Clair, Arthur, 42
Sterne, Laurence, 74
Steuben, Baron von, 138, 165, 178
Steuben, Friedrich Wilhelm von, 14,
    95–96, 115
Stevens, Edward, 52
St. John, Henry, 195
    See also Viscount Bolingbroke
Strategies
    for changing conditions, 36
    of leaders, 23–29
Strength, 173–177
Stuart, Gilbert, 171
Subordinates, 118–119
*A Summary View of the Rights of British
    America* (Jefferson), 208–209
Superiors, dealing with, 113–117
Supplier commissions, 127

Taft, William Howard, 229
Talleyrand-Périgord, Charles Maurice
    de, 148
Tallmadge, Benjamin, 17–18
Tarantino, Quentin, 155
Tariffs, 34, 64–65
Taxes, 64–65
Tax protest, 58–60
Taylor, Zachary, 172
Temper, 219–225
Theater, 74–75
Thompson, Fred, 208
Tobacco, as demanding crop, 29–31
Traitors, 130
Travels in North America
    (Chastellux), 32
Treason, 18–19, 128–129
Treasury department, 82
Treasury secretary, 64–65, 90
Treaties, 19–20
Trenchard, John, 195

Trenton, second battle of, 68–69
Troublemakers
    getting rid of, 99–105
    hanging themselves, 105
    working with, 105–111
Truce, 48–49
Truman, Harry, 230
Trump, Donald, 191

Uniform design, 172

Valley Forge, 14, 45
Van Buren, Martin, 229
Vice President
    Adams, John, as, 3
    Jefferson as, 158–159
Virgil, 27
Virginia, 29, 137–138
    assembly, 91
    Convention, 201
Virtues, 185–186

Wadsworth, Jeremiah, 148
Ward, Artemas, 94
War of Independence. *See* American
    Revolution
Washington, Augustine (father), 186,
    193
Washington, Bushrod, 233
Washington Crossing the Delaware, 57,
    171
Washington, George. *See also* Mount
    Vernon
    Adams, Abigail, impressed by,
        169–171, 177–179
    Adams, John, succeeding, 228
    allies defending, 139–142
    aloofness of, 228–229
    American Revolution causes
        understood by, 195
    American revolution strategies
        available to, 24–29
    amiability described of, 179
    amiability of, 177–180
    appearance of, 171–172

associates protecting reputation of,
    225
Boston attack suggested by, 56
Braddock defeat described by, 181
bravery of, 180–184
cabinet members trusted by, 65–66
civilian superiors and, 117
civility grounding needed by, 159
as commander in chief, 2, 11–15
composed countenance of, 69–70
Congress contacting, 144–145
congressmen relationships with,
    114–116, 162–163
Congress report of, 124
Constitutional Convention
    attendance decision of, 34–35
Conway Cabal against, 100–102
Conway not liked by, 99–100
council of war called by, 57–58,
    61–62
credit crunch of, 30–31
drunkenness reprimanded by,
    150–151
education of, 192–198
enemy nations dealt with by,
    134–135
as exacting employer, 67
Fairfax property surveyed by,
    186–187
Fairfax teen love of, 149
family business of, 4–5
farming read about by, 196–197
Federalist Papers comments of,
    195–196
financial independence of, 191–192
first immunization campaign by,
    45–46
first inaugural address by, 73–74,
    199–200
first treaties negotiated by, 19–20
French allow retreat of, 136
French and Indian War with,
    113–114, 137–138
French officers attitude toward, 217
French revolution and, 109

Washington, George, *continued*
  Genet incident and, 109–111
  as gentleman outlaw, 50–51
  government influence of, 133–134
  Greene, Nathanael,
      recommendation of, 227–228
  Greene, Nathanael, supporting, 56
  Hale mission approved by, 16–17
  Hamilton headache to, 93–94
  heroic phase of, 215–216
  horseback skills of, 175–176
  House of Burgesses speech of,
      202–203
  Indian wars and, 40–41
  Inland navigation interest of, 218
  inland navigation interest of, 39–40
  Jefferson comments on, 5, 27,
      71–72, 78
  Jefferson political enemy of, 232
  keeping-mouth-shut strategy of,
      77–79
  Knox refusing, 145–146
  Lafayette defending, 101–102
  Lafayette's affection from, 142–143
  as leader, 5–6
  leadership characteristic of, 162–163
  leadership failure of, 129–130
  leadership roles of, 236
  letter of truce sent to, 48–49
  Littlefield dancing with, 147–148
  management style of, 62–63
  marrying well, 188–189
  Mason break with, 92–93
  memoir suggestion to, 192–193
  military initiation of, 1–2
  Mount Vernon inherited by, 29–31
  Mount Vernon office of, 168
  mutiny diverted by, 82, 126,
      141–142, 161–162
  "my brave fellows" phrase of, 163
  national university sought by,
      197–198
  new congressional session and,
      52–54
  New Englanders and, 97–98

  New York recaptured by, 218–219
  no confidence vote on, 139–140
  obstinacy shown by, 213–214
  officer testimonials hailing, 178–179
  operation 'Culper' code name by, 18
  "passions of men" statement of,
      235–237
  patience/power formula of, 60
  people crossing path of, 165–166
  Philadelphia returned to by, 54
  physical prowess of, 173–177
  politics read by, 194–195
  pre-Revolutionary experience of, 66
  presidency surrendered by, 158–159
  as President, 3
  president-elect comments from,
      181–182
  presidential outburst of, 219–221
  problems faced by, 81–83
  public speaking ability of, 200–205
  Randolph confrontation with,
      130–131
  reputation of, 182
  retirement of, 232–233
  retreat of, 124
  "rules" received by, 156
  sanitation battle of, 12–15
  self-education of, 197
  Shenandoah Valley first purchase of,
      187
  Shenandoah Valley first visit by, 157
  Shenandoah Valley surveyed by, 38
  as skillful spymaster, 19
  slave labor of, 68
  smallpox experienced by, 43–46
  smart people known by, 87–94
  spectacles gesture of, 76–77
  theater enjoyed by, 74–75
  traitor document received by, 130
  uniforms designed by, 172
  in Valley Forge, 45
  wealth and, 189–190
  western land opportunity of, 37–42
  writing qualities of, 71–72
  writings of, 209–210

Washington, Lawrence, 186, 193
Washington, Lund, 97
Washington, Martha, 135, 183, 233
Wayles, Martha, 189
Wayne, Anthony, 42, 115, 148
Weaknesses, 199, 213
Wealth
    as character reference, 190–191
    leadership and, 189–190
    Washington, George, and, 189–190
Wealth of Nations (Smith), 196
Weedon, George, 151
Weems, Parson, 76, 173
Welch, Jack, 147
Westerners, 39, 60
Western land, 37–42

Whiskey Rebellion, 82
    deliberately provoked, 130
    as tax protest, 58–60
Whitefield, George, 200
White, Joseph, 118, 166
Wilderness, fighting in, 136–137
Wilkinson, James, 40, 101
Willis, Lewis, 173
Wilson, Woodrow, 198, 204
Wirt, William, 202
Wolcott, Oliver, 130–131
Wolfe, Tom, 188
Writing qualities, 71–72

Yellow fever, 51–54, 82
Young, Arthur, 196